T0072457

Everything You Need to Know
about OCD

'As a comedian, I am only too aware about jokes concerning OCD. When I was a psychiatric nurse, I knew that it was no laughing matter. People with OCD are often misunderstood and lack access to appropriate information and services. This book attempts to help by setting out everything about OCD, what may cause it and how it is treated. Using personal stories of people with OCD, it gives advice to families as well as the individual. The final section gives details of how you may help yourself to face up to and overcome OCD. A must-read for anyone whose life has been impacted by this illness.'

Jo Brand, comedian

'A timely intervention from a leading expert on OCD.'
David Adam, Sunday Times bestselling author of, The Man
Who Couldn't Stop: The Truth About OCD

'As an OCD sufferer myself, reading this book was like being wrapped in a warm blanket. Lynne manages to explain this complex condition with both deep insight and caring understanding. And reading the many brave stories from fellow sufferers made me feel that I'm not alone in the battle to control this dreadful mental illness. This book, I believe, will help enormously to do just that!'

Ian Puleston Davies, Actor and Patron of OCD UK

'Experiencing OCD can be incredibly isolating and painful, it is a condition surrounded by misconception and confusion. This wonderful book by Lynne Drummond really is a one stop shop for all things OCD. It answers every question you could possibly have about OCD and stops you feeling alone - it is wonderfully validating. Lynne's outstanding knowledge of OCD is clear throughout and she covers some of the more difficult conversation surrounding OCD with compassion and kindness. I wish I'd had access to this book when I was struggling.'

Catherine Benfield, Founder of 'Taming Olivia'

'This is an excellent book that provides in a clearly accessible form all the latest thinking and science on how OCD manifests and how to treat it. It is written by a world-leading specialist in the field who has been studying OCD and treating OCD patients for decades. I thoroughly recommend it.'

Nick Sireau, Chair and founder of Orchard

'OCD is a devastating condition which causes so much anguish and distress and is often misunderstood. This comprehensive new book by Dr Lynne Drummond is so easy to read and understand, and is packed with information for those living with OCD and their families. There is an extensive self-help section which describes the methods you need to embrace to overcome your condition. It is possible to overcome OCD and this book guides you through the evidence-based treatment methods so you can do it yourself. If you want to understand OCD and be inspired to take the road to recovery, then this is the book for you.'

Trilby Breckman, Clinical Director of TOP UK

'Dr Lynne Drummond has made it her mission to use her vast clinical experience, wisdom and skill as a consultant psychiatrist and psychotherapist to help people suffering from obsessive-compulsive disorder (OCD) by offering teaching and advice, and promoting the cause of OCD wherever possible. In this gem of a book, Everything You Need to Know about OCD, an updated and expanded version of her previous prizewinning volume, she has pulled it off once again. In this book, Professor Drummond delivers authoritative guidance on how to recognise the symptoms of OCD and what to do about it, in terms of treatments that work, with a particular focus on self-management. In so doing, she manages to combine the most up-to-date research advances with a pragmatic, common-sense approach, all articulated with the clarity and compassion for which she is renowned and illuminated by a wealth of personal "stories" that bring the book to life. Her final chapter, entitled "When the Treatment Doesn't Go According to Plan or Even If It Does, What to Do Next", is just brilliant, encapsulating her forward thinking and positive approach to what can turn out to be one of the most crippling of illnesses. The book is aimed at all those living with OCD, but will be valued by a much wider readership, including clinicians, carers and all those interested in understanding more about this intriguing disorder.'

Professor Naomi A. Fineberg, Professor of Psychiatry,
University of Hertfordshire

'*Everything You Need to Know about OCD* is a cutting-edge and comprehensive, yet very clear and widely accessible, book on best treatment approaches for OCD. The book's target audience includes both the lay public (OCD sufferers, family members and the general public) and clinicians (various healthcare workers and therapists, including behaviour therapists, occupational therapists, psychologists and psychiatrists). The author, Lynne Drummond, is a very rare physician with extensive expertise in both psychological and biological treatments of OCD. Her longstanding clinical and research experience is combined with a unique ability to communicate effectively and in simple terms on this topic. The book will undoubtedly increase awareness, enhance recognition and diagnosis, highlight and increase expertise in psychological and medical treatment options, and provide a roadmap for concrete self-help approaches to manage intrusive obsessive thoughts and control compulsive behaviours.'

Eric Hollander, MD, Director, Autism and Obsessive Compulsive
Spectrum Program, Albert Einstein College of Medicine and
Psychiatric Research Institute at Montefiore-Einstein

'Dr Lynne Drummond has extensive experience in both the psychotherapy and pharmacotherapy of OCD. In this volume, she summarises current state-of-the art approaches to treatment, so that people living with this condition can immediately and practically benefit. The chapters focused on different kinds of OCD symptoms are particularly useful, as these will help people with OCD to tailor their treatment plans according to their specific needs.'

Professor Dan Stein, Head of Psychiatry and Mental Health,
University of Cape Town

Dr Lynne Drummond, a UK psychiatrist who has dedicated her career to the assessment and treatment of OCD, has written another brilliant book for those who suffer from this disorder. The book provides a clear description of OCD and its varied presentations, an overview of pharmacological and psychological treatments and specific guidance on how to treat different types of OCD symptoms. Dr. Drummond writes with warmth and clarity, making the information very accessible to anyone. The book really comes to life with the many case descriptions which adeptly illustrate different symptom presentations of OCD. The latter portion of the book focusses on step-by-step self-help treatment plans to overcome specific symptoms and regain control of your life. This book is an essential resource for OCD sufferers, their carers and treatment providers. Although this book is not intended to instruct mental health providers, I would highly recommend this as a starting point for anyone new to treating this disorder. This book truly is everything you need to know about OCD.

Professor Michael Van Ameringen, Department of Psychiatry and
Behavioural Neurosciences, McMaster University; Co-Chair, International
College of Obsessive Compulsive Spectrum Disorders; and Anxiety Lead,
Canadian Network for Mood and Anxiety Disorders

'This book represents the distilled wisdom and knowledge from one of the world's leading experts in the assessment and treatment of OCD. Dr Drummond shares her decades of expertise in OCD through discussions of the nature of the condition, as well as the range of evidence-based treatments. In an accessible, and understandable way, Dr Drummond provides practical suggestions for individuals with a range of OCD symptoms. I am sure this book will be useful to clinicians and individuals with OCD, continuing Dr Drummond's career as a leader in the area.'

Dr Mark Boschen, Clinical Psychologist, Griffith University

Everything You Need to Know about OCD

Lynne M. Drummond

*Honorary Consultant Psychiatrist at South West London and St George's NHS Trust
and Visiting Professor at University of Hertfordshire*

Laura J. Edwards

Freelance Writer

CAMBRIDGE
UNIVERSITY PRESS

University Printing House, Cambridge CB2 8BS, United Kingdom

One Liberty Plaza, 20th Floor, New York, NY 10006, USA

477 Williamstown Road, Port Melbourne, VIC 3207, Australia

314–321, 3rd Floor, Plot 3, Splendor Forum, Jasola District Centre, New Delhi – 110025, India

103 Penang Road, #05-06/07, Visioncrest Commercial, Singapore 238467

Cambridge University Press is part of the University of Cambridge.

It furthers the University's mission by disseminating knowledge in the pursuit of education, learning, and research at the highest international levels of excellence.

www.cambridge.org
Information on this title: www.cambridge.org/9781009001946
DOI: 10.1017/9781009004176

© The Royal College of Psychiatrists 2022

First published 2022

A catalogue record for this publication is available from the British Library.

Library of Congress Cataloging-in-Publication Data
Names: Drummond, Lynne M., author. | Edwards, Laura J., author.
Title: Everything you need to know about OCD / Lynne Drummond, Consultant Psychiatrist, South West London and St George's Mental Health NHS Trust, Laura J. Edwards.
Description: First edition. | New York : Cambridge University Press, 2022. | Includes bibliographical references and index.
Identifiers: LCCN 2021055380 (print) | LCCN 2021055381 (ebook) | ISBN 9781009001946 (paperback) | ISBN 9781009004176 (epub)
Subjects: LCSH: Obsessive-compulsive disorder.
Classification: LCC RC533 .D778 2022 (print) | LCC RC533 (ebook) | DDC 616.85/227–dc23/eng/20211128
LC record available at https://lccn.loc.gov/2021055380
LC ebook record available at https://lccn.loc.gov/2021055381

ISBN 978-1-009-00194-6 Paperback

Contents

Downloadable resources can be found at www.cambridge.org/ocd-drummond

Preface

In 1979, I was a young junior doctor working in General Medicine in the east end of Glasgow, and I was studying for my Membership of the Royal College of Physicians. My ambition was to be a psychiatrist, but I had been advised to gain post-graduate experience in other aspects of medicine first. In May of that year, I was accepted by the Bethlem and Maudsley training scheme in psychiatry and so ended up in a new city and in a new hospital. It was here that I began working on Professor Isaac Mark's ward. This ward was a pioneering and world-leading research and clinical facility helping people with obsessive compulsive disorder (OCD) using the then, somewhat controversial treatment, of Graded Exposure and Self-Imposed Response Prevention (ERP). My experience on this ward cemented my decision to work in psychiatry, and after witnessing the impressive results of the exposure treatment, my particular interest in OCD was born.

After my time working in Professor Marks' ward, I moved on through other experiences. I began to realise that many people working in mental health did not understand OCD, nor the principles of treatment. Having experienced how devastating OCD could be to individuals and families, I was surprised at finding my passion for this subject was not only not shared by others, but was often dismissed as being 'unimportant'. I maintained my interest throughout my training years and was lucky to also work at St Mary's Hospital in Paddington, where Professor Stuart Montgomery was a world expert on the use of drug treatment for OCD. Although I have always predominantly been interested in behavioural and cognitive therapies and, indeed trained in these in their very early days, I believe in an eclectic approach. I believe all approaches, both pharmacological and psychological, which can be shown to be helpful to the patient with OCD, should be available and discussed with the patient, to produce a truly individualised treatment plan tailored to the individual and their circumstances. Working with Professor Montgomery also helped me further my understanding of OCD and introduced me to even more experts in the field who would later become close colleagues.

In 1985, I was fortunate to be appointed to run the OCD service at what was later to become South West London and St George's NHS Mental Health Trust. Initially we had very few staff and only five inpatient beds. Indeed, I was only allocated one and a half days a week for this work. Immediately I decided that, with such limited resources, we should concentrate on those people with the most severe conditions who had not been helped by previous interventions. Despite it being obvious to me and the people who worked with me how desperately ill some of our patients were, we were still often regarded as working in a niche area and tended to be dismissed as dealing with a minor condition. One of the major problems is that many people do not take OCD seriously. Many people describe themselves as 'a little bit OCD' when what they mean is they are fussy about an aspect in their lives such as cleanliness or being well organised. Of course, the symptoms of OCD are experienced to a minor degree by all of us from time to time, but this is very different from the life-changing and restricting problem of OCD. If your 'obsessions' and 'compulsions' are useful to you and help you in achieving your life-goals, then it is unlikely you have OCD. In OCD, the obsessions and compulsions impair your ability to achieve what you wish. This somewhat flippant attitude towards OCD has too often also been perpetuated by the media, with some TV programmes presenting OCD as a joke and not the serious condition it is. It was also apparent that, despite being so desperately unwell, these people could and did improve and could go on to live happy and fulfilling lives. We also saw that if the most ill patients who were admitted to our ward could improve so dramatically, this was often even truer for those with less profound conditions. Despite our success, I found we regularly had to fight for our survival. The demands for our services were huge but they were often disregarded by commissioners. The ignorance about the severity of OCD and its sometimes life-restricting and health-limiting impact which is so widespread in the population, including healthcare professionals, also extends to many who commission mental health services and fund research.

In 2005, the National Institute for Health and Clinical Excellence (NICE) set out the expected treatment for OCD. In response, we proposed a way in which these services could be cost-effectively delivered throughout the UK. NICE published our proposals but in reality little else happened. Not long after this, our local commissioners proposed closure of our inpatient service and a move over to a more primary and secondary care service. I was devastated, as I knew this meant that many desperately ill people would not receive the treatment they needed. Together with Professor Naomi Fineberg, we initially approached the Department of Health for direct funding. They suggested we invite the services at Bethlem and Maudsley to join us and in 2007, the National Services for OCD and Body Dysmorphic Disorder (BDD) were born. This meant we could increase our outreach work and I began regularly to try and teach mental health professionals throughout the UK about OCD and how to treat it. Demand for our services grew, but it became very clear that there was huge variability in the level and quality of services for people with OCD across the country. Theoretically, the development of the Primary Care Psychological Services should have improved the situation for people with OCD. In some ways it did, but in far too many areas patients were not being offered the gold-standard exposure treatments, but a much more generic anxiety-management instead. To compound this situation, psychology and psychiatry were often divorced from each other which leads, I believe, to a fractured and broken system whereby the total needs of a patient are often not fully addressed.

I have made it my mission to try and improve this situation by offering teaching, advice, and promoting the cause of OCD wherever possible, including via the media. In addition, by working with psychiatrist colleagues across the UK, we have pushed the importance of knowledge of OCD up the Royal College of Psychiatrists' agenda. Since 2019, we have successfully had skills for treating OCD accepted as necessary basic skills for all Community Mental Health teams.

In 2018, I published my book *Obsessive Compulsive Disorders: All You Want to Know about OCD for People Living with OCD, Carers and Clinicians* (Cambridge: Cambridge University Press and The Royal College of Psychiatrists). This book was designed to inform people with OCD, their families, friends, and their healthcare workers about OCD and how it should be treated. It was a success, and in 2019 it won the Royal College of Psychiatrists/Cambridge University Press best-seller award. Following feedback from people who had read the book, I realised that a more detailed description of treatment and how to set up a successful treatment programme were necessary. This would mean that some people with OCD could set up a treatment programme for themselves and start to work through their problems without the input of a trained professional or whilst awaiting such treatment. To this end, this new book, *Everything You Need to Know about OCD,* was born. I hope you find it helpful and useful as you try to gain support for this difficult problem. Please always remember that, no matter how difficult and hopeless you may feel it is to overcome your OCD, there is light at the end of the tunnel. Overcoming OCD is never easy, but with the right treatment or combination of treatments, I would go as far as to say that there is a solution for each and every person. it Please never give up as you can and will overcome this eventually.

Acknowledgements

I firstly need to acknowledge all the brave and truly amazing people with OCD who I have had the privilege to meet over the past five decades. You have taught me all I have learned about OCD and I have appreciated your determination, dedication, bravery, and also, on many occasions, your sense of humour. Just because this is a serious condition, does not stop you often seeing a funny side and I admire you for this.

I would like to thank three very special people. Firstly, Professor Isaac Marks, my mentor and guide, not only in the early years, but also throughout my career to the present day. Isaac, you have guided me in so many ways and at so many different stages of my career. You have served as a role model even though I could never achieve a fraction of what you have done. Thanks also to Professor Stuart Montgomery, who taught me to look at the science of psychopharmacology. Thank you, Stuart, for pointing me in the right direction so many times and for your continued work in this field. I enjoy continuing to work with you as a wise and much respected colleague. I also need to thank my good friend, colleague, and general supporter when I need it, Professor Naomi Fineberg. Thank you, Naomi, for often pushing me when I have needed it and for your indefatigable energy, wit, humour, and wisdom. I may often have been tempted to give up the fight, but your example spurred me on and you deserve to be the world-renowned and respected expert you have become.

1

• • • • • • •

What Is OCD and Is It Really a Problem?

This chapter will examine a brief overview of obsessive compulsive disorder (OCD) and its defining features. Public perception of OCD over time will then be appraised, from the low awareness that existed throughout much of the early twentieth century to the present, when it is almost fashionable to claim that an individual is 'a little bit OCD'.

The chapter will then examine what distinguishes 'normal' obsessions and compulsions from those that are detrimental to the individual and their functioning. Finally, the chapter explores how obsessions and compulsions may have evolved and how they may give the individual a biological advantage.

What Is OCD?

Obsessive compulsive disorder (OCD) is one of the most overlooked and frequently misdiagnosed conditions. People often talk about a friend or family member being 'obsessed' by a particular football team, a hobby, or a girlfriend/boyfriend. In addition, someone who is organised, works hard, and is generally neat and tidy may describe him- or herself, or be described by others, as 'slightly OCD'. The behaviours in these cases are often very different from the extreme symptoms with which many patients with OCD suffer.

A person with OCD has two major symptoms: obsessions and compulsions. Obsessions are troublesome and persistent thoughts, images, or impulses which appear in a person's mind and result in anxiety, horror, or disgust. Because these thoughts are often so unpleasant, the person will resist them and try to ignore them or force them away. Unfortunately, trying to push the thoughts away often results in them recurring more frequently. These obsessive and intrusive thoughts are generally the worst thoughts that the individual can imagine. For example, a religious person may have blasphemous thoughts; a gentle and loving parent may have images of harming their child; or a person with high moral standards may have worries that they have been acting in an inappropriate or sexual way towards another, despite evidence to the contrary.

Obsessive thoughts cause the person to be very anxious and uncomfortable. Normally, when a person is frightened, they will attempt to escape from the situation. In the case of anxiety-provoking thoughts, it is impossible to escape from them; as a result, a number of compulsions develop. Compulsions are thoughts or behaviours which are designed to reduce or prevent the harm of the obsessive thought. However, either they are not realistically linked with the obsession, or they are clearly excessive. Compulsions tend to reduce anxiety, and because high anxiety is unpleasant, the decrease in anxiety following the performance of a compulsion is rather like a reward to the individual. If you reward any behaviour, you increase the chances of it happening in similar circumstances in the future. This means that by causing a reduction in anxiety, the tendency to perform compulsions becomes stronger and the more they are repeated. In addition, compulsions will only slightly reduce anxiety over a short space of time, and so individuals will repeat the compulsive behaviours until they feel 'right' or until another thought distracts them.

Anne's Story

Anne is a 30-year-old married woman who used to work as a teaching assistant. She has always been a conscientious and **capable** woman, and she worked hard at her job. After giving birth to her daughter Lily at age 28 years, Anne became increasingly worried that she might 'poison' Lily with dirt and germs, which would result in Lily becoming ill or dying. Most mothers worry about cleanliness around a baby, but in Anne's case, this quickly got out of control. She was not content with using sterilising fluid on Lily's utensils; rather, she would repeat the action many times. In addition, she began to wash her hands increasingly, until she was eventually washing them more than 100 times a day. Once Lily was mobile and walking around, Anne began to clean every area where Lily might play and then began to prevent Lily from playing outside. Anne realised that her concerns were excessive, but due to her overwhelming anxiety, she was unable to ignore her thoughts and she felt the urge to 'play safe' by performing her compulsive rituals.

In Anne's situation, her compulsions are linked to her desire to be a good mother, but her worries and her 'decontamination' compulsions are excessive and beyond normal cleanliness. This **overconcern** about Lily is restricting Lily's ability to play, learn, and explore the world.

Amy's Story

Amy is a 25-year-old woman who fears that she might cause a catastrophic fire if she does not ensure she has turned off all electrical appliances and the gas cooker. After using appliances, she repeatedly checks that they are switched off, returning up to 50 times. In the past two years, she has tried to avoid using all electrical or gas appliances and asks her mother, with whom she lives, to use these for her. If she does have to use an appliance, she will repeatedly ask her mother for reassurance that she has not caused a fire. Her mother will reassure her, but a few minutes later, Amy will ask again, and this can continue for many hours until Amy has a new worry. If Amy's mother refuses to answer her questions, Amy becomes extremely tearful and upset, and her mother will then relent and give her the reassurance.

Amy's story shows that compulsions can sometimes take the form of reassurance seeking. Just like checking, counting, and decontamination compulsive rituals, these activities can also slightly reduce anxiety. Because high anxiety is unpleasant, this reduction in anxiety is similar to a reward. If any behaviour is 'rewarded', the chance that it will reoccur in similar circumstances increases. This means that the compulsions increase the more they are repeated. By providing reassurance, Amy's mother is trying to help her daughter and alleviate her distress, but is accidentally making the situation worse.

Jim's Story

Jim is a 35-year-old man who has always wanted to ensure that he does the 'right' thing, and he prides himself on holding high moral standards. He was popular in school and left school having passed his exams. There were no **obvious** signs of OCD during his early life and he had close friends, although he had never formed a lasting sexual relationship.

Jim has worked as a security guard since leaving school, and he managed well until four years ago. At that time, Jim read about some high-profile celebrities who had been involved in child sexual abuse. Jim was appalled and shocked by these revelations and was clear that he believed such behaviour was 'evil'. However, he began to check that he himself had not inadvertently sexually assaulted a child. These concerns have led him to completely avoid any place where there may be children. Parks, roads with schools or nurseries, and even buses at peak times before and after school have become 'out of bounds' for Jim. If he does unexpectedly see a child, he will tightly squeeze his hands into fists, cross his arms across his body, and stand totally still until they leave.

This behaviour is an attempt to ensure that he does not 'lurch at the child and assault them'. Once they have passed, he still doubts himself and repeatedly taps his right foot on the ground in multiples of 20 until he feels sure he remained motionless on the spot when the child went past. Occasionally, he has been stuck in this position for 15–20 minutes after seeing a child.

Jim realises that this behaviour is unconnected with his fears, and he understands that he has not attacked a child. Nonetheless, the fear is so great that he feels compelled to perform the compulsive foot tapping. Occasionally, he has placed himself in danger as a result of this behaviour by becoming 'stuck' in the middle of busy roads. The OCD has also resulted in Jim having to stop working due to his attempt to avoid children.

In the case of Jim, it is clear that the obsessional thoughts are completely abhorrent to him, and he is the opposite of someone who would enjoy sexually abusing children because he finds the thought so awful. His behaviours to avoid this are excessive and, in the case of the foot-tapping compulsion, are not actually connected with the obsessive fear. In addition, Jim's story demonstrates his increasing avoidance and restriction of daily activities due to OCD.

People with OCD tend to progressively avoid objects or situations which provoke the obsessive thoughts. Due to this avoidance, their lives can become increasingly more restricted and limited. This is demonstrated through the personal stories in this chapter. Anne increasingly handed over some of her childcare responsibilities to either her mother or her husband as her fears progressed. Amy increasingly stopped using electrical appliances and demanded her mother cook and switch off appliances for her. Jim's life became increasingly restricted as he avoided all areas where children and young people might be present.

But We All Have Some OCD, Don't We?

Most of us experience some kind of obsessions and compulsions. Many people will, for example, throw salt over their left shoulder in response to spilling salt, due to a European belief that this will scare the devil away. Others will salute or cross their fingers if they see a solitary magpie, which has traditionally been linked with sorrow. These behaviours are similar to obsessions and compulsions, but they tend not to be repetitive and also do not cause extreme distress or interfere with a person's ability to perform normal activities of daily living.

Obsessive thoughts have been experienced by many of us when standing on the top of a high building or on the platform as a train is about to arrive and we suddenly have the thought or urge that we may throw ourselves over the side. This thought is unpleasant, and we may take a step back. Similarly, most of us have experienced sudden violent or inappropriate sexual thoughts. Generally, we will have these thoughts and then dismiss them as being 'stupid' or 'inappropriate' and forget about them. It appears that most people with OCD are not able to do this. Many will have a thought and find it so overwhelmingly unpleasant or worrying that they try very hard to never have that thought again. Of course, once you try *not* to have a thought, the thought will continue happening as you keep it in your mind.

The fact that all of us experience some obsessions and may perform some compulsions shows that along with many other psychological and mental disturbances, OCD is on a spectrum. Although it is not difficult to recognise that people who are spending almost all their time preoccupied by their obsessive fears and compulsive rituals have a problem, people often ask the question, 'When is OCD a problem that needs help?' The answer to this question depends on the individual. OCD traits seem to be at least partially genetically inherited. Some of the traits that many OCD patients have – being conscientious, meticulous, and punctual – are clearly an advantage in life. There is no mystery in the fact that many sufferers of OCD have been highly successful as doctors, nurses, accountants, lawyers, secretaries, journalists, and in many other professions which require high attention to detail and the ability to concentrate well for hours on end.

It is easy to see that there may be a biological advantage to humans to have some obsessive traits. Avoidance of excrement and disgust, for example, are traits which humans share with many other animals. From the Stone Age (or even earlier), an individual who avoided faeces would clearly have a biological advantage over one who did not. Similarly, someone who was persistent and meticulous would also often have an advantage in survival terms over someone who was not. However, it is when these traits become overwhelming and take over every other aspect of the individual's life that the issue becomes a problem.

Geoff's Story

Geoff is a 25-year-old man whose parents were both doctors; his mother worked as a general practitioner, and his father was an orthopaedic surgeon. The family has three children. The eldest child, George, is a solicitor working in a successful law firm. Molly, the middle child, is an academic historian working at a prestigious university. Geoff was similarly a high-achieving scholar in the early years of his schooling but began to fail to achieve predicted grades once he reached the age of 13. His parents were concerned at the time, and Geoff was seen by a child psychologist.

Not wishing to admit to the problems he was experiencing, Geoff denied any difficulties, despite the evidence to the contrary. The family was offered therapy, and Geoff's teachers believed he was experiencing 'adolescent rebellion'. In fact, Geoff had become concerned that he had to get everything perfect and correct or else he would feel a failure. He was not able to describe what 'being a failure' may constitute except that it was a 'terrible, bad thing' and that his family and friends 'would not respect' him. Occasionally, he admits that he believes that not being perfect would lead to him being abandoned by everyone he loves. He finds this thought so frightening that he becomes paralysed with fear, checking that everything he does is performed 100 per cent correctly. For example, he was meticulous at school with his handwriting and, consequently, he was predicted to easily pass his school examinations with the highest grades. However, he failed or gained borderline grades due to his meticulous attention to detail, resulting in his inability to complete the examinations within the allotted time.

As the years passed and his fear of failure continued, his symptoms worsened. Currently, he is unable to perform any activity without extreme distress. Washing and bathing take up to eight hours as he tries to ensure that he washes his body perfectly. Consequently, he has given up his daily bath and now showers when he believes he 'has the time'. This has meant that he has not bathed for more than six months. Similarly, his fingernails and toenails are long and curled because he cannot bear to make a mistake when trimming them. His hair is matted and unkempt; he cannot visit the hairdresser as he would worry that the barber had not cut his hair perfectly straight. Geoff has a long, straggly beard because he is unable to attempt shaving; he makes a sharp contrast with his pristine and well-groomed parents and siblings.

SUMMARY

The history of Geoff shows that his high-achieving and slightly perfectionist family members all managed to succeed in life in spite of, or maybe because of, these characteristics. Geoff, on the other hand, became so caught up in perfectionism that it has impaired his ability to function in activities of daily living and his ability to work. It is clear to everyone that Geoff's fear of performing an action imperfectly means that he is far from perfect – the situation he is fearful of! This 'all-or-nothing' or 'black-and-white' thinking is frequently observed in people with a desire to achieve perfection. They seem unable to compromise and are happier to accept the state of total failure rather than try to perform an action and risk not doing it perfectly. In other words, they seem unable to find the 'happy medium' and be 'good enough' rather than perfect. Realistically, perfection is not a normal human state, and anyone who seeks to achieve it is likely to fall short to some degree. It is more realistic to try to arrive at a happy compromise of being 'fit for purpose'!

KEY POINTS

- Obsessive compulsive disorder (OCD) consists of obsessions and compulsions.
- Obsessions are thoughts, ideas, images, or impulses which are deeply unpleasant and result in increased anxiety or distress.
- Compulsions are thoughts or actions which are designed to reduce or prevent the effect of the obsession. However, either they are not realistically related to obsessive fear or they are clearly excessive. Many patients seek repeated reassurance from their friends, family, or others as a form of compulsive behaviour.
- Avoidance is also frequently seen in people with OCD. People will often progressively avoid objects and situations which may provoke the OCD thoughts. The consequence of this avoidance is that the individual may live an increasingly restricted life and may end up unable to work or socially very isolated.
- The symptoms of both obsessions and compulsions are found in the general population amongst people who do not necessarily suffer from OCD. The difference between obsessions and compulsions in OCD and these more 'normal' obsessions and compulsions is that they do not take over the person's life, nor do they restrict the person's ability to achieve their life aims.

2

• • • • • • •

Who Gets OCD and How Would Anyone Know if They Had It?

We will now examine who can develop OCD and why this might happen. We will look at population data on OCD. The role of inheritance, genetics, and possible environmental factors will be discussed, as well as the idea of developing resilience. Next, we will explore OCD throughout the life cycle. OCD is a common disorder in childhood and seems to have some differences compared to adult-onset OCD. Following a discussion of OCD in childhood or early adult life, we will look at how the pattern changes throughout the years and into middle and old age. A frequent time for development of OCD in younger women is at times of pregnancy and childbirth. This will be discussed in detail in Chapter 7.

This chapter will also examine how culture may have an effect on the presentation of OCD. For example, all religions involve ritual and symbolic behaviours which have some similarities to OCD but generally do not take over a person's life. When OCD features religious ideas, other members of the same religion can often distinguish that the person with OCD is taking this to an extreme.

Who Gets OCD?

In Chapter 1, we briefly discussed the role that inheritance may play in developing OCD and how some obsessive traits may be helpful in developing a successful life path. In the case of OCD, the obsessions and compulsions become overwhelming and interfere with the person's life objectives, aims, and ambitions. OCD can affect people of any gender and of any social class, race, nationality, or religion.

Many years ago, OCD was thought to be a rare condition. Large population studies performed in the 1980s showed that this was untrue and that two or three per cent of the population suffer from OCD during their lifetime. Of course, estimating the prevalence of OCD is not an easy task. Many people with OCD are ashamed and embarrassed by their condition and will go to great lengths to try to hide it rather than admit to problems. It has been found that some people with OCD may resist seeking help for decades. In addition, population studies may run the risk of including people with mild obsessions and compulsions which do not interfere with their lives, and this may falsely increase the numbers. Generally, it seems that the figure of two or three per cent of the population is accurate for most societies.

Population studies generally suggest that women with OCD outnumber men with OCD by a ratio of 1.5:1. The interesting twist in this fact is that with regard to hospital, clinic, and professional referrals, more men than women are referred for help. This may be because men tend to have more severe conditions compared to women. Alternatively, it might be that men's absences from work are more likely to be noticed than women's absences. Women more frequently have washing compulsions and avoidance, whereas men more frequently have checking compulsions or complex thought compulsions. Of course, these trends, based on large populations of people with OCD, do not mean that a woman cannot have the most profound OCD with thought compulsions or that a man cannot have washing rituals; they simply demonstrate overall trends in the population.

The average age of onset of OCD is approximately 20 years. However, there does appear to be a peak of development of OCD around or just before puberty and then a much larger peak of onset in early adult life. Men are more likely to report that their OCD started in their early teens, whereas women more commonly have an onset in their early twenties. These figures are averages, and OCD does occur at extremely young ages and also at older ages. It is quite rare for OCD to develop without any earlier symptoms after the age of 40 years, and in such cases, further tests are usually advisable to ensure there are no other complications.

Until recently, it was thought to be unusual for children to suffer from OCD. Now it is known that OCD is, in fact, one of the most common mental disorders in childhood and may affect up to five per cent of children and adolescents. The clinical presentation in childhood is similar to that seen in adults. Again, boys tend to develop the condition earlier than girls. The prognosis for OCD in childhood is generally better than that for adults.

Maternal OCD

Most women are concerned about the wellbeing of their child. This concern is often the most obvious during pregnancy and immediately after the birth of a baby. However, pregnancy and childbirth is also a common time for women to develop OCD. Some mothers develop contamination fears and are extra careful that their child is kept in a scrupulously clean environment or away from any perceived contaminants. The effect of this may be to limit the usual play of young toddlers. Others may develop fear of harm occurring to the family and repeatedly check windows, gas and electrical appliances, doors, and light switches. Others may have distressing intrusive images of harming their child which can have an effect on the relationship with the child. In short, the type of OCD which develops around the time of pregnancy and childbirth is as varied as any OCD. Psychological treatment is discussed in the relevant chapters and there is no difference in the type of psychological therapy used to treat pregnant women or new mothers. With medication, however, it is always best to obtain a more specialist opinion. The drugs most commonly used for OCD (see Chapter 4) are known as selective serotonin reuptake inhibitors or SSRIs. These have a small risk to the baby in pregnancy and breastfeeding. Overall, the current knowledge suggests that there is no association with these drugs and deformities or illness in babies exposed to them. The major risk is that they can make bleeding more likely, and this could present a problem during delivery if the mother bleeds heavily. Due to changes in the mother's body during pregnancy, the normal dose of SSRI may be less effective. There is some suggestion that babies of mothers who take SSRIs are more prone to an increase in breathing difficulties and may be more jittery for a while after birth. For breast feeding, sertraline seems to be the drug of choice, as it has been shown to have little effect on the child. If possible, you may be advised not to take drugs at all, but the decision needs to be made individually, weighing up the small risk to the baby against the risk to both of more severe OCD. Extreme OCD can have a detrimental effect on the child as well as the mother, and so it is important for both that treatment is obtained as early as possible. The decision about medication can only be made with full discussion with your doctor. Children should be able to socialise and play normally and to meet friends. In the main, children are resilient, but the full wellbeing of a child must always be considered.

If Someone in My Family Has OCD, Does That Mean I Will Get It?

The issue of genetics and psychological problems and mental illness is a complex one. Most conditions are not caused by a single gene but, rather, are 'multifactorial'. In other words, the characteristics may run in families, but not everyone in a family will suffer from the condition. The same is true for OCD. What also appears to be true is that even if an individual inherits a very strong chance of suffering from OCD, it is not guaranteed that he or she will develop the condition. Increasingly, research seems to show that the way in which genes express themselves can be modified by external events. Some people, even within the same family, appear more prone than others to developing problems. This resilience seems likely to be partly inherited and partly a result of upbringing and early life experience. In the past, parents often took responsibility for causing their offspring's psychological problems due to poor parenting. This is clearly unfair and not the case. Parents share some of their genes with their offspring, and so parenting styles are partly influenced by their own genetic makeup and personality. Second, although it appears likely that a warm, loving family environment may provide the offspring with somewhat greater resilience, this can never be absolute. People from the very best families who have received an abundance of warmth, love, and the best parenting can still develop psychological problems. Genes are still the main deciding factor.

Not even the happiest and most loving family experience can completely prevent OCD from occurring in some individuals. The pattern of age of onset for OCD reflects this idea. Most adult patients with OCD develop it in early adult life and often in association with a major negative life event. In these cases, it may be reasonable to assume that the individual had a high genetic susceptibility to OCD and that, due to the individual's resilience, it took a major life event for OCD to be manifest; that the individual had moderate genetic susceptibility to OCD and poor resilience; or that the individual had a low susceptibility to OCD, and an extremely traumatic life event, coupled with low resilience, which resulted in OCD. Therefore, it can be seen that factors which may determine whether or not an individual develops OCD include their genetic makeup, resilience (which is likely to be due to both genetics and early life nurturing), and the scale and impact of the negative life event.

A smaller but still significant number of adults with OCD develop it before puberty. These individuals are slightly more likely to be male rather than female. It has also been noted that they may have some specific neurological signs which do not interfere with normal functioning but may suggest high genetic loading for OCD.

What Will Happen If You Do Develop OCD?

Many children who develop OCD go on to recover; OCD is one of the most common psychological problems seen in childhood. Most children will experience a phase of OCD-like behaviours which will resolve in time. Other children go on to develop OCD, but the prognosis is extremely good. Apart from the small group of individuals who go on to develop long-standing OCD into adulthood, most children who are treated for OCD respond well and recover completely. Treatment for childhood OCD is mostly psychological, but short-term drug use can also be helpful for some children.

The course that OCD takes when untreated is variable. Some people may have occasional, discrete episodes interspersed with periods during which they are symptom-free. These episodes are often precipitated by stress surrounding a major life event, such as bereavement, illness, pregnancy, or loss of a job. Some people with apparent very late-onset OCD may develop this after retirement, but careful examination of the life history can show that there may have been previous short-lived episodes of OCD or strong OCD tendencies which were controlled by the discipline of working. Other people develop OCD and it remains at a similar level for many years until successfully treated. Another group of people may have OCD which is consistently present, but which waxes and wanes throughout the years; sometimes these variations are related to life circumstances at the time, and sometimes they are apparently unrelated. Finally, a small group develops OCD which becomes increasingly restrictive over the years. The content of the obsessions in all types of OCD may change throughout the years, or in some cases it will remain consistent.

Because many people with OCD often do not seek help for years or even decades, fewer of them are married or in cohabiting relationships than would be expected based on their age. Many people with OCD live alone, and a significant number live with their parents. OCD can sometimes be a strain on families and relationships because they feel the need to comply with the OCD 'rules' of their family member. The prime consideration must always be the wellbeing of any children. Everyone involved with a person with OCD needs to ensure that children are free to have as happy and carefree lives as possible and can play normally inside and outside the home and interact with their peers. Some people with OCD live with aging parents, who are called on to perform functions to help their children at an age when they would normally be more independent.

Fred's Story

Fred is a 45-year-old man who has suffered from OCD with fear of contamination for 25 years. He lives with his 85-year-old parents. Due to his OCD, Fred believes he is unable to shower himself because he thinks he may not do it 'sufficiently'. He insists that his parents shower him once a week. These showers must be performed according to Fred's strict OCD 'rules'. When his parents refuse to comply with these 'rules', Fred becomes angry and threatening.

Fred's story shows how the family, as well as the sufferer, can become completely enveloped in OCD. It is never acceptable for an individual to be coerced into performing OCD compulsive rituals for another person. Violence and threats cannot be tolerated. The problem is often that family members of the person with OCD may feel guilty about their son's or daughter's plight, wrongly thinking it is their 'fault'. Most parents do not like to see their offspring suffer and so will start to perform some of the compulsive rituals for them in the hope of easing the distress. Unfortunately, this help can escalate until the whole family is 'imprisoned' by the OCD, which can increase the symptoms of the person with OCD. Family members are best to encourage a patient to seek professional help and treatment, for both their own sake, and the person with OCD.

As well as fewer people with OCD being married or living with a partner, fewer are employed compared to the general population of the same age. Some people have OCD and work in jobs in which some minor OCD traits may appear to be an advantage. These traits can also frequently get out of control.

Jenny's Story

Jenny, a 20-year-old student nurse, has recently become extremely concerned that she may cause an infection to spread to a patient in her current placement on an elderly ward. The hospital has strict policy guidance about staff hand washing and the use of protective gowns and gloves when handling bodily fluids. However, Jenny fears these do not go far enough. She insists on wearing a new pair of gloves for every activity, which is beyond the hospital guidance on infection control. If she has to prepare a sterile trolley for a doctor to perform a blood test, she will take up to an hour to ensure it is clean and sterile. Rather than just cleaning the surface once, she will repeatedly clean the trolley until she believes it is 'just right'. Although at first the more senior staff believed Jenny would settle into the job and become less anxious, the charge nurse is now planning to fail her for this placement due to her slowness and overly meticulous behaviour.

George's Story

George is a 30-year-old architect. He is studious and hard-working and is generally appreciated by his boss. For the past ten years, George has been overly concerned that he may make an error which would result in either a catastrophic problem with a building he has been working on or lead to him losing his job. George arrives at work at 7:00 a.m. every morning, which is two hours before he is due at work. He rarely leaves work before 7:00 p.m., and even then, he tends to take home files and work on his computer at home, checking and rechecking his calculations repeatedly. On weekends, he generally works 15–18 hours a day, checking and rechecking his work. Due to these excessive hours, he often fails to eat or drink sufficiently and has found that he feels permanently exhausted and cannot sleep well at night. Despite working the extra hours, George has not yet been noted to have any difficulty by his work colleagues, who are unaware of the number of hours he is working.

These examples demonstrate how OCD can impact the working environment. In Jenny's case, she is too slow and careful to perform her job usefully. George is performing well and the amount of time he works is currently unknown by his superiors, but his excessive working hours are impacting on his general health and wellbeing.

Is OCD New and Caused by Modern Society? What about Religion and Culture?

OCD is not a modern-day disease of the Western world; rather, there is evidence of its existence in historical figures as well as across all cultures. John Bunyan, the author of *Pilgrim's Progress*, was born in 1628, and it has been suggested that he may have suffered from OCD. In his spiritual autobiography, Bunyan, a strict Christian, describes blasphemous thoughts repeatedly entering his mind. He found these thoughts deeply abhorrent and repeatedly tried to distract himself or to 'put this right' by saying he did not mean these thoughts. A more modern example is that of the famous film producer, aviator, aircraft manufacturer, successful businessman, and playboy, Howard Hughes. He suffered from obsessions concerning his health and fear of death. Despite being a multimillionaire, he became increasingly concerned about his health and developed an extreme lifestyle. Ultimately, he lived the life of a recluse, living in a bare room with no clothes and eating and drinking at starvation levels. This self-neglect may have led to a hastening of his death at the age of 71 years.

OCD has been found in very different cultures throughout the world. There have been reports of OCD with similar characteristics and a similar prevalence amongst the Han population in China and the ultra-Orthodox Jewish population in Israel, as well as similar reports from Iran, India, and Western countries. The detailed content of the obsessions may vary from culture to culture – for example, it has been noted that the ultra-Orthodox Jewish person with OCD tends to have obsessions related to religious teachings – but the forms these obsessions take are indistinguishable throughout the world.

In the past, it was often argued that certain religious upbringings may lead to OCD. There is no evidence that this is true. There does seem to be a tendency for people with OCD to be attracted to more dogmatic branches of religions, in which there is a firm stance on what is 'right' and what is 'wrong', rather than more philosophical beliefs, in which there is less certainty. OCD is not, however, related to any specific religion; it has been reported in Christians, Muslims, Jews, Hindus, Buddhists, Confucians, and Taoists, as well as atheists and agnostics. It was once thought that the religions themselves may precipitate OCD. This was first reported in Italy, where a higher proportion of people with OCD were found in religious orders than in the outside population. However, it seems more likely that people with OCD were more attracted to the certainty and security of religious life rather than the religion itself being a causal factor. All religions have ritualistic and symbolic aspects which may resemble OCD. Some people with OCD believe that their religion requires them to carry out their OCD behaviours. Overall, it seems that whereas some people with OCD-like tendencies or even real OCD may be attracted to the stricter forms of religion, there is no evidence that any religion causes OCD. Religions with a more rigid 'black-and-white' approach to life seem to be particularly attractive to some people with OCD compared to religions with a more philosophical approach. People who practise religions and adhere to various religious rituals can generally be distinguished from people who perform their OCD compulsions to excess within their religions.

Emma's Story

Emma is a 45-year-old woman with a 30-year history of OCD. She worries that she may have harmed others and constantly checks to ensure that this is not the case. In addition, she constantly asks for reassurance from family and friends that she has not committed the heinous act she is currently worrying about. If she reads about a terrible murder in the papers or sees a news bulletin describing such an event, she will check that she was not in the vicinity of the event and will then ask for repeated reassurance from her husband or others around her at the time that she did not commit the act. This is extremely difficult for her husband, who frequently is asked for reassurance for four or five hours at a time after he returns home from work. In the past, Emma frequently telephoned the police to 'confess' her guilt, even though she based her confessions on only sketchy media reports about the crimes. She realises that she has no memory of the events but worries that she may have forgotten them. The police no longer pay any attention to her 'confessions', but on one occasion they took up the floorboards of her house because she was worried she may have murdered a man and hidden him there.

After many years of this behaviour, Emma resisted all offers of therapy but was befriended by a member of a local church. Emma began to attend the church, whose members believed in spiritual healing. Part of the spiritual healing involved not only other church members praying intensely for one to be healed but also public confession of one's sins. Emma became a regular attendee at these confession sessions, where she tended to dominate the proceedings with her current worries of crimes she may have committed. At first, the church was welcoming and tried to accommodate her. Soon, the members realised that she had a serious psychological problem. The minister approached her and suggested that she get referred for treatment. She was also told that although she was still most welcome to attend church, she was no longer welcome at the public confession sessions.

The story of Emma shows how a particular aspect of religion can become very attractive to someone with OCD. It also demonstrates that regular worshippers are able to identify a person who is taking the religion too far and needs help. People have been advised to seek help from a variety of religions when following religious rituals excessively. It may be useful for the therapist to work in conjunction with the local priest, mullah, minister, vicar, or rabbi with the consent of the person with OCD to ensure that treatment is truly in accordance with appropriate religious beliefs.

KEY POINTS

- Although once thought to be a rare condition, OCD affects two to three per cent of the population and is therefore a very common disorder.
- Both men and women can be affected by OCD, and overall, the gender ratio is approximately equal.
- Most people develop OCD in early adult life and often, but not always, following a negative life event.
- A smaller but significant number of adults with OCD developed it in childhood, usually just before puberty.
- OCD is also a very common childhood problem.
- Children with OCD have a better prognosis than adults, and the vast majority respond extremely well to treatment.
- OCD tends to run in families, but it is not a straightforward inheritance pattern. Both genes and life experiences may have a role in precipitating OCD symptoms.
- OCD can present during pregnancy or after childbirth and is known as Maternal OCD.
- Maternal OCD is very similar to any other type of OCD in its symptoms.
- Treatment of Maternal OCD is identical to any OCD with respect to psychological treatment, but drug treatment is best discussed with your doctor. However, the risks of drug treatment are very small.
- OCD is not a new condition, and historical figures throughout the ages have been described with what we recognise as OCD.
- OCD can often appear to be similar to religious rituals. Members of a faith can generally distinguish when an individual is taking the religion 'too far'. Strict religious orders of any faith may attract people with OCD, but there is no evidence that religion causes OCD.
- It may be useful for therapists to work collaboratively with a prominent member of the person with OCD's religious group if he or she would like this to occur.

3

· · · · · · ·

Types and Presentation of OCD

Obsessive compulsive disorder can present in many forms, but the most common symptoms of OCD feature one or more of a number of 'themes'. These themes will be described in detail and illustrated with examples of people's personal experience. The main themes are:

- Contamination fears
- Fear of harm to others due to failure to act appropriately
- Fear of harm to self or others due to your own actions (or thoughts)
- Perfectionism
- Worry about losing something
- Symmetry
- Slowness
- Ruminations

The idea of 'magical thinking', whereby a person fears that by thinking a thought they make it more likely to occur, will also be described. Thought–action fusion, whereby a thought is believed to be morally equivalent to an action, will also be examined.

The final part of this chapter will examine other conditions which can occur alongside OCD, including physical complications arising from self-neglect such as infection. Other psychological problems and their relationship with OCD will also be explored and will include examination of depression, anxiety disorders, the obsessive-compulsive spectrum disorders, autistic spectrum disorders, and schizophrenia.

Types of OCD

There are several themes which encompass all types of obsessive thoughts and compulsive rituals. The content of these thoughts may change over time in a person. The common themes of OCD also change depending on current news items and what is happening in the person's environment. For example, fear of contamination may frequently feature fear of HIV, whereas this would not have been the case prior to the 1980s. Similarly, someone who was previously concerned about general dirt and germs for fear of becoming ill may change this to specific fears relating to their offspring once they have children.

Contamination Fears

Contamination fears are one of the most common forms of OCD. In these cases, the person worries that either they will fall ill or they will cause others to fall ill, or they may feel 'unclean' and not 'right' if they believe they have been contaminated by dirt or germs. Some people fear specific infections such as HIV or bacteria that may cause vomiting, diarrhoea, or tuberculosis; for some people, the fear is a worry about general dirt and germs.

Joyce's Story

Joyce is a 36-year-old mother of twins aged six years. Following a difficult pregnancy, the twins were born prematurely and had to be nursed in a special care baby unit. Understandably, this was a very difficult time for Joyce and her family as there was a risk the twins would not survive. Both twins did recover, and now they are typically energetic and healthy children. However, Joyce has an extreme concern that she might **cause** them to become ill unless she keeps everything in their home scrupulously clean. Consequently, she washes her hands up to 100 times a day, cleans the wood floors in her house with a diluted bleach mixture daily, and has a prolonged and exaggerated showering regime which takes up to an hour. She has been unable to cook for the children since they were babies because she is so fearful she might infect them. Fortunately, her mother lives locally and prepares the children's evening meal when they return from school and also their lunch when they are not at school. Joyce allows the children to pour their own cereal and milk in the mornings as long as she has disinfected the cupboard and refrigerator the day before. Joyce recognises these worries are excessive and unfounded, but she still feels extremely anxious.

The story of Joyce's OCD development shows how it arose following a very difficult time when there was a real risk to her children's lives, but now her fear persists and is mainly focussed on dirt and germs which she worries that she may spread to the children. She is able to trust her mother and others, including her husband and the teachers at school, not to infect the children, and she realises that her fears are both irrational and exaggerated.

Mick's Story

Mick is a 25-year-old man with a ten-year history of OCD featuring fear and avoidance of dirt and germs. At school, he was bullied for wearing glasses and being short for his age. He developed what he called 'self-preservation' strategies which were to always ensure he was extremely clean. Over the years, this developed into an extreme fear of his own urine and faeces and avoidance of any situation in which he might come into contact with other people's waste products, such as public toilets. Mick takes up to an hour to pass urine as he needs to ensure that no drop of urine has landed on himself or his surroundings. Moving his bowels takes up to two hours as he feels the need to ensure that his bowels are completely empty and that he is perfectly clean. Due to his problems, Mick restricts his food and fluid intake to reduce the number of times he needs to visit the toilet. Unlike many people with fear of urine and faeces, Mick denies he is anxious about becoming ill or spreading infection, but he explains his feelings of disgust about his bodily functions and how he feels 'morally superior' when he has completed his decontamination compulsive rituals to his satisfaction.

The story of Mick shows that very similar obsessions with urine and faeces can actually be related to very different thought processes. In Mick's case, his fear is very akin to that of people with perfectionistic OCD in that he fears being 'imperfect' or unclean.

Marie's Story

Marie is a 45-year-old woman with a long history of OCD dating back to her early twenties. The form this has taken has varied over the years. Initially, she had a fear of general dirt and germs, but during the past five years this has altered to a fear of contracting the HIV virus. In the past, Marie controlled her anxiety by drinking alcohol excessively to the point that she was consuming cheap wine or any other alcohol she could afford every day. While in a drunken state, she would sleep with men she had just met in exchange for them cleaning her bathroom and toilet. Five years ago, she had a health scare when she vomited blood and was told that she would die within five years unless she stopped drinking alcohol. She was sent for alcohol detoxification followed by rehabilitation, and she has been teetotal since that time. Once sober, she had an HIV test, which was found to be clear. However, Marie's OCD then focussed on concerns about contracting HIV. Avoiding public toilets and places where there might have been drug users (for fear of used syringes and needles), Marie began to limit the areas in London which she would visit. Her fear has now spread so that anything red, which she associates with blood, causes extreme anxiety. The local genito-urinary medicine clinic has asked her not to attend as she has been requesting weekly HIV tests.

The story of Marie shows how the content of OCD can change over time. She still has contamination fears, but these are now specific to HIV. Marie does not perform excessive decontamination compulsive rituals, but instead she tends to avoid areas that she fears may be frequented by drug users. She also avoids places where there may be openly gay people. In addition, she seeks medical reassurance by asking for repeated blood tests to check if she has HIV.

Fear of Harm to Self or Others Due to Acts of Omission

Fear of causing harm to self or others by failing to perform safety checks, or by failure to act, is another common obsessive theme. Some people fear their house may be burgled, which leads them to repetitively check doors and windows. Others fear they might inadvertently leave an electrical or gas appliance switched on which could result in harm and which leads to repetitive checking of electrical and gas appliances or even light switches. Some people with OCD assume extreme responsibility for others and may repeatedly report minor issues to the authorities.

Ayesha's Story

Ayesha is a 30-year-old married woman who has an eight-year history of fear that her house might be burgled. She lives with her husband and five children in a four-bedroom detached house in an affluent suburb. Her concern is that a burglar might enter the house while the family is sleeping or relaxing and that this will result in an attack on her children, her husband, or herself. As a result of this fear, Ayesha repeatedly walks around the house checking and pulling on the doors and windows to ensure they are firmly closed. Repeatedly checking in this way has caused her to break door handles on several occasions due to the force she uses. She even walks around the house four or five times each night after a prolonged session of checking before going to bed. These night-time checks tend to wake the family, and consequently the entire family is exhausted. Interestingly, Ayesha does not feel the need to check the doors or windows repeatedly when the entire family goes out together – for example, on holiday – as it is only when a family member is in the house that she fears they will be physically harmed. When on holiday, her symptoms tend to improve for a few days, but then she becomes worried about the security of the new environment and she starts to check doors and windows there.

Another example of someone with a fear that harm may occur is Amy (see Chapter 1), whose fear of causing a fire by failing to switch off electrical or gas appliances led to excessive checking and then avoidance of using such appliances as well as reassurance-seeking from her mother. Some people have more widespread fears.

Mohammed's Story

Mohammed is a 55-year-old man who lives on his own in a small flat. His mother, who is in her eighties, lives on an adjacent street. Mohammed worries that some type of disaster might happen to someone in his vicinity if he does not remain vigilant. An example of Mohammed's fears is that sometimes when he hears the squeal of car brakes at night, he will immediately leave his house to see if there has been an accident. If he does not find evidence of an accident (which has usually been the case), he travels to adjacent streets and often remains outside in all types of weather for two or three hours.

He is well known to the city council for repeatedly reporting overhanging trees, loose paving slabs, and kerbs which he considers too high and a risk. He is also well known to the fire brigade for reporting any perceived risk of fire, including piles of leaves in the street. This overly zealous behaviour has led him to come into conflict with the police, who consider him to be a time-waster, and he has been cautioned for wasting police time. Due to his concern that he will get into further trouble with the police if he continues to call them, Mohammed now reports all his findings to his mother and asks her repeatedly for reassurance that he is doing the correct thing by not reporting them to the police.

Mohammed's telephone calls to his mother can last several hours at a time, and he calls any time of the day or night. If his mother does not answer the telephone, Mohammed goes to her house and knocks on the door until he gets a reply. Once at the house, he generally refuses to leave until she agrees to accompany him to check on his latest concern. This behaviour is having a marked effect on an elderly and frail lady. Mohammed realises that the demands he makes on his mother are unreasonable, but he feels unable to resist.

The story of Mohammed shows how people who have severe OCD can come into conflict with the police, local authorities, or the neighbourhood in general. Whereas the underlying desire to prevent harm to others will appear an honourable one, the effect it causes in terms of wasted police time, when taken to excess, is also very clear. It also demonstrates how difficult OCD can be for the family of the individual. Mohammed's mother's health and wellbeing are being severely compromised by Mohammed's behaviour. When local health services have been involved, Mohammed was told that he should not call his mother more than once a day for a maximum of 30 minutes and should only visit her house at pre-arranged times. His mother was advised to call the police if unannounced visits were to keep re-occuring, and to consider raising an injunction against Mohammed. As a loving mother, she had resisted doing this as she did not want to cause Mohammed to get into more trouble.

Fear of Harm to Self or Others Due to Acts (or Thoughts) of Commission

Some people have intrusive thoughts, urges, or images of a terrible event happening or that they fear they may have committed or may perform.

These obsessions are similar to the sudden thought many people occasionally get when standing on a train platform to throw themselves in front of the train. The individual does not want to do this, but they feel as if their body may do it anyway.

A very distressing variant is images of harm occurring to loved ones. In these cases, the thoughts or images are very clear but are totally abhorrent to the individual.

Sabine's Story

Sabine is a 20-year-old woman who was studying law at Manchester University but has had to postpone her studies this year due to her overwhelming OCD. A year ago, soon after she started university, she began to have vivid and extremely distressing images of her close family members being involved in an accident, severely injured, or terminally ill. If she learns about an accident while watching television or listening to the radio, she immediately has a picture in her 'mind's eye' of the same thing happening to someone she loves. Stories of beheadings in the Middle East have led her to have intrusive images of her mother undergoing the same fate. Similarly, she recently saw a poster regarding cancer research and immediately had abhorrent intrusive images of her sister, thin and emaciated and dying painfully from cancer.

Although she realises that these types of thoughts are untrue, Sabine worries that her having the thoughts makes it likely that these events may occur. To guard against these terrible images coming true, Sabine will repeatedly say 'no' out loud whilst trying to imagine the same family member looking well or happy. Whilst performing these compulsive rituals, she will stand totally still and often remain in this position for up to 30 minutes, until she can achieve an image of the healthy person without any 'traumatic' images. As a result of these symptoms, Sabine avoids watching television, listening to the radio, or reading newspapers. Whilst at university, she avoided mixing with other students due to fear that they might mention something which would provoke her compulsive rituals. This resulted in her restricting attendance at lectures and tutorials, and when the module concerning criminal law was timetabled, Sabine was unable to attend any of these lectures, as this would provoke more images. It was agreed with the university that she should suspend her studies until her situation improves, and now Sabine has returned home to live with her family.

The story of Sabine demonstrates a fairly frequent finding in OCD which is known as 'magical thinking'. Although realising that the images are not true, Sabine fears that having the abhorrent images makes them more likely to happen. Although people will recognise that such thoughts do not make the reality more likely, there are in fact minor variants of this 'belief' found in most cultures. Many people are superstitious about naming certain good or bad events for fear that by speaking them out loud or even thinking them, they can alter the likelihood of their occurrence. For example, people often try to touch something made of wood whilst saying 'touch wood' after stating that something may happen. The reason for touching wood is to try to 'undo' the negative impact that thinking or stating aloud an outcome may have. The vast majority of people do not really believe that stating an outcome will affect the likelihood of its occurrence; nonetheless, many feel compelled to act in this way.

In Chapter 1, the story of Jim was told. Jim has unwanted thoughts and fears that he may be a paedophile, and he spends much of his waking time avoiding anywhere there may be children, as well as checking that he has not had any chance to touch children. In reality, Jim is extremely different from a person who is a paedophile and would be a risk to children. First, Jim finds the idea of sexually abusing children abhorrent, whereas people who do abuse children do not find their thoughts abhorrent, and indeed will often have excuses as to why their behaviour is 'appropriate'. Second, Jim goes to extreme lengths to avoid children, particularly anywhere he might be alone and in close proximity to children. Again, this is very different from the actions of a paedophile. Due to the intensity of his thoughts, Jim does worry that his health workers have made the wrong diagnosis and that unless he can make them understand, he may uncontrollably grab a child, even though this is something he would hate to do. Due to these thoughts, he has, on several occasions, tried to kill himself. Jim's entire history is different from that of a real child abuser. Unfortunately, people who have these obsessions can often be misunderstood when they claim they are worried about abusing children. In reality, people like Jim are almost the opposite of anyone who is a danger to children, because they will go to extreme lengths to ensure they are not.

Jim's story also demonstrates a phenomenon known as 'thought–action fusion'. This refers to an individual believing that having a thought is morally equivalent to performing an act. Although the thoughts of sexually abusing a child are totally repugnant to Jim, he still feels morally responsible for the distressing and hideous thoughts which come into his mind. In some religious teachings, it is stated that the individual must have pure thoughts to be free of sin. In the case of OCD, the effort of trying not to have these thoughts means that a person will have more of the thoughts. To demonstrate this, try to think about anything at all, but *do not* think about a pink hippopotamus *under any circumstances!* Once given this instruction, most people will immediately have an image or thought of a pink hippopotamus, and the more they try not to think of it, the more pressing it becomes. A similar circumstance occurs if you ever have a tune that you cannot stop playing over and over in your head, even when you actively dislike the tune and try to suppress it. You may try to not think of the tune, but the more you try, the more insistent it seems. The story of Eilidh also demonstrates how trying *not* to have a thought actually tends to increase its frequency.

Eilidh's Story

Eilidh is a 35-year-old woman who has frequent blasphemous thoughts which come into her mind and are shocking and abhorrent to her. Worried that these thoughts will result in her suffering eternal damnation, Eilidh tries to undo these thoughts by praying. She often spends up to five hours a day involved in these 'undoing prayers'.

Eilidh clearly has OCD, and the more she tries not to have blasphemous thoughts, the more they persist. Her story also demonstrates thought-action fusion, as she believes that she should be able to control her thoughts all the time and that the more she tries not to have blasphemous thoughts, the more they persist, and this is further evidence that she is 'evil'.

Perfectionism

It is not within human nature for things to be perfect at all times. Anyone who aims at total perfection in all things at all times is doomed to fail. Most of us can figure out when things are 'good enough' and will let that suffice instead of total perfection. It may be fair enough to believe in the old adage, 'If a thing is worth doing, it's worth doing well', but when someone tries all the time to be perfect, the end result is usually extreme tardiness and failure to achieve very much at all. The story of Geoff (see Chapter 1) illustrates a person with perfectionism, who due to this became crippled and unable to perform much at all. When referred to the clinic, he had not bathed for months and was unkempt and in a poor state of health and self-care because he could not tolerate being just 'good enough'. It is clear that Geoff was far from perfect in his current state. As noted, this 'black-and-white thinking' in OCD is reasonably common. Someone who tries to have a perfect house may at times find it too much to deal with and end up living in squalor.

Perfectionism often results in extreme slowness. The issue of obsessive slowness is discussed later in this chapter.

Loss of Objects

Fear of losing items or even fear of losing part of oneself is another frequent obsessive fear.

Ian's Story

Ian is a 35-year-old man who works as a kitchen porter. Although he has a long history of minor and occasional obsessive thoughts and compulsions, he had always been able to control these and get on with his life, until five years ago when his grandmother died at the age of 87. Ian had always been very fond of his grandmother and found it difficult to come to terms with her death.

Soon after her death, he began to worry about losing objects. Mostly this has taken the form of worrying that he may drop things from his pockets. Before leaving for work, he checks his trouser and jacket pockets to ensure they have no holes. Indeed, as a result of his checking behaviour, he has created holes in some of his clothing. When his trousers develop holes, he does not repair them as he believes the stitching may not be as robust as the original. Once he places items in his pockets, he counts how many items he has placed there and writes the number on his arm in ink. If this number wears off during the day, Ian will become extremely anxious. He also places three tissues folded in a set pattern on top of these objects to prevent them from falling out of his pockets. Although still able to work, Ian is concerned that this preoccupancy is interfering with his concentration at work.

The story of Ian demonstrates the fear of loss of objects. Although this fear apparently began in his thirties, it appears that Ian has a long-standing history of minor obsessive fears. The story of Geraldine is another example of a fear of losing things.

Geraldine's Story

Geraldine is a 45-year-old woman who lives alone. She has a long history of OCD, starting in her teens when she would worry about inadvertently losing personal information which might be used against her. This fear developed throughout the years until she would not **leave** the house with any pieces of paper in case they might provide information which would be detrimental to her or her future security. Unable to express what information this might be, she remained very fearful, even though she realised that this fear was unrealistic. Due to these problems, she has been unable to work as frequently as in the past because she feels unable to leave her house. She has also been unable to form close personal relationships as she fears that allowing someone into her house might result in her losing some information. Due to her inability to throw items away, she lives in a house which is in a severely hoarded state, and she is in danger of causing an avalanche of papers whenever she moves around. As she is living in a housing association flat, Geraldine is at risk of facing eviction due to the state of her property and the fire and health hazard it presents to herself and other residents.

Geraldine's story demonstrates how an imagined and unrealistic fear of losing personal information has meant that she now lives in real and tangible danger of losing her home and also placing her life at risk. This story also raises the question of hoarding.

Hoarding can be a symptom of many physical and psychological problems and will be discussed fully later in this book. There is also a condition, recently categorised as hoarding disorder. Unlike the situation with Geraldine, people with uncomplicated hoarding disorder do not have any underlying OCD fears, although many may have somewhat perfectionist personalities.

Some people go further than both Ian and Geraldine in their fear of losing objects and are unable to throw out urine and/or faeces without checking that they are not losing anything else first. This problem clearly has health and environmental implications and needs to be tackled with utmost urgency.

Symmetry

Problems with wanting to arrange objects symmetrically are frequently seen in people with autistic spectrum disorder which includes Asperger's syndrome. These topics are discussed towards the end of this chapter. Frequently, such apparent desire for symmetry in these patients is not true OCD, as the patient does not have any obsessive thoughts but just feels uncomfortable if things are not symmetrical.

Issues with symmetry can also arise in people with OCD. In these cases, a lack of symmetry is usually related to an obsessional thought.

Brian's Story

Brian is a 30-year-old man who works as a shop assistant in a major electrical store. He is good at his job and was recently promoted to supervisor. Since the promotion, he has started to worry that a disaster might happen and that he might forget to perform an important duty which may lead to his being dismissed. In order to prevent this disaster from happening, Brian feels the urge to arrange all items around him in pairs which are exactly parallel to each other. To enable this to hap- pen, there must always be at least two of every item in the store. Recently, he was reported to his manager as a customer wanted to buy a toaster. The toaster was one of two remaining in the store. If the customer bought the toaster, this would mean that only one toaster would remain. Generally, Brian will hide the single object until another one is delivered to the store. In this case, he was unable to hide the toaster because a new member of staff was 'shadowing' him for the day. Brian refused to sell the customer the toaster, claiming it to be faulty. The customer asked to buy the second one, which Brian also refused to sell. Suspicious that something was not right, the customer complained to the store manager.

In addition to demonstrating how someone can develop symmetry compulsions, Brian's story demonstrates the paradox of OCD. Brian is fearful of losing his job, but by acting on his compulsions aimed at reducing this likelihood, he actually increases the chances that he will be dismissed.

Slowness

In the past, obsessive slowness was suggested to consist of purely compulsions without any obsessive thoughts. In fact, people with OCD do have worrying obsessive thoughts, although these may have become forgotten with the passage of time. Most people with obsessive slowness have a desire to be perfect.

Lucia's Story

Lucia is a 19-year-old woman who lives with her extended family in a three-bedroom house. The family consists of three siblings, her parents, and her elderly grandmother. The house has one bathroom with a toilet in the same space.

Three years ago when Lucia was working towards her school exams, her mother noticed that Lucia seemed to be taking increasingly longer to perform simple tasks. She was working excessively and was taking longer to eat meals and spending a prolonged time in the bathroom. Her family initially thought that the behaviour was due to the stress of her examinations and that she would return to normal after they were over. In fact, Lucia performed much worse than expected on the examinations, and since then she has become slower in every action.

Currently, Lucia is unable to do more than basic self-care. Every morning she spends up to three hours getting dressed and then a further three hours in the toilet. Because it would take too long to complete, Lucia has not showered in months. Eating her meals, which her mother prepares for her, takes two hours, and so on many days she only manages one meal a day. She has started to restrict her drinking of fluids as going to the toilet takes her so long. The family is in crisis as Lucia's prolonged occupation of the bathroom and toilet means it is difficult for them to get to work. Her brothers often go to the local gym to shower, and the family has started using the public toilet in the local park. If anyone knocks on the toilet door, Lucia takes even longer to come out. Lucia says that unless she performs everything perfectly, she thinks she will be despised by her family and friends. She therefore feels the need to repeat every action until she is convinced she has performed it perfectly. If interrupted, for example by a knock on the toilet door, she has to go back to the beginning of her sequence of actions to ensure they are performed perfectly.

Lucia's story shows the paradox of perfectionism: in trying to be perfect, she is far from perfect and is a burden to her family. Indeed, the risk of being despised and arguing with her family is increased by her attempts to be perfect. Lucia realises that in trying to live up to her perfectionistic attempts, she is alienating her loved ones, but she feels helpless to stop. This story also emphasises how people with OCD can endanger their health by not eating and drinking sufficiently to ensure their health.

Ruminations

Any compulsion can be either an action or a thought. For example, some-one with contamination fears may either perform compulsive washing rituals or mentally go through evidence to disprove to themselves that what they have done is really a risk. When the compulsive ritual is an internal mental ritual, then the whole phenomenon can be described as rumination. Because this term often leads to confusion, I personally prefer to describe the content of the obsession rather than describe the OCD as 'rumination'.

Billy's Story

Billy is a 40-year-old man who spends up to six hours a day in obsessive ruminations. For the past 20 years, he has felt the need to rehearse his actions throughout the day at work to ensure he has not acted inappropriately or caused offense. During the day, he works well as a clerk and is good at his job. He tends to isolate himself from his workmates and does not mix with them socially, even at lunchtime and during coffee breaks. He isolates himself because the more contact he has, the more likely he is to worry he may have been socially inappropriate.

Billy lives alone in a rented flat and has been unable to maintain friendships since the onset of his worries. Once alone at home, he replays every social interaction he has had during the day and repeats it until he can reassure himself that he has not been inappropriate or caused offense. This behaviour generally takes six hours but can last longer if he thinks he may have done something 'wrong'. He describes himself as lonely and wishes he had a family but finds that due to the worry which follows any social interaction, he cannot mix with friends after work, and it has stopped him from seeking a partner.

Ruminations often cause confusion. The problem is that ruminations appear to be a person just thinking the same thing over and over. Ruminations can occur with depression when the individual is consumed by negative and worrying thoughts. Indeed, just as slowness was previously thought to be an example of pure compulsions without obsessions, ruminations have often been described as an example of obsessions without compulsions or 'pure obsessionality'. In OCD, however, ruminations consist of two parts: the anxiety-provoking, distressing obsessive thought followed by the anxiety-reducing compulsive thought. It can sometimes be difficult to distinguish these two types of thought as they can happen in quick succession so that even the person with the OCD thoughts can become confused about the nature of the thoughts. Careful analysis in OCD, however, will usually reveal that there are indeed these two components. Only rarely do there not seem to be clear compulsions, but in these cases, there is some other activity aimed at suppressing the thoughts which acts as an anxiety-reducing activity.

Are There Any Physical Risks in OCD?

Many people with severe OCD do neglect themselves and do not lead a healthy lifestyle, which can lead to a number of health problems or even an early death. One of the most frequent complications of contamination OCD is that the person washes to excess. This breaks down the skin's natural defences against infection. Again, the paradox of OCD is that people who fear contamination place themselves at greater risk of having a serious bacterial infection, as a direct consequence of 'decontamination' compulsive rituals.

Self-neglect is frequently seen in severe OCD. Key issues which may arise from self-neglect include a risk of very low vitamin levels. As many people with OCD have restricted diets and spend a large amount of time indoors, low vitamin D is often found. This can lead to serious bone problems. Other vitamin deficiencies include vitamin B deficiency, which most commonly results in tiredness, and vitamin C deficiency, which usually causes an increased risk of infections. Many OCD sufferers who self-neglect do not have an adequate intake of iron, which leads to anaemia and extreme tiredness. A lack of fruit and vegetables in the diet leads to constipation. People who are worried about 'contamination' from faeces may deliberately make themselves constipated. Complications of constipation can include development of diverticular disease in which the gut becomes misshapen and prone to infections and impaction, which can be a surgical emergency when constipation is extreme and the bowel becomes completely blocked. If constipation is accompanied by excessive straining or excessive cleaning of the area, prolapse of the bowel, whereby part of the bowel hangs below the body, has been reported as a complication of OCD. Another frequent problem with severe OCD is that the individual restricts their fluid intake either deliberately or because they are so preoccupied by their OCD that they forget to drink. In its most severe form, this can lead to irreversible kidney damage.

Many people with OCD go through periods of feasting followed by fasting due to their OCD symptoms. This generally can lead to rapid weight loss and weight gain. In addition, many OCD sufferers have restricted physical activity. Such behaviour can predispose individuals to an increased risk of diabetes, heart disease, and stroke. Recent studies of both people with OCD and also those with hoarding disorder have found they are more likely than the general population to have high levels of fat in their blood which can also make them more likely to have heart disease or stroke. This can be treated if discovered and prevent further consequences.

Do Any Other Psychological Problems Frequently Occur in People with OCD?

Depression

Most people with moderate or severe OCD also have accompanying depressive symptoms. This is unsurprising when you consider how restricting and debilitating OCD can be. Fortunately, most people with OCD who are treated will also find their depression improves in parallel with the OCD symptoms. However, this is not true for a smaller but significant number of people who require additional treatment for the underlying depression.

Other Obsessive Compulsive Spectrum Disorders

Conditions such as body dysmorphic disorder, hoarding disorder, Tourette syndrome, skin picking, and hair-pulling disorder are often described as obsessive compulsive spectrum disorders. Each of these conditions frequently occurs alone but can also coexist with OCD. These conditions are described in detail in Chapter 8. When an individual has more than one of these conditions, treatment generally needs to address both areas.

Other Anxiety Disorders

Many people with OCD may also have another anxiety disorder. Generalised anxiety is most frequently seen. Fortunately, this can usually be treated in parallel with OCD treatment. Examples of anxiety disorders frequently seen with OCD include phobic anxiety and social anxiety disorder, along with more generalised anxiety problems or panic disorder.

Post-Traumatic Stress Disorder

We have already seen that many people develop OCD after traumatic life events. For some people, these events were so traumatic that they have symptoms including vivid nightmares and flashbacks of the original trauma. Sometimes the OCD can mask the post-traumatic stress disorder (PTSD) symptoms, which can then worsen during psychological treatment. If someone has severe PTSD, such as can arise following childhood sexual abuse or following a traumatic incident such as a rape or a situation in which the individual believes their life is in peril, it is helpful for them to undertake treatment for the PTSD before moving to psychological therapy for OCD.

Autism Spectrum Disorder

In autism spectrum disorder (ASD), which includes Asperger's Syndrome, the individual has difficulty in understanding and interpreting the feelings and motivation of other people. This makes the world a very confusing place. Many people with ASD are more interested in inanimate objects than people, as they find other people, apart from their closest loved ones, bewildering. Many people with ASD have stereotyped behaviours which can appear similar to OCD rituals. In addition, some people with ASD have the need for a rigid routine or for objects to be in a specific place. These symptoms, although appearing similar to OCD, do not have the same rationale as OCD. The individual does not wish to alter these.

In addition, a high proportion of people with ASD also have some OCD symptoms. The individual will, in the case of OCD symptoms, recognise these as troublesome and may wish to alter them. In these cases, the OCD can be treated in the same way as with a person without ASD, provided the therapist gains the person's trust.

Alcohol and Drug Misuse

Obsessive compulsive disorder causes distress and anxiety. Some people seek solace and relief from anxiety by using alcohol, sedative drugs, or even illicit drugs to try to cope with the anxiety. Unfortunately, these are not the 'quick fix' that they may appear to be. Inevitably, increasing amounts of alcohol or drugs are necessary to achieve the same effect, and the person starts to suffer from complications of excessive usage. Some individuals, most frequently with contamination fears, who wish to restrict their toilet visits, may consume large amounts of anti-diarrhoeal medicines. This is also very dangerous. Anti-diarrhoeal medicines which contain codeine can lead to increasing escalation of the dose to achieve the same effect.

Ultimately, these drugs can cause liver and brain damage.

Eating Disorders

Certain types of eating disorder have been particularly linked to OCD. Some of these individuals may not have a 'true' eating disorder but may be dangerously thin due to self-neglect. People who are starving often develop symptoms very similar to OCD. Thus, it is not surprising that some of those with very low weight due to a condition such as anorexia nervosa may also develop OCD symptoms. In these situations, it is important that the individual first gains weight until they are within the normal range before embarking on any treatment for OCD. This is necessary for three reasons.

First, as weight is gained, the OCD symptoms may disappear spontaneously. Second, any psychological treatment for OCD is stressful, and people with a tendency for self-starvation will tend to lose weight when stressed, which may be life-threatening. Finally, the drugs which can be useful for OCD do not work for people of very low weight.

Bulimia and obesity may also accompany OCD. In the case of bulimia, separate treatment for this is generally advisable before embarking on psychological treatment due to the risk that the stress of therapy will provoke worsening of the binges. Drug therapy may be helpful for both the OCD and the bulimia. In the case of obesity, treatment for OCD may help reduce self-neglect and improve the diet and increase the individual's activity once the OCD is less restricting.

Schizophrenia

A significant minority (approximately 1 in 10 to 1 in 25) of people with schizophrenia may also have symptoms of OCD. The incidence of OCD seems particularly common in people with resistant schizophrenia who are treated with drugs such as clozapine. There is evidence that in genetically susceptible individuals, clozapine can induce OCD. The problem is that clozapine is usually prescribed for people who have failed to respond to other antipsychotic drugs. Treatment with serotonin reuptake inhibiting drugs can be useful to control the symptoms of OCD. In a person with stable schizophrenia, psychological treatment of OCD may also be tried.

Personality Disorders

A significant number of people with OCD may also have obsessive compulsive personality disorder. These people have a tendency to be hard-working, perfectionistic, and frequently intolerant of others who are perceived as not living up to their high standards. This seeking of extremely high standards, unlike in perfectionistic OCD, is not seen as problematic by the individual. It is often difficult to clarify the extent of the personality traits and the extent of the OCD. In general, treatment for OCD should improve the distressing OCD symptoms. Sometimes people think they do not wish to change certain beliefs and behaviours but find that when undergoing OCD treatment, the beliefs they held rigidly are not as useful as they once thought, and they can change with therapy.

Other personality disorders can also coexist with OCD. These personality disorders are frequently found in people who have experienced a difficult childhood. Emotionally unstable personality types are people who have difficulty regulating and tolerating their emotions. They may harm themselves through taking deliberate overdoses, cutting, or other self-harming behaviours when their emotions are too severe for them to tolerate. It is generally useful for such individuals to receive some help to try to cope with their emotions before beginning psychological therapy for OCD, although drug treatment may help the symptoms.

KEY POINTS

- OCD often presents in several forms and with various themes, as described in this chapter.
- Magical thinking, whereby an individual believes that thinking of an event may make it more likely to occur, is frequently found in OCD.
- Thought–action fusion is also a frequent occurrence in OCD. In this, the person believes that having a thought is the moral equivalent of performing the deed.
- Ruminations are obsessions followed by compulsions, but the compulsion is also a thought rather than an act. The compulsion may take the form of a 'putting it right' thought or image which cancels out the obsessive thought.
- There are many physical risks and complications in OCD. These are generally caused by either excessive cleaning, which can render the individual prone to infections, or due to self-neglect. Other physical complications of OCD can be extremely serious and can range from prolapsed bowel due to excessive straining, to kidney damage due to water restriction and a higher risk of diabetes, heart attacks, and stroke due to erratic eating patterns and lack of physical activity.
- Many other psychological problems exist alongside OCD. Depression, anxiety disorders, and other obsessive spectrum disorders are the most frequent. Harmful dependence on alcohol and other drugs can develop in individuals with OCD. Other conditions include PTSD, autism spectrum disorder, eating disorders, schizophrenia, and personality disorders. Personality disorders may complicate OCD. People who have difficulty tolerating strong emotions are likely to find psychological treatment of OCD extremely difficult. In such cases, it is usually advisable to treat the emotional issues first.

4

• • • • • • •

Drug Treatment

This chapter starts by examining how, in the 1970s, the discovery that clomipramine, a drug used to treat depression, can greatly improve the symptoms of OCD led to the development of the 'serotonin' theory of OCD. Although clomipramine works well with OCD symptoms, it does have a number of potential side effects. The development of newer drugs which act on the same parts of the brain but have fewer side effects – that is, selective serotonin reuptake inhibitors (SSRIs) – will then be discussed in 'Serotonin Reuptake Inhibiting Drugs' later in this chapter. This section will examine the possible benefits of these drugs and also discuss potential side effects as well as whether they are addictive and whether they can alter someone's personality.

The chapter will then explore the options for people who have OCD which does not respond to SSRIs or clomipramine, examining two main approaches to this problem. The role of dopamine blocking agents in OCD will be described, including discussion of how these act on a different part of the brain compared to SSRIs and clomipramine. We will then explore how some people with OCD fail to respond to the normally prescribed dosages of SSRIs but may respond to higher dosages. This needs to be undertaken carefully and with the close supervision of an expert.

The final part of this chapter will examine new research in the area which may be helpful for the future, including the possible role of drugs acting on the glutamatergic system of the brain.

Medication can improve the symptoms of OCD in six out of ten people. The first drugs that are likely to be given to someone with OCD are those which act on the serotonin system (see 'What Are the Advantages and Disadvantages of Medication and Exposure and Response Prevention?'). These drugs include clomipramine, which is an older drug, and the newer SSRIs.

History of Drug Treatment for OCD

Until recently, OCD was thought to be an untreatable condition. Many people with the most severe symptoms were in institutions. There was no description of OCD in the medical literature until the 1930s. People with OCD were offered sedative drugs to reduce their distress and anxiety. Electric shock treatment (also known as electroconvulsive therapy or ECT) was also tried for OCD, and although this is often extremely effective for some types of depression, it had no effect on obsessions or compulsions. More extreme treatments, such as a form of brain surgery called prefrontal lobotomy, reduced the symptoms of OCD, but at the cost of a possible profound change in the individual's personality.

What Are the Advantages and Disadvantages of Medication and Exposure and Response Prevention?

Medication is easily prescribed by a general practitioner (GP). However, it can take two or three months before the real benefits are seen. There is little evidence regarding how long medication needs to be taken for. The research evidence suggests that in many cases, it must be taken for a long time to prevent relapse. Indeed, some people may need to take medicine for the rest of their lives. In most cases, if a person has been well on medication for a year, it may be worthwhile to attempt to reduce or even stop the medication. This should be done gradually and with the guidance of a GP or psychiatrist. If symptoms recur, a person may need to restart at the higher dose again.

Sometimes people can mistake the recurrence of symptoms as being due to 'withdrawal effects' of the medication. If medication is reduced slowly, there should be few, if any, withdrawal effects. However, it is important to reduce slowly over several months and preferably under medical guidance, as even with care, a small percentage of people can have problems unless they are very carefully supervised. The whole issue of withdrawal effects of these medications is currently being researched and new guidance is likely to be released in the future. The important issue, however, is to reduce slowly and under medical supervision. The potential side effects of medication are described in this chapter.

Psychological treatment involving exposure is difficult. It involves commitment and requires the individual to face the objects, situations, and thoughts which they find anxiety-provoking or extremely unpleasant. For some people, this is just too difficult. Others find that they would prefer to take medication. Some people who find it difficult to face the fear may be helped by first completing a few sessions of cognitive therapy (see Chapter 5). Once people have learned the techniques of exposure and response prevention (ERP), then if they relapse in the future, which frequently occurs when going through a difficult time, they should be able to reintroduce some ERP for themselves before the symptoms become severe.

Some people will need a combination of medication and ERP treatment. These are usually people with more difficult-to-treat OCD who have not responded to either treatment alone. However, some specialists believe that it may be better to use a combination of medication and ERP from the outset of treatment with all people with OCD. This is controversial but is being studied.

Clomipramine

A breakthrough in the treatment of OCD occurred in the 1960s and 1970s when modern-day exposure treatments started to be designed and applied to people with OCD with great success. At approximately the same time, it was discovered that the antidepressant drug clomipramine had a specific anti-OCD effect. This effect has been shown to be independent of and unrelated to its antidepressant effect. This finding led to a number of studies which showed that other antidepressants available at the time did not have such a beneficial effect on OCD. Clomipramine belongs to a class of drugs known as tricyclic antidepressants (TCAs), which work on a number of chemicals in the brain. TCAs have been demonstrated to work on the five major chemical systems in the brain which transmit information between brain cells. These chemicals are known as neurotransmitters. Clomipramine has a particularly powerful effect on the serotonin neurotransmitter system (also called the 5-HT system). It was dis- covered that clomipramine increased the levels of serotonin in specific areas of the brain. Clomipramine works by blocking the neurotransmitter serotonin from being rapidly taken back into the brain cells, resulting in an increase in serotonin. This increase in serotonin is believed to be the cause of the anti-OCD effect. The parts of the brain that are affected by low levels of serotonin in OCD are located in the front of the brain in an area known as the orbitofrontal area.

Although clomipramine is effective in reducing some of the symptoms of OCD, it is not without problems. Because the drug acts on a range of other neurotransmitter systems in the brain, clomipramine has a large number of potential side effects. The more common side effects of clomipramine include the following:

- Drowsiness
- Dry mouth
- Dizziness
- Headache
- Constipation
- Difficulty passing water
- Sexual problems
- Weight gain
- Blurred vision

Much less commonly seen are more serious side effects, including the risk of seizures. However, not everyone will experience side effects with clomipramine. The risk of experiencing side effects can be reduced by introducing the drug at a low dose with gradual increases.

Recently, concern has been raised about certain drugs used to treat OCD which may have a specific effect of slowing down part of the heart cycle, which extremely rarely may lead to sudden death in susceptible individuals. Clomipramine is known to sometimes cause this slowing, which is known as prolongation of the QTc. This can be checked by performing an electrocardiograph (ECG) test. Most people will not have this effect, and the ECG will be normal. Again, a gradual increase in the dose prescribed and monitoring by a GP will prevent any untoward effects.

Another major disadvantage of clomipramine is that it is extremely dangerous in overdose. An effective dose for OCD is often up to 225 mg clomipramine per day. Rarely should it be prescribed at a dose greater than 250 mg per day, although occasionally doses up to 300 mg are used. An accidental or deliberate act of self-poisoning with clomipramine is very dangerous and can be quickly fatal because the drug can have devastating effects on the heart and other organs.

Serotonin Reuptake Inhibiting Drugs

After clomipramine was determined to be effective in treating OCD due to its effect on the serotonin system, drugs which had a more specific effect on the serotonin system without affecting other systems in the brain were sought. This led to the development of the SSRIs, which are generally better tolerated and have fewer side effects compared to clomipramine. SSRIs act on OCD symptoms and also have beneficial effects on depression and other psychological problems, including some anxiety disorders and eating disorders. Fluvoxamine was the first SSRI shown to be effective in the treatment of OCD. Although it has fewer side effects than clomipramine, fluvoxamine may cause slightly more side effects than the other SSRIs.

Initially it was thought that clomipramine might be more effective than the SSRIs in the treatment of OCD, but this has not proved to be the case, and there is strong evidence that they are equally effective. As such, there are few situations that justify prescribing clomipramine for OCD because the SSRIs are as effective, with fewer side effects, and are much safer in overdose. However, some people still prefer clomipramine, which is more sedative and also may help sleep.

Possible side effects of SSRIs include the following:

- Feeling energised, agitated, restless, or, occasionally, drowsy
- Feeling nauseous
- Not wanting to eat
- Difficulty sleeping
- Diarrhoea
- Dizziness
- Dry mouth
- Sexual problems
- Headache
- Blurred vision

Again, not everyone experiences side effects with these drugs. Unfortunately, it is not possible to predict who will experience which side effects with any given drug. Starting at a low dose and increasing slowly (every one to four weeks) tends to reduce the risk of experiencing side effects. Although some of the possible side effects of SSRIs are similar to those that can be experienced with clomipramine, the frequencies of these are usually lower with SSRIs. For example, problems with sexual function have been reported in up to 80 per cent of people taking clomipramine but in less than 30 per cent of those on SSRIs. Another factor is that the common side effects of SSRIs, such as feeling nauseous and not wishing to eat, usually wear off one or two weeks after starting the medication and do not seem to recur when doses are increased (see 'Commonly used drugs for the treatment of OCD').

Stopping either clomipramine or SSRIs leads to the risk of relapse but also, in some people, withdrawal effects. For this reason, if you are on a high dose of medication, you should withdraw from this over several months and preferably under the guidance of a medical practitioner. There is some evidence to suggest that, for a few people who stop their medication and relapse, restarting it may not always result in as much improvement as the first time.

What Drugs Are Most Commonly Used to Help OCD?

Commonly used drugs for the treatment of OCD

Drug name	Trade name	Usual dose to be effective in OCD	Notes
Clomipramine	Anafranil	Starting with 50 or 100 mg and increasing gradually over a few weeks to 225 mg at night.	This is an older drug which tends to be sedative and have more side effects than newer drugs.
Fluvoxamine	Faverin	50 mg in the evening initially and increased gradually to 300 mg.	Although it has fewer side effects than clomipramine, it may have slightly more than the other SSRIs.
Fluoxetine	Prozac	20 mg in the morning and increasing every 2–4 weeks up to 60 mg.	
Paroxetine	Seroxat	10 mg in the morning initially, increasing every 2–4 weeks to 50 mg.	

(*cont.*)

Drug name	Trade name	Usual dose to be effective in OCD	Notes
Sertraline	Lustral	50 mg in the morning, increasing by 50 mg every 2–4 weeks to 200 mg.	
Citalopram	Cipramil	10 mg in the morning, increasing every few weeks up to 40 mg.	Most evidence is for dosages of 60 mg citalopram, but it is only licensed up to 40 mg due to concern about specific heart slowing. (See 'Are These Drugs Safe'.) This means that it is possible to take a higher dose but this will need to be discussed and agreed with your doctor.
Escitalopram	Cipralex	5 mg in the morning, increasing every few weeks to 20 mg.	There is some evidence for dosages of 30 mg of escitalopram, but it is only licensed up to 20 mg. This means that it is possible to take a higher dose but this will need to be discussed and agreed with your doctor. At higher dosages, there is some evidence that this may prevent relapse of OCD.

Do These Drugs Really Work?

No one can say that there is a perfect drug or that all drugs will always work for everyone. However, clomipramine and SSRIs do work. Approximately two-thirds of people with OCD will respond to treatment with these drugs. Most people who respond to treatment with these drugs have a 25–35 per cent reduction in their symptoms, but some obtain greater improvement. The tablets take longer to work than many people expect. Although helpful results can occasionally be seen earlier, many beneficial effects are not seen until two or three months after taking the highest dose of the medicine. Improvements can continue thereafter, with further improvement for up to two years after starting the medicine.

If someone does not respond to one medication, it is worthwhile trying another. It is not clear why some people respond to one SSRI rather than another, but it is definitely the case. Thus, for example, if a person with OCD has not improved on 60 mg fluoxetine, it can still be beneficial to switch the person to sertraline or another SSRI.

Although some people may eventually be able to stop treatment with SSRIs or clomipramine, those with the most severe conditions may need to remain on them long term. It has been shown that one in three people who have responded to SSRIs will relapse within a few months of stopping the treatment. Always remember that stopping these medications should be done extremely slowly over several months whilst monitoring any return of symptoms and preferably under the supervision of a medical practitioner.

Are Clomipramine and SSRIs Addictive?

These drugs are not addictive but should not be stopped suddenly. They have an effect on brain chemistry, and stopping them abruptly can lead to a number of side effects. To stop the medication, it needs to be tailed off gradually over a few months. As such, this should be done under the guidance of a GP.

Are These Drugs Safe?

There is concern that people taking certain drugs may have a specific slowing of the heart rate known as a prolongation of the QTc interval, which is demonstrated on ECG. In turn, the concern is that a miniscule number of individuals with this abnormality may have sudden death due to heart arrhythmia. The development of these abnormalities seems to increase with higher dosages of drugs.

Drugs that are most commonly associated with prolonged QTc interval are those used as antipsychotics (discussed later), clomipramine, as well as citalopram and escitalopram. Sertraline seems to have the lowest risk of causing an increase in the QTc interval. It is advisable for anyone on an antipsychotic drug, clomipramine, or a higher dose of SSRI to have an ECG test annually and also when the drugs are changed.

Otherwise, clomipramine and SSRIs are generally safe drugs when taken in accordance with instructions from a GP.

Will Clomipramine or SSRIs Alter My Personality?

The short answer to this question is 'no'. As already explained, in people with OCD, there appear to be low levels of serotonin in specific areas of the brain. This shortage seems to precipitate the OCD symptoms. Clomipramine and SSRIs aim to address this and increase the serotonin levels. Often, the individual's basic personality is intact but the person is free of the problematic OCD symptoms.

What Should I Do about Treatment with Clomipramine or SSRIs if I Am Pregnant?

This should always be discussed with your doctor. In general, medication is best avoided, particularly during the first three months of pregnancy. However, the risk of relapse of the mother's OCD has to be weighed against the small risk to the baby. This should be fully discussed with a GP, who should explain in detail the risks and benefits. In later stages of pregnancy, there does seem to be an extremely small risk of problems such as breathing difficulties.

Regarding breastfeeding, it is generally thought that the benefits of breast-feeding to both the baby and the mother outweigh any potential risks of drug treatment for OCD. Paroxetine and sertraline are the most commonly recommended SSRIs because they are found in lower concentrations in breast milk, thus resulting in low infant exposure. In general, when a mother is lactating, fluoxetine and citalopram should be avoided or used with caution because more of these drugs are passed onto the baby. This is not an absolute rule, and if the mother has been taking fluoxetine or citalopram during pregnancy, it is usually possible to continue to do so during breastfeeding, with guidance from specialist medical professionals.

What If These Drugs Don't Work?

The most common reason people do not obtain a beneficial effect from SSRIs or clomipramine is that they have not been taking a sufficiently high dose for a long enough period of time. These drugs must be taken for up to two or three months before a beneficial effect is experienced. In addition to taking the medication in a sufficiently high dose, it must be taken regularly. Some people take the medication on sporadic days when their symptoms are most troublesome. Unfortunately, this does not work. The beneficial effect is dependent on a sufficiently high dose that is taken regularly. Missing one dose as a rare event may have no negative effect, but the medicine should be taken almost every day.

Some people fail to benefit even after taking the recommended dose of medication for three months. In these cases, it is worthwhile to try another SSRI because some people respond better to one SSRI rather than another. If this does not work, two other drug treatment approaches can be attempted.

First, and most commonly, drugs known as dopamine blockers can be added to the SSRI or clomipramine regimen. A second approach, which is most likely to be performed by a specialist OCD service, is to increase the dose of SSRI above the recommended limit. Due to its toxicity, clomipramine should not be increased above the recommended dose range. A number of other treatment approaches have been suggested, but there is insufficient evidence to recommend these.

Adding a Dopamine Blocker

Unlike SSRIs, which act at the front of the brain, dopamine blockers act at an area towards the back of the brain which is linked to an area known as the basal ganglia (Figure 4.1). It has long been recognised

Figure 4.1 Diagram of areas of the brain targeted to treat OCD.

Illustration © Dorling Kindersley; annotations by L. M. Drummond

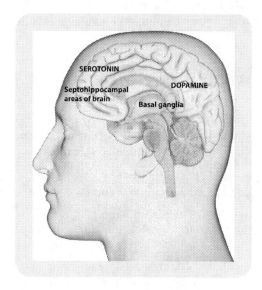

that certain abnormalities of the basal ganglia and their connections can result in obsessions and compulsions. Examples include some movement disorders, such as chorea. In addition, the medicine used to treat Parkinson's disease (another disease of the basal ganglia) can also result in obsessions and compulsions. Dopamine is a neurotransmitter, but in the case of OCD, it appears that this is too active and needs to be reduced. The dopamine blockers bind to the nerve cells and dampen down the effect of dopamine. Dopamine blockers are also used to help treat conditions such as schizophrenia and other psychoses, and they are sometimes called 'antipsychotics'. The dose of drug used in people with OCD, however, is much lower than that used for schizophrenia. For example, it is not unusual for a patient with OCD to receive just 0.5 mg of risperidone with beneficial effect, whereas doses of up to 10 mg are more commonly used for schizophrenia.

Side effects with dopamine blockers are much less frequently seen than with the much higher doses used for schizophrenia. There is concern about the long-term side effects of movement disorders, but they are only rarely seen in people treated for many years with high-dose antipsychotic medication and are much less likely to occur with the tiny doses used for OCD. Older dopamine blockers are known as conventional antipsychotics, and these tend to have more side effects. In addition, more acute movement disorders are sometimes seen with use of these dopamine blockers, but generally only at higher doses. Most of the dopamine blockers can also cause prolongation of the QTc interval, as discussed previously in relation to clomipramine and SSRIs. For this reason, people taking these drugs should be monitored by ECG. Aripiprazole, a newer drug, does not cause any heart conduction changes. Other potential effects are raised levels of the brain chemical prolactin. This chemical is secreted by mothers who are breastfeeding. In extreme cases people produce milk whilst on usually high doses of these drugs and more commonly on the older types of dopamine blocking drugs. Other side effects can be a reduction in sexual desire and infertility and, in severe cases, if untreated, in weakening of the bones. . However, these side effects are less likely to occur with the low dosages used in OCD and in people prescribed the newer so called 'atypical' drugs. A simple blood test can also detect if there are any issues with prolactin levels.

'Newer atypical drugs which have been used in OCD' are shown in the next table. In general, large-scale clinical trials of these drugs have not been performed, but there is evidence that they can be helpful. There is more evidence for some of these dopamine blockers than for others with regard to their use in OCD. However, the studies have generally all been small. Overall, there is probably more positive evidence for risperidone than for other drugs.

Overall, approximately one-third of people who have not responded to an SSRI or clomipramine will experience improvement with the addition of a dopamine blocker. A large study also found that the addition of psychological therapy for OCD, which comprises a form of treatment known as cognitive behaviour therapy (CBT), was more effective than adding a dopamine blocker. CBT for OCD is described in Chapter 5.

Higher than Licensed Dosages of SSRIs

We have already mentioned that in order to be effective, doses of SSRIs for OCD need to be higher than those required for depression. This observation that the improvement with OCD is correlated with higher dosage has led some people to prescribe above licensed dosages of drugs. This prescribing at a higher level would normally only happen under the close medical supervision of a specilaist service. Of course, the upper limits of licensed drugs are sometimes overly cautious. It was previously noted that the licensed upper recommended doses of the drugs citalopram and escitalopram have been reduced in recent years. Similarly, the upper recommended licensed dose of fluoxetine is 60 mg in the UK but 80 mg in the US and several European countries.

Newer atypical drugs which have been used in OCD

Drug name	Trade name	Usual dose for OCD	Common side effects	Notes
Risperidone	Risperdal	0.5 mg up to 1–2 mg if helpful	Drowsiness; dizziness; can occasionally cause weight gain.	This is the atypical drug with the greatest number of studies to demonstrate its effectiveness in OCD.
Aripiprazole	Abilify	2.5–5 mg	Can cause an increase in activity and even anxiety; drowsiness is less common; can cause loss ofappetite.	This does not have any effect on the heart.
Olanzepine	Zyprexa	2.5–5 mg	Drowsiness; dizziness; weight gain common.	Weight gain is common with olanzapine; therefore, this is not advisable for those who are overweight.
Quetiapine	Seroquel	25 mg	Drowsiness; dizziness; difficulty sleeping; increased appetite and weight gain	Weight gain is generally less than that with olanzapine.

One of the drugs which has been studied in higher doses is sertraline. Whereas 200 mg is the usual recommended dose for OCD, a study that examined patients prescribed between 250 and 400 mg found that, in general, they had greater improvements compared to those on lower doses (see Rabinowitz et al. For this reason, if an individual has not responded to SSRIs or clomipramine and has had adequate trials of psychological therapy (see Chapter 5), then the person can try a dose of SSRI above the normally recommended doses. This strategy, however, should never be used for clomipramine, which can be extremely dangerous at high doses. The prescribing of above normal recommended doses is most likely to occur in a specialist OCD centre. The ECG should be checked before each dose increase to ensure there is no change to the heart. In addition, it is often useful to check the blood levels of these patients.

In our centre, we routinely check the blood levels of patients who are on high doses. The most commonly used drug is sertraline. Despite dosages of up to 400 mg of sertraline per day, our results routinely demonstrate blood levels within the recognised range, and they are frequently at the lower end of this range. In other words, although one might expect people taking these very high doses of drugs to have blood levels at the high end of the range or even higher, our finding is that this is not the case. For these blood levels to be either within the therapeutic range or below it, despite taking above the normally recommended doses of SSRIs, means that either these people have a problem absorbing the drug or they must rapidly break down the drug in the body. In fact, it often appears that these people rapidly break down the drug. Sertraline and similar drugs are broken down in the liver. It appears that some people have a very active metabolism in their liver and so break the drug down into non-effective components more rapidly than the majority of the population. These people are often described as 'rapid metabolisers' of sertraline or other drugs. This rapid metabolism may be inherited, because certain genes have been identified which seem to be associated with this finding. People who are rapid metabolisers can be big or small, old or young, slim or obese. The ability to rapidly break down sertraline and other SSRIs is entirely unrelated to body size.

The Glutamate System

In addition to SSRIs and clomipramine, other drugs have been used to try to improve outcomes for people with OCD. Trials have been performed in which an SSRI was combined with other antidepressants, and some have used a combination of an SSRI and clomipramine along with various combinations of other drugs. Very few studies indicate that any of these methods can be recommended.

One interesting new area of research is the glutamate system. Throughout the brain, messages are sent from one cell to another via neurotransmitters. We have already discussed how in OCD, the neurotransmitter serotonin appears to be in the circuits at the frontal areas of the brain, and there seems to be an excess of the neurotransmitter dopamine in the areas connecting to the basal ganglia towards the back of the brain. The neurotransmitters are secreted into the spaces between cells by one neurone and taken into the cell by the next cell, thus transmitting the messages through the brain. Also in the spaces between the neurones are cells known as glial cells. One of the functions of glial cells is to secrete glutamate, which modifies the effects of the neurotransmitters. In short, the role of the glial cells and glutamate is complex and varies in different areas of the brain. In general, there is not a total lack or an excess of glutamate, but this may vary in differing regions of the brain. Glutamate is a modulating agent rather than a neurotransmitter.

Drugs which act on the glutamate system

Drug name	Comments
Topirimate	An anti-epileptic drug which has been shown to have possibly modest improvements in obsessions in OCD.
N-acetylcysteine	A modified form of a normal nutrient; may be useful for people with compulsive hair pulling (trichotillomania).
Riluzole	The first drug acting on glutamate to be tested in resistant OCD; does not currently appear to be effective, but there is ongoing research in this area.

(*cont.*)

Drug name	Comments
Memantine	A drug first used for Alzheimer's disease; preliminary reports suggest it may be helpful in OCD.
Ketamine	An anaesthetic agent and a drug of human abuse; no evidence of long-lasting benefit in OCD, but further trials are being conducted.
Pregabalin	A drug which has been approved in the UK for treatment of generalised anxiety disorder; may also be a helpful additional drug in resistant OCD.
Lamotrogine	An anti-epileptic and also mood-stabilising drug; preliminary trials in OCD have shown variable results.
Glycine	An amino acid (i.e., a nutritional supplement); it has a low level of toxicity and may be helpful for some people.

A number of drugs act on the glutamate system, which may be potentially useful in people with OCD who have not responded to normal methods. Clozapine, a powerful drug used in schizophrenia when standard methods of treatment are ineffective, has an effect on the glutamate system. In Chapter 3, we discussed how certain patients who appear to be genetically predisposed to do so may develop OCD symptoms after starting on clozapine.

Certain drugs which act on the glutamate system have been suggested as being potentially useful for OCD. These have not been subjected to extensive research and thus are still in the experimental stage. Examples of drugs which have been tested to determine if they are useful in treatment-resistant OCD are shown in 'Drugs which act on the glutamate system'. Further studies are needed before drugs acting on the glutamate system can be generally recommended for people with difficult-to-treat OCD.

KEY POINTS

- Clomipramine was the first effective psychopharmacological treatment discovered for OCD. Despite being effective, it can have a number of disabling side effects and is also extremely dangerous in overdose. Selective serotonin reuptake inhibitors (SSRIs) were developed later and have fewer side effects.
- The following SSRIs have been shown to be beneficial in OCD:
  - Fluvoxamine
  - Paroxetine
  - Fluoxetine
  - Sertraline
  - Citalopram
  - Escitalopram
- Doses required for successful treatment in OCD are often considerably higher than those used for depression and most other conditions.
- Approximately 60 per cent of people prescribed an SSRI or clomipramine will have significant improvement in their OCD symptoms.
- The beneficial effects of SSRIs and clomipramine can take up to three months of regular treatment at full dose to manifest. Continued gradual improvement can be seen up to two years after starting the drug.
- Whereas some people may be able to stop treatment with SSRIs or clomipramine, those with the most severe conditions may need to remain on them long term.
- Stopping SSRIs or clomipramine should be done gradually and slowly and under the supervision of a medical practitioner.
- If an individual does not respond to one SSRI or clomipramine, it is worthwhile switching to another because they often respond to the new one.
- If two trials of SSRIs or clomipramine fail to produce improvement, there are two further strategies that are generally employed: adding a dopamine blocker or increasing the dose of the SSRI beyond usually recommended levels.

- Dopamine blockers improve symptoms in approximately one-third of people who have not responded to SSRIs or clomipramine. Adding dopamine blockers to an SSRI or clomipramine is less effective than the addition of CBT for OCD.
- Other drugs have also been examined to determine if they can help people who do not respond to SSRIs or clomipramine. Drugs that act on the glutamate system in the brain are one avenue of research.

5

. . . .

Exposure and Response Prevention for OCD

This chapter will introduce the concept of graded exposure and self-imposed response prevention (ERP). It will describe the vicious cycle of compulsions and reassurance-seeking behaviours and the way they are rewarded by a reduction in discomfort. However, although these behaviours reduce discomfort, it is reduced only slightly, and the effect is often short-lived. Overall, therefore, the compulsions and reassurance-seeking serve to prolong and worsen the obsessive-compulsive symptoms. Later in this book, we will be discussing the practice of ERP in greater detail.

Avoidance of discomfort-inducing situations is also frequently found in OCD. This avoidance can lead to further worsening of the condition and an abnormal lifestyle which might, at its most extreme, threaten general health.

The treatment using ERP will be explained in full. Personal stories explaining the principles of ERP treatment will be given. We will also examine the success and likely outcomes of treatment with ERP.

The reasons why an ERP programme may not work in any specific case will be examined, and tips for moving forward in subsequent ERP programmes are presented.

Finally, the role of other therapies, including cognitive strategies as well as counselling, psychotherapy, and family therapy, will be mentioned.

In Chapter 1, we examined the key features of OCD – the anxiety-inducing obsessions and the discomfort-relieving compulsions. We also examined how most of us experience obsessions and compulsions from time to time. We all know people who set extremely high standards for themselves. These people often have the obsessive traits of high achievement, meticulousness, punctuality, and extreme neatness or cleanliness. Indeed, traits such as striving for perfection and meticulous hygiene can be seen to have a survival advantage. This advantage may help keep these traits in the gene pool. However, in OCD, these tendencies have become an end in themselves, with the sufferer feeling compelled to perform compulsions even to the detriment of everything else in their life. For example, whereas general hygiene in the kitchen can be viewed as an excellent quality, in the case of an OCD sufferer, this may have developed such importance that every waking hour is spent cleaning the kitchen. For example, a woman with OCD and contamination fears had financial difficulties due to her inability to perform any paid work as well as her excessive spending on cleaning materials. Both she and her young son were undernourished because too much time was spent cleaning to the detriment of actually cooking any food.

We also discussed how obsessions are thoughts, images, or impulses that appear in the sufferer's mind and are distressing and anxiety-provoking. Everyone has worrying or anxiety-provoking thoughts from time to time, but with obsessions they are so pervasive or so worrying that the sufferer feels the need to try to not have a specific thought ever again. Of course, the effort of trying not to have a specific thought means that the thought occurs more frequently. For example, a religious person may have blasphemous thoughts. These are abhorrent to the person, so extreme effort is made to try to prevent them from recurring. However, trying to suppress them is part of a vicious circle of constantly monitoring these thoughts and consequently increasing them. Much of the sufferer's time and effort are devoted to resisting the obsessions. Later in the illness, less time might be spent resisting as the individual learns this is not successful.

Common obsessions include the following:

- Fear of contamination (particularly dirt and germs) due to the worry that harm may occur to self or others.
- Fear of harm occurring to self or others due to an act of omission – for example, fear that the family may be attacked if the doors or windows are left open, leading to excessive checking of these.
- Fear of harm occurring to self or others due to an act of commission. For example, an individual worries that they may run 'amok' and harm someone in the presence of knives. This often causes some fear in professionals dealing with the individual. In OCD, this is not a true urge or desire; rather, the sufferer does not want to perform the act at all and is frightened by the thought.
- Blasphemous religious obsessions. These are repugnant to the individual.
- Fear of loss of objects or inadvertent disclosure of information. For example, an individual may be unable to throw away household rubbish due to a fear that secret information may get into the wrong hands to the detriment of the sufferer. This can result in a house becoming virtually uninhabitable and filled with empty packets and papers.
- Hoarding. Recently, it has been recognised that many people with hoarding disorder do not have OCD. However, there is still a group of individuals who hoard objects for a variety of reasons related to their obsessional fears. For example, a man wanted to keep up to date on all book reviews. He therefore bought four newspapers a day and would repeatedly read over these reviews. He was unable to cut out the reviews for fear he might have missed some of the information. His house and garage were completely full of

newspapers, and he had consequently rented a flat, resulting in financial hardship. The new flat was rapidly becoming uninhabitable due to continued hoarding of newspapers.

- Perfectionism is a common theme for OCD sufferers. Because nobody is perfect, these individuals are bound to fail. This failure leads to anxiety. Instead, the opposite of perfection often occurs, as the sufferer cannot even start to perform the action for fear of failure. For example, a woman felt the need to have a perfectly tidy house. She managed to achieve a pristine environment for a brief time. However, as the exacting standards became impossible to maintain, she was found living in squalor in an extremely anxious state.

- Symmetry was discussed in Chapter 3. These features can often be found in people with the developmental disorders of autism spectrum disorder and Asperger's syndrome. Some people with OCD also have a desire to ensure everything is symmetrical.

- Slowness, which was also discussed in Chapter 3, is usually related to perfectionism.

Obsessions are usually recognised by the OCD sufferer as being a product of their own mind. Importantly, however, obsessions are anxiety-provoking and often abhorrent. Therefore, an OCD sufferer who has obsessive concerns that they may sexually abuse young children will *not* do so. A true paedophile enjoys the thoughts of abuse and finds them sexually rewarding rather than repugnant. In general, people with OCD realise that although very anxiety-provoking, their obsessional thoughts are either irrational or 'over the top'. After many years of dealing with OCD, this insight into the irrationality of obsessive thoughts can be blurred. In addition, if someone has recently been exposed to a situation that provoked their obsessions, they will at that point believe their obsessive thoughts. However, during periods of calm reflection, many people will admit the irrationality of their obsessions.

In Chapter 1, we also discussed compulsions. These are thoughts, words, or deeds which are designed to reduce or prevent the harm of the obsessive thought. However, either they are not realistically connected to the obsessive concern or they are clearly excessive. For example, an individual may feel the need to repeat prayers in sets of three following a blasphemous thought; the person may perceive this as a 'good' number. Thus, stopping at a number not divisible by three would cause further anxiety.

Sometimes, however, the compulsions are not connected with the obsessions in any logical way but, rather, are examples of 'magical thinking'. Most people have performed irrational magical, superstitious acts in order to prevent bad things occurring. In OCD, however, these behaviours are more extreme. For example, one man had the thought that catastrophe might befall his close family members. This was extremely anxiety-provoking to him, and he developed a compulsion which involved him standing on his right leg and hopping up and down in multiples of 12 until he felt that he had 'undone' the bad thought. In addition to compulsions, some OCD sufferers repeatedly seek reassurance from others as a way of abating anxiety. This works in an identical way to compulsions. For example, whenever she returned home, a young woman had a fear that she might have inadvertently pushed a child onto the road whilst she was out. She would therefore avoid going out alone, insisting that a family member accompany her. Whilst out and on returning, she would constantly seek reassurance that she had not performed these acts by asking the observer to account for every movement and every minute of her time.

Although compulsions reduce anxiety, they do so inefficiently. They tend to reduce anxiety only slightly, and their effect is short-lived. For example, a man who has a fear of contracting diarrhoea from dirt and germs may wash his hands in a stereotyped way after every time he touches a door handle used by others. This activity will reduce his anxiety a little, but it will not be long before he believes he may not have washed his hands sufficiently well and he feels the urge to repeat his hand-washing routine. The end result is that people with OCD spend most of their time being highly anxious and distressed.

Compulsions are anxiety-reducing and/or discomfort-relieving activities which reduce anxiety and discomfort, albeit inefficiently.

The Exposure Principle for Treating OCD

Psychological treatment for OCD is highly effective, and the outcomes obtained with this treatment will be discussed later in this chapter. The treatments with the highest rate of success, however, involve facing the objects and situations which cause the obsessions, discomfort, and fear and to do so without performing compulsions. This may sound extremely difficult, if not impossible, to some people. However, it is certainly not necessary or even desirable to face all these at once. In any treatment programme, the person with OCD needs to examine the objects, situations, and thoughts which are likely to provoke obsessive thoughts. These are likely to range from those that are less fear-provoking to the most frightening. It is useful to then score these situations on a scale. I tend to use a 0- to 8-point scale, where 0 represents no anxiety at all, 2 represents mild anxiety, 4 represents moderate anxiety, 6 represents severe anxiety, and 8 represents the highest anxiety possible and complete panic. It is then possible to construct these situations into a 'hierarchy' or ladder where easier tasks can be performed first. These tasks should be performed without resorting to also performing anxiety-reducing compulsions. It must be remembered that old habits die hard, and many people find themselves performing compulsive rituals after exposure. This is fine as long as further exposure at the same level then occurs. Once an exposure task has been performed, the person with OCD will normally experience heightened anxiety for approximately two hours. This is normal in the early stages, but eventually the anxiety will naturally abate as long as compulsions are not performed. The key 'golden messages' of exposure treatment are as follows:

- Anxiety is really horrible and unpleasant, but it will not harm you.
- Anxiety will eventually reduce if you stick to the exposure task.
- Continued practice of the exposure task will mean that it becomes easier.

It has been found that to be effective, exposure combined with resistance of performing anxiety-relieving compulsions should:

- be continued until the anxiety reduces consistently by at least a half (initially this may take two hours);
- be practiced frequently – ideally three times a day; and
- be performed reliably: the person should not move onto more difficult items on their hierarchy until they have mastered the easier ones. (Sometimes people are impatient, and while just starting treatment they will suddenly perform a task at the top of the hierarchy. This results in panic, and the individual can become disheartened and disillusioned.)

The treatment just described is known as exposure and self-imposed response (or ritual) prevention or ERP.

Eleanor's Story

Eleanor has a ten-year history of fear of contamination by dirt from dog faeces. Her obsessional thoughts are that she might catch a variety of diseases, which could then be passed on to others and which would result in her feeling responsible for this plague. This problem caused her to avoid any situations in which she had seen dogs in the past. Even if she saw a dog through her window, she would feel anxious and resort to cleaning rituals. Her anxiety-reducing rituals consisted of stripping off all her clothes which were then considered contaminated and washing them. She would bathe in a set pattern and would repeat this ritual washing in multiples of four, which she considered a 'good' number.

Eleanor was seen in clinic by a therapist. Having obtained a full history of her problems, the therapist explained:

When you are in contact with anything which makes you feel 'contaminated', you experience extreme anxiety. A high level of anxiety is uncomfortable and so you will try to escape or avoid that experience. Escaping from the situation is not possible if you already feel contaminated. In order to reduce your anxiety, you have developed the anxiety-reducing compulsive rituals of washing in a set pattern in multiples of four. When you perform these compulsions, your anxiety reduces. Because high anxiety is uncomfortable, this reduction in anxiety is like a reward. You are therefore rewarding your compulsive behaviour. If we reward any behaviour then we increase the chance of it recurring in that situation again. For example, if a dog sits up and begs and is rewarded with a treat, then you increase the chance of it sitting up and begging again. In the case of obsessional rituals, however, although they reduce anxiety, there are two problems:

1. They only reduce anxiety a small amount.
2. The anxiety reduction is short-lived, and you then have to repeat the compulsion.

In practice this means that you are constantly experiencing very high levels of tension and anxiety. I am going to ask you to stop performing any compulsions at all. Although this sounds difficult, I think you will soon find that your anxiety eventually reduces much further than when you are repetitively performing your compulsions. You may on occasion find yourself performing your compulsions before you realise it. That is fine as long as you stop once you realise and then 'recontaminate' yourself.

This example demonstrates that the keystone of treatment for OCD is exposure to the anxiety-producing obsessions or the objects and situations which produce these thoughts. Self-imposed response prevention is also used as a way of prolonging exposure and removing the compulsions. The important thing to remember is that the person with OCD needs to face the fear in a reliable, regular, and graded fashion. In addition, the person needs to stop performing compulsive activities whilst facing the fear. The model for how the compulsions serve to worsen Eleanor's anxiety and how facing her fear without compulsions will result in reduced anxiety is shown in Figure 5.1.

Sometimes people with OCD make the mistake of also trying to produce a list or hierarchy of compulsions. Generally, this will not work, and it is often easier for OCD sufferers to stop the behaviour completely or replace the compulsive behaviour with a new, more adaptive

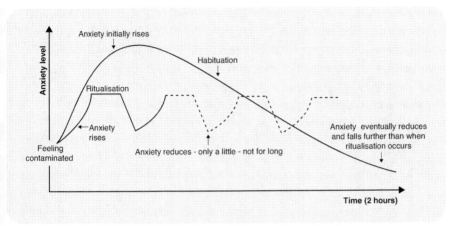

Figure 5.1 Eleanor's diagram.

Reproduced from Drummond, L. (2014). CBT for Adults. London: Royal College of Psychiatrists

behaviour. In Eleanor's situation, she would wash her hands and arms to midway between the elbow and wrist under running water and using antibacterial handwash gel. The performance of this compulsive hand washing would take three to four minutes, and it was repeated in multiples of four. She therefore had to be taught a new way of hand washing which involved putting the plug in the sink, using soap, and washing her hands to her wrists only for 15–20 seconds. (Singing the tune 'Happy Birthday to You' is sometimes used to time the hand wash because it is 15–20 seconds in length.) These new hand-washing activities could be performed whenever Eleanor went to the toilet or before meals. Her exposure tasks, therefore, were scheduled immediately after meals so that she did not reassure herself that she would soon be washing her hands.

Another problematic area was Eleanor's showering. Like many people with OCD and contamination fears, Eleanor did not take baths because she did not like sitting in 'contaminated' water. Instead, she would wash in the shower and then rewash her entire body in multiples of four. At the commencement of therapy, it was agreed that Eleanor should not shower but was to daily stand in the shower without washing for five minutes. A form of bathing that involved washing her body just once was also implemented but with the proviso that she leave one part of her body unwashed at each bath. Thus, one day she was instructed not to wash her right arm, the next day not to wash her left leg, and so on. This was done so that Eleanor experienced the idea of not being, in her view, 'completely clean'.

Eleanor set herself the overall goal of returning to her previous job as a fitness instructor. She had not worked for ten years due to her concern about dog faeces. In addition, she also wished to be able to go out with friends without fearing that she would have to return home if she saw something 'dirty'. She produced the hierarchy of situations to be tackled shown in 'Eleanor's hierarchy for ERP'.

Eleanor's hierarchy for ERP

Exposure item	Anxiety rating 0 = No anxiety; 8 = Panic
NB: All of the items are rated as if to be performed without compulsive hand washing and compulsive bathing/showering.	
Look at pictures of dogs and touch these pictures and then touch myself including my hair and lick my fingers.	1
Look at films of dogs and touch the screen and then touch myself including my hair and lick my fingers.	3
Go out of the house to the local shop and touch items such as the door handle to the shop. (Once I saw a woman with a dog excrement bag touch this handle.) No precautions and touch items in my house afterwards.	5
Touch my legs below the knee even though I have been walking outside as I fear they are closer to the ground and more likely to be contaminated. Without washing, touch myself including my hair and lick my fingers.	5

(*cont.*)

Exposure item	Anxiety rating 0 = No anxiety; 8 = Panic
Go to the local park and touch the children's play equipment and then touch myself including my hair and lick my fingers.	6
Touch items handled by other people without washing and then touch myself including my hair and lick my fingers.	6
Touch the floor and then touch myself including my hair and lick my fingers.	8
Stroke a dog and then touch myself including my hair and lick my fingers.	8
Pick up dog faeces using a plastic bag and dispose of this in the appropriate disposal bin and then touch myself including my hair.	8

In the hierarchy, it is noticeable that Eleanor was told that she would need to touch herself and also lick her fingers afterwards. This is because it is not effective if someone were to touch a feared item and then sit still not touching anything else until their next meal or next visit to the toilet to wash their hands. In such a situation, the anxiety is unlikely to reduce, and the person would not have fully engaged in the exposure. Similarly, if they performed compulsive washing rituals after the exposure, the anxiety would not improve in the long term. By touching herself and a variety of objects in her home, Eleanor was ensuring that the effects of the exposure last longer and the anxiety reduces. Indeed, by licking her fingers, she was also ensuring that the 'risk' of her exposure could not be 'undone' by compulsive rituals. Of course, the term 'risk' is no real risk, and most people without OCD would have few or no problems completing most of these items. Some do seem extreme, however, and will be discussed later. This reduction in anxiety is also known as habituation. Habituation can refer to the reduction in anxiety following an exposure session which initially can take up to two hours. The term habituation is also used to describe how, when the same exposure task is repeated several times, the anxiety does not reach as high levels as before and does not last as long as it did initially. It is this habituation between sessions which can be used to record progress, and it is the reason why the expo- sure task should be repeated regularly (ideally three times a day).

Sometimes it is helpful to record the homework tasks in some type of diary. This can be as simple as a piece of paper or even a mobile telephone. The easier the diary is to complete, the more likely it is to be completed by an individual. For this reason, it is usually best to keep these as simple as possible. Such a diary only needs to include a list of the exposure tasks and the day and time these are performed. A rating of anxiety at the beginning and after two hours of exposure (without performing any compulsions, reassurance-seeking, or other safety behaviours) is also useful.

Why Some of These Exposure Tasks Appear Extreme and Not 'Normal'?

One of the surprises and criticisms people have when an exposure hierarchy is worked out with them is that it seems 'over the top' and that most people would not perform the acts that they are being asked to do. This is undoubtedly true, but the reason is quite simple. If a person has OCD and also fear and avoidance of certain objects and situations, once the therapy stops, there will be a tendency for the behaviour to return. If the person with OCD is still performing tasks in an obsessive-compulsive manner, then this is a slippery slope which can rapidly return to OCD. I often describe the treatment as being like a pendulum, with one direc- tion being increasing obsessional behaviour which I call 'OB' and the other direction 'slobbishness' or 'SLOB'. 'NORMAL' is in the middle of these two. If in ERP treatment we aim for somewhere in the 'SLOB' range, then when this treatment comes to an end and the person with OCD slips back slightly, they are still within a 'normal' range. Also, by performing tasks that are 'over the top', the person really challenges the obsessions and their veracity. Although most people with OCD realise that their obsessions are extreme and not based on reality, there can be a lingering doubt. Really smashing the obsessional thoughts by acting in a way so contrary to them and subsequently discovering that the feared consequence does not occur, is a very powerful learning experience, and it provides a memory which can be useful if obsessions threaten to creep back into the person's thoughts.

Reassurance-Seeking

Some people with OCD use reassurance-seeking instead of or in addition to compulsive rituals. These people will repeatedly ask friends or loved ones for reassurance. Obviously not wishing to see their loved one distressed, most people will respond with reassurance. Reassurance, however, is similar to any other compulsive behaviour, and the more it is given, the more it is required.

Katy's Story

Katy is a 40-year-old woman who lives with her elderly mother. For the past 15 years, she has worried that she may have inadvertently caused offence to someone by something that she has said or done. During the past five years, this worry has increased so that she avoids going out except when accompanied by her mother. On her return, she repeatedly asks her mother for reassurance that she has not been rude or offended anyone. This can be repeated more than 50 times and can go on for several hours.

Katy's treatment involved a hierarchy of social situations which she faced up to. Her mother was asked to say, 'I'm afraid that I have been told by the clinic not to answer questions like that'. Over several weeks, Katy began to increase her journeys alone. At first, her mother had difficulty remembering not to give reassurance, but the more she managed to do so, the more she noticed that it curtailed Katy's demand for reassurance.

Katy's story shows how persistent and disabling OCD can be for both the person with OCD and their loved ones. Having a standard response available whenever her daughter asked for reassurance made it easier for Katy's mother to not offer reassurance. The fact that this response reminded them both that reassurance is not helpful in the long term, and that this had been discussed with them, may also have been useful. In addition, putting the onus on the clinic rather than on herself may have made it easier for Katy's mother to resist giving reassurance. Obviously, it is ultimately the responsibility of the person with OCD not to ask for reassurance. The person with OCD should agree in advance with their friend or relative how many times they can ask for reassurance before the other person gives the reassurance. This is because it is unfair for the other person to be badgered constantly, and the person with OCD does need to accept responsibility for their treatment. Needless to say, threatening and violent behaviour are totally unacceptable and should be dealt with in the appropriate way, including calling the police if necessary.

Reassurance can also be sought from other agencies, such as doctors' offices, or even by repeatedly searching the Internet. In the case of seeking medical reassurance, this is particularly a problem for people with health anxiety. This will be discussed in Chapter 8.

Other Examples of Treatment of OCD Using ERP

Contamination Fears

Mike's Story

Mike is a 30-year-old electrician who has always had minor obsessive-compulsive difficulties. Five years ago, he was visiting the Metro Centre with his wife and went to the toilet. While in the toilet, he noticed some dried blood on the cubicle door. Following this incident, he became convinced he had contracted HIV from the blood. He visited his local genito-urinary clinic to have an HIV test. Unsurprisingly, his test was negative, but this did not reassure him, and so he started returning to the clinic on a weekly basis 'in case they'd missed something'. In addition, he became concerned about anything that he may have touched since he went to the Metro Centre or which he believed may have become 'contaminated' in another way.

These problems grew, and eventually he was forced to stop seeking reassurance from the genito-urinary clinic and his general practitioner (GP) after the clinic refused to see him again and his GP threatened to discharge him unless he stopped making emergency appointments to see him regarding HIV. Although Mike was very anxious after this, the anxiety eventually lessened, but he continued to perform extensive 'decontamination' compulsions. These involved asking anyone who visited him who had been outside (and thus potentially in contact with somebody who may have been at the Metro Centre) to take off all their external clothes, which were placed in plastic bags. They were then asked to wash and bathe extensively. The clothes were sprayed 10–15 times with antibacterial spray before being washed in hot water several times. Clothes were often thrown away if he did not believe they were 'clean'. Mike had been unable to work for the past five years, and due to the stress of his compulsive rituals, he had started staying in bed for the past six months. Because getting out of bed resulted in so many urges to start his 'decontamination rituals', he was frequently incontinent of urine in the bed. In addition, he restricted his fluid consumption to avoid visiting the toilet. At the time of assessment, he was drinking only 500 ml of fluid a day. Bathing took him up to five hours; consequently, he bathed only once a month. His wife was tired and distraught and was considering divorce.

The first stage of treatment was to fully assess Mike and to determine his obsessional fear at the root of his problems. This was identified as 'a fear of catching HIV, primarily from the Metro Centre or from anyone who has been in contact with the Centre'. This fear resulted in extensive avoidance of leaving the house and significant decontamination compulsive rituals concerning items which were brought into the house. In addition, there were widespread decontamination compulsions concerning the house and Mike's personal hygiene. Due to the extreme nature of these problems, Mike was avoiding basic personal care of washing and bathing. He was also restricting his fluid intake to reduce his use of the toilet.

The next stage of therapy was to ensure Mike understood OCD and the principles of treatment. It was explained how he would be asked to face his fear and 'contaminate' himself without engaging in his 'decontamination' behaviours. The first issue that needed to be addressed, however, was his avoidance of drinking sufficient fluid. It was explained to Mike and his wife that such fluid restriction could lead to permanent damage of the kidneys. Although we would normally expect Mike to produce a hierarchy of fears, it was believed to be so important to address his fluid intake that any therapy would need to start by tackling this issue. Mike agreed he would drink 1–1.5 litres of fluid a day if he could use tissues to touch any item in the bathroom. Both the therapist and Mike's wife agreed to this, but he was told that he must also go to the toilet at least every three hours during the day to avoid any incontinence. Before the therapist saw him again, he was asked to produce a list of situations which would cause him to feel 'contaminated' and anxious and to give these an anxiety rating, with 0 representing no anxiety and 8 representing panic. It was explained that these anxiety ratings needed to rate how he would feel if he did not engage in any compulsive rituals or any avoidance to 'put right' the fear. Although he was initially allowed to use tissues when visiting the toilet, this was to ensure his health, and eventually he would be asked to forego the use of tissues.

Mike was very anxious about what he may be asked to do but did realise that his concern about the Metro Centre was 'completely over the top'.

At the therapist's next visit, Mike produced the following hierarchy of fears:

Exposure item (without washing/ decontamination rituals)	Anxiety level predicted (0–8 scale)
Touch walls, doorknobs, taps, etc. in the house without hand washing after or decontaminating before	3–4
Touching clothes that have been outside	4

(cont.)

Exposure item (without washing/decontamination rituals)	Anxiety level predicted (0–8 scale)
Using bathroom and toilet without 'decontaminating' first and by touching flushers and bathroom taps using bare hands	5
Walking to High Street and seeing other people; return home without changing clothes or bathing immediately	5–6
Travelling on public transport	8
Travelling to Metro Centre	8

At the next session, it was agreed that it was important to work on changing the compulsive behaviours and establishing a reasonable self-care routine. First, it was confirmed that Mike had been drinking enough fluid during the previous week and was looking far less unwell than at the first meeting. Next, the therapist enquired about his bathing and the reason it took so long. As well as cleaning everywhere before getting into the shower, Mike also had a set 'routine' of showering whereby he washed starting from the top of his body and worked down. If he believed an area had not been washed 'properly', he would repeat the routine. These repetitions often occurred eight or nine times so that each part of his body was red and raw. To break this pattern, the therapist instructed him to take a shower twice daily but that he was to stand under the shower for a maximum of five minutes and was not to use soap or try to 'wash' any area. He was also asked not to clean the shower before use. Mike agreed to try this and predicted his anxiety score for this activity would be 6 or 7. The therapist also showed him a new way to wash his hands that involved plugging the basin of the sink and filling it a quarter full of water. 'Normal' hand-washing taking 30 seconds or less was then demonstrated. This involved only the hands and not the forearms as Mike had previously been doing. Mike was then asked to try this with the therapist watching. He was asked to wash his hands only after going to the toilet and at no other times. It was agreed that at the next session, the therapist would visit

Mike's house, and they would 'contaminate' themselves by touching items in the house which Mike believed were contaminated.

When the therapist next visited the house, Mike was delighted to inform them that he had bathed in the prescribed fashion all week, continued to maintain his fluid levels, and washed his hands as demonstrated. The therapist praised him and then demonstrated how Mike should expose himself to 'contamination'. This involved touching the 'contaminated' object with both hands; rubbing the hands together and then touching his hair, upper torso, lower torso, legs, lips, and mouth; and then licking his hands to ensure that he felt 'contaminated'. Mike was extremely anxious about this but was reminded of the habituation curve and agreed to give it a try. In fact, he did extremely well, and during the session he agreed to go further and touch the toilet flusher and taps without washing. He was praised and was asked to continue performing these exposure exercises three times a day for the next week.

Treatment continued in this way. Mike was asked to touch the toilet seat and contaminate himself in the prescribed manner. The principle of performing tasks which appear excessive was discussed previously. It is often useful to overlearn these tasks to prevent reversion to previous behaviours after therapy ends.

After nine sessions, Mike agreed to accompany the therapist to the Metro Centre. They travelled around the Metro Centre, touching as many items as possible. They went into the toilets and touched the taps and toilet flushers and the door. Then they went to the burger shop and ate a burger without washing their hands. Mike was anxious, but he settled as the day progressed. This exposure session lasted a total of four hours, including travel on public transport to get to the Metro Centre.

Is ERP Dangerous?

Some people worry that exposure exercises such as those described previously are 'risky' and that it is unethical to ask someone to risk contracting an illness by not washing. The risk of contracting HIV by such activity is almost zero, but there is a very small possibility of contracting another less serious infection. Of course, during a situation such as the recent pandemic with COVID-19, it is imperative that everyone follows government and World Health Organization advice regarding hand washing and other infection control measures. This issue is discussed fully in Chapter 13. It is important to remember that all of us perform risky behaviours every day, for example when we drive a car or cross a road on foot. Patients with OCD can be restricted in all aspects of their lives for decades. If asked to weigh the tiny risk of catching a minor illness against suffering from OCD with its life-impacting consequences, most people will conclude that the risk of ERP is overshadowed by the life-destroying effects of OCD.

It must also be remembered that the body has protection to fight infection. The skin forms a thick barrier to infection. It is covered with normal, useful bacteria which help prevent harmful bacteria from spreading. Excessive washing, as seen in many people with OCD and decontamination compulsions, actually destroys some of these bacteria and can make skin infection more likely. The use of antibacterial gels and sprays (or, even worse, antiseptics and bleach) adds to this effect and greatly increases the risk of infection. Excessive washing also serves to thin the skin, and many people with hand-washing compulsive rituals have open cuts and sores on their hands and other parts of their bodies where they wash excessively. This results in a direct route for infection into the body and also greatly increases the risk of infection. In fact, studies have been performed at the University of Sydney whereby people were asked to touch things commonly perceived as 'dirty' by people with contamination OCD. When hands that touched these 'dirty' items were compared with hands that did not touch these items, there were no differences in the types and numbers of bacteria. This finding is part of the 'evidence' presented to people who undertake danger ideation reduction therapy (discussed later).

Indeed, the best hand-washing technique in most normal situations is to wash hands for the duration it takes to sing 'Happy Birthday to You' in one's head or, in other words, for 15–30 seconds.

Treatment of Checking Compulsions

Jill's Story

Jill is a 30-year-old woman with a ten-year history of minor obsessive fears. Five years ago, she moved away from her parental home into her own studio flat and started a new job as a legal secretary. Since moving into her flat, Jill has become very anxious that a disaster will occur, resulting in her losing all her belongings. She therefore feels the need to check her cooker and all electrical appliances to ensure they are switched off, and repeatedly checks her doors and windows before leaving for work. Initially, these checks took only a few minutes, but the time required has gradually increased so that they currently take up to two hours. Recently, she has even become concerned about leaving the freezer on whilst she is out. Having had a minor flood in her flat and being forced to throw food away, she has emptied the freezer and now only uses the refrigerator as a store for milk and butter and switches this off when not in the house. Realising that this problem is getting out of control, Jill decided to seek help.

Jill's problems were still under control but were starting to impact her ability to work as well as her ability to feed herself because she needed to buy fresh food every day. Initially, she set up a hierarchy of her fears, which were as follows:

Exposure item	Anxiety rating (0–8 scale)
Not checking light switches when leaving the flat	2
Not checking television and computer are switched off when leaving the flat	3
Not checking the refrigerator	4
Leaving the refrigerator and freezer switched on whilst leaving flat	5
Not checking hair straighteners when leaving flat	6
Not checking windows when leaving flat	7
Not checking front door when leaving flat	8

It was decided that Jill would start therapy herself by not checking the light switches, television, and the computer when leaving the flat. She easily performed these tasks but then became stuck. Feeling just too scared to move on to the other items in her hierarchy, Jill believed she could not move forward. It was agreed that she would take a day off work and meet with the therapist. On the day she was to do this, Jill was to get ready to go out but was not to check any of the items on her hierarchy. She would telephone the therapist on her mobile phone, who talked her through walking out of the flat without checking. Jill would then travel to the clinic with the risk that a disaster had happened to her possessions.

Although this was a difficult exercise, Jill managed to complete it. She was tearful and shaking whilst at the clinic, but this settled after two hours. During this time, she was encouraged to think of the 'worst-case scenario' whereby she returned home to find her flat burgled or burned to the ground. Following this session, Jill has been able to continue this routine on a daily basis. Some days are more difficult than others and she has a stronger urge to check, but despite a few setbacks, she persists and finds that her overall anxiety is reduced to mild levels.

Perfectionism and Slowness

Colin's Story

Colin is a 45-year-old man who lives with his wife and two children. He previously worked as a clerk for a building firm but had to leave this job five years ago due to an inability to complete his work on time. Since being at home, he has become increasingly slower at performing a range of tasks so that now he can take up to six hours in the bathroom. This problem impacts the family, and he has recently started sleeping during the day and waking at night to avoid restricting family access to the bathroom due to his OCD. Colin believes that everything he does needs to be performed 100 per cent correctly or else he will be a failure. Being a failure means that his family and friends will abandon him. In discussion, he agrees that he is more 'fussy' that other people. Although he still likes the idea of being 'perfect', he realises that he is far from it in his current state and is thus willing to try to change and to be 'good enough'. The first phase of this treatment is to deliberately perform actions incorrectly. Colin believed he would like to start with this problem rather than tackle his bathing and toileting problems (even though this means he has to attend the clinic having had little sleep). Colin produced the following list of 'wrong' items and the anxiety they would cause:

Exposure item	Anxiety rating (0–8 scale)
Wearing odd socks all day	3
Wearing T-shirt inside out and back to front	4
Making a cup of tea and adding the milk first (Colin believes the milk should always be added afterwards, although he realises others disagree.)	4
Leaving one arm unwashed in the shower	3
Leaving one leg unwashed in the shower	4
Not combing hair	4
Shaving with electrical razor without looking in the mirror	4
Eating dessert before main course	3

Because Colin may be tempted to perform each of these exposure items perfectly, he was instructed that as soon as he got up, he was to throw a die three times until he obtained three different numbers. The three numbers represented the three items that he had to perform each day. He was to continue otherwise as normal. In addition, he was asked to only perform his programme 75 per cent correctly rather than strive to be the 'perfect patient'.

Colin managed to perform the 'imperfect' programme with approximately 70 per cent compliance. He performed all the items on the list several times over a few weeks. However, he was still spending many hours in the bathroom before being able to get out and was also spending up to two hours in the toilet every time he went to pass water. Colin stated that the reason he took so long was that he felt the need to perform tasks until they felt 'just right'. This involved, for example, sitting on the toilet seat and altering his position several times over many minutes until he felt he was completely balanced and symmetrical. Because the list of items such as these that Colin performed was so numerous, it was agreed to tackle this in one go. The therapist agreed to visit Colin's home for a morning and talk him through getting up and dressed in no more than two hours. Before this meeting, Colin had been asked to practice items such as sitting asymmetrically on the toilet seat.

When the therapist arrived at Colin's house, he was dressed in his pyjamas. The first task was to get him to eat his breakfast. Every day, Colin's breakfast consisted of cereal and milk with a cup of tea. He was encouraged to sit down and, without arranging his cutlery perfectly next to the cereal bowl, pour the approximate amount of cereal and milk he required without measuring these. Then he was to drink his tea rapidly. He was to perform these eating and drinking activities without a break to ensure he was doing them correctly. Once he had eaten, he needed to go to the toilet and shower. Obviously, the therapist did not accompany him but, rather, remained outside the bathroom and encouraged Colin to sit imperfectly on the toilet seat and to take a shower without checking that he washed every part of his body perfectly. It was decided that he should then get dressed before shaving. Colin would normally check that his clothes were perfectly ironed and would make sure that he put them on his body so that they were perfectly straight. He was encouraged to take a risk and put his clothes on in a more 'haphazard' manner before moving on to shaving and brushing his hair. Shaving was to take no more than four minutes and hair brushing 30 seconds. Colin found hair brushing very difficult as he tried to copy the technique of the therapist, who showed Colin how he brushed his hair.

The entire process took two hours. Colin said that he did not feel 'right' following this but was happy to continue. The therapist had made an audio recording of the entire session on Colin's mobile phone. Colin was asked to listen to the recording every day for the next week and to keep to the schedule.

When Colin returned to see the therapist a week later, he had not only achieved this goal but also was taking less than one hour and so had abandoned the tape. He was taking only five minutes to go to the toilet during the day and was feeling much happier.

Currently, Colin is still aware that he occasionally has urges to be 'perfect', but mostly manages to resist these. He is happier and is going out with his family without demanding that they perform actions perfectly as well. He is thinking about attending adult education classes to retrain as a gardener.

Colin's story again demonstrates the main principle of treating OCD by using ERP. In Colin's situation, his basic fear is the consequence of being less than perfect. Therapy was designed to encourage him to perform actions imperfectly and, by so doing, find out what happens when he is 'imperfect'. In reality, of course, all of us are imperfect, and in Colin's case, his constant seeking for perfection meant that he was able to do very little and was thus far from perfect as an employee (he had to stop working), as a father (he rarely saw his children), and as a husband (he rarely saw his wife and was unable to be a 'partner' in the relationship). Once he abandoned striving for perfection, he was much more successful in all areas of his life.

Obsessions with Covert Compulsions (Ruminations)

People often become confused about so-called obsessive ruminations. This is because they are used to the idea that anxiety-provoking obsessive *thoughts* are followed by anxiety-reducing compulsive *behaviours*. However, compulsions can be behaviours, thoughts, or images. As such, any ERP therapy must identify the anxiety-provoking thoughts whilst stopping the anxiety-reducing compulsive thoughts.

Ethan's Story

Ethan, a 42-year-old unmarried ex-schoolteacher, has a 15-year history of distressing obsessions which occupied 10–12 hours a day and led to his early retirement from work. Whenever he saw anyone, he would have the thought,

'I would like to have sex with him/her'. This thought was repugnant to him because he was a devout 'born-again' Christian who did not condone extra-marital sex, and because homosexuality, paedophilia, and incest, which his thoughts implied, were abhorrent to him.

To reduce his anxiety, he had developed the habit of repeating the Lord's Prayer and then saying 'Jesus, forgive me' seven times. If he was interrupted by any sound or movement in his environment, he would have to repeat this process until it was performed perfectly. This problem led him to seek the life of a recluse, and he had even stopped attending church. He had contemplated suicide to rid himself of the problem, but he believed this was an even greater sin.

Initially, treatment took the form of graduated, prolonged exposure to situations he avoided. However, he made only limited progress because he could not stop himself from automatically starting his 'praying ritual' which helped to maintain his anxiety. It was decided that he needed to experience prolonged exposure to his anxiety-provoking thoughts without ritualising. This was achieved by having him record these thoughts (e.g., 'I want to have sex with her' and 'I want to have sex with him') on his smartphone. Ethan was then asked to play these thoughts to himself via the phone's earpiece for at least one hour three or four times a day while in the company of other people (e.g., while riding the bus).

Initially, Ethan found this so aversive that he had difficulty complying. Therefore, the therapist advised him to start with the volume turned down low and to increase the volume as he became more confident. This procedure worked extremely well, and within two weeks, Ethan reported that he had little anxiety and was able to go out at other times and not just when performing his programmes. Despite having the thoughts, he no longer carried out the ritual. After two months, he was able to return to work as a 'supply' teacher. At six-month post-treatment follow-up, he reported that he had a girlfriend, he was planning to marry, and he laughed at the thoughts which he now considered to be 'stupid'.

Two issues appear to be of particular importance in this treatment. First, it appears to be most effective if the recording is made by the person with

OCD rather than by another person. Second, it appears to be more effective if it is played through an earpiece. The effect of these two strategies is that it seems virtually impossible for the person with OCD to perform compulsive thought rituals whilst their own voice is repeating the obsessive thought. The fact that it is their own voice and is heard in their head means it is difficult to concentrate on much else initially.

Treatment of OCD with Hoarding Problems

Hoarding disorder will be fully discussed in Chapter 8. The symptom of hoarding, however, can occur in people with OCD. Joan's story illustrates how hoarding can be part of OCD and how it can be tackled.

Joan's Story

Joan is a 42-year-old woman who lives with her husband and two teenaged children. She has suffered from a series of obsessive worries all her life, but these had not been overly problematic until the birth of her youngest child 15 years ago. This had been a difficult delivery, and Joan had suffered massive bleeding during labour. There was concern about the baby, and he was taken to the paediatric intensive care unit overnight. Although there was no long-lasting effect on his health, Joan understandably found this to be a very difficult experience. Following the birth, she developed postnatal depression. This depression was eventually noted and treated with antidepressants nine months after the birth, but Joan was left with residual obsessive fears. Joan fears that she may inadvertently disclose information which will lead to her losing her children. She is not worried about verbally giving away information but, rather, that she may write something down which is incriminating and, as a written word, would be more difficult to explain away.

Initially, this problem meant that Joan felt the need to meticulously check all pieces of paper in the house for fear they may contain some detrimental information. All labels, receipts, letters, and papers which came into the house were repeatedly checked. During the past eight years, this problem has become increasingly worse, and Joan is now unable to throw out any written material, including empty food packets. The family lives in a large detached four-bedroomed house, but it is quickly becoming uninhabitable due to Joan's hoarding. Initially, the double garage was filled from floor to ceiling, but now the spare bedroom is becoming full, and Joan wants her sons to share a bedroom so that she can continue to hoard her items. During the past three years, in addition to paper items, Joan has also been collecting pieces of paper and detritus left on the pavement in case these also contain damaging revelations about her. Joan realises that these thoughts are ridiculous and untrue, and she also realises the stress she is causing the family, but she still has an overwhelming fear when faced with pieces of paper.

When Joan came to the clinic and discussed her problem, it was agreed that the first issue to be tackled would be working on preventing more items from being brought into the house. With anybody who hoards, it must first be established that no more items will be brought into the house while the clearing of items is taking place. Otherwise, the exercise of clearing the house is pointless because the hoard will rapidly reaccumulate. Obviously, in a situation such as Joan's, some items will continue to come into the house in the form of letters and food packaging. It was thus decided that therapy would start with an exposure programme involving Joan's fear of revealing information.

It was very difficult for Joan to create a hierarchy of her fears because all of them related to her fear of revealing detrimental information. Throwing away a food packet was as anxiety-provoking as throwing away a piece of paper with her writing on it because she believed both may contain damaging information. Eventually, it was agreed that the therapist would write the following on several pieces of paper, 'I declare that I am a bad mother and that my children should be taken away from me'. These pieces of paper were then signed by the therapist. This exercise was designed to be anxiety-provoking for Joan but also demonstrated that the therapist was prepared to take the same or greater risk herself. Joan and the therapist then walked into the main High Street of town and deposited these pieces of paper in litter bins, on a table in a fast-food restaurant, and on a table in a local library. Joan found this very anxiety-provoking but agreed that she would not return to the High Street to collect these papers later. She also agreed to go out every day and to throw away blank pieces of paper in the way the therapist and she had done during the session.

The next week, Joan was feeling very pleased and had already been able to throw away printed paper. She was praised for doing so. It was agreed that in light of this, therapy should move on to throwing away some of the hoarded items. Initially, Joan wanted to check all the papers she threw away. The therapist reminded her that this checking was likely to lead to more checking and more anxiety. Eventually, she agreed to start throwing away items in the garage which had been there for more than two years. During the first session, the therapist and Joan managed to discard six large rubbish sacks full of paper. Joan agreed to let the therapist take these to the local tip so that she could not check them later. She also agreed to put out at least two sacks per day for her husband to discard on his way to work.

Over the next few weeks, Joan cleared most of her house. Dealing with newer post was difficult initially, but she was reminded of the principle that she should read any post, act on it immediately if necessary, and then discard it.

Does ERP Really Work?

Studies throughout the years have repeatedly shown that approximately 75 per cent of people with OCD who are offered ERP will improve. The rate of improvement is generally measured using a scale known as the Yale–Brown Obsessive–Compulsive Scale (Y-BOCS). To be identified as a 'responder' to either drugs or ERP (see 'What Are the Advantages and Disadvantages of Medication and Exposure and Response Prevention?' in Chapter 4), an improvement of more than 35 per cent on the Y-BOCS should be found from the start of treatment to the end of treatment. In reality, this is probably an underestimate because the Y-BOCS is not very sensitive to anything other than large improvements in symptoms. An improvement of 35 per cent on the Y-BOCS is often found to be accompanied by an improvement in life functioning of 50 per cent or more.

It has proven impossible to predict precisely who responds the most to treatment with ERP. Certainly, children appear to respond better than adults. Obviously, if a person has had a mild problem for a short time, they may also be expected to respond well to treatment. However, this is not an absolute rule. Many people who have had profound OCD problems for many decades can still respond to ERP. This may be because they are more motivated to carry out the treatment to overcome the OCD which has blighted their lives. A study involving some of the most profoundly ill people treated in our inpatient ward and severely ill people treated in the community examined outcomes and found few clear predictors of success at the beginning of treatment.

The main factor which determines how much improvement a person can gain from ERP seems to be how well they can adhere to the treatment programmes and face their fears without the anxiety-relieving compulsions.

A recent review which examined all the recent studies using ERP concluded that ERP was an effective treatment but that more research would be helpful in this area to understand how this is working.

What Are the Reasons Why ERP May Not Work?

There are several very obvious reasons why ERP may not work. First, the person has to be committed to change. If they do not wish to stop the OCD then, obviously, they will not be motivated to apply the treatment. It is often extremely difficult for the family and friends of someone with OCD to understand why the person with OCD would not want to overcome this potentially devastating condition. Humans generally dislike change and tend to feel secure with what they know. Asking someone to give up the OCD symptoms, which are so familiar to them, can feel threatening and scary. Sometimes the treatment can seem worse than the OCD. Indeed, OCD seems to give some individuals comfort and security; losing the label of OCD would mean that they have to face the problems of the world, such as working fora living, moving out of the parental home, or forming new relationships. In this case, OCD gives them a reason to not engage with these challenges.

When a person with OCD does not wish to change, then ERP will not work. Very often, friends and relatives of the person with OCD believe that the therapists have failed their loved one if they cannot persuade him or her to engage in therapy. The best course of action in this case is to make sure they understand what therapy entails and the likely benefits. They may then decide not to engage in therapy at the current time. Throughout the years, I have seen many people who did not wish to engage in ERP when I first met them but, sometimes years later, came back and completed therapy and are now doing extremely well. In other words, the door should always be left open for the individual to accept ERP therapy in the future; it is never too late, and it is the individual with OCD who must decide when the time is right for them.

On the other hand, some people have therapy and then wish to have more and more. ERP works by the person with OCD eventually learning to be their own therapist. If the individual has had a reasonable trial of therapy of approximately 20–40 sessions, then there should be a gap of six months to one year before any more therapy is prescribed. It is counter-productive to become fixated or 'addicted' to the therapy! A gap in therapy allows the individual to think about their goals of therapy and how best to apply ERP and to try to implement some of this themselves.

Another important reason for ERP not being successful is that it is not prescribed or performed in a regular, prolonged, predictable manner. For the best results, ERP should be practised three times a day and for sufficient time to allow the anxiety to reduce consistently by at least 50 per cent.

Sometimes the wrong programmes are being applied. For example, someone may be performing ERP in the clinic but not be able to continue it at home. In such cases, it can be useful to return to easier items on the hierarchy and determine if they can then perform these at home. In other cases, it may be helpful for the therapist to go with the person to perform ERP in the home setting or wherever the symptoms are maximal.

Another issue arises when there is confusion over fear-provoking obsessions and anxiety-reducing compulsions. Exposure should be performed without the compulsions, because the compulsions essentially neutralise the effect of exposure.

It can often be tempting to gradually reduce compulsions or even place these on a hierarchy. In reality, this rarely works because it is extremely difficult to cut down on such behaviours. It is much better and easier in the long term to stop the compulsive behaviours entirely. In the case of washing compulsion or other compulsions which are also necessary behaviours, the compulsive activity should be stopped and a new form of more 'normal' behaviour introduced and practised.

Sometimes anxiety does not reduce after exposure due to certain medications or even alcohol. Tablets such as lorazepam (Ativan), diazepam (Valium), and chlordiazepoxide (Librium) are sometimes prescribed for people with OCD, even though these should only be used for short periods of time up to a maximum of six weeks. It can be tempting for the individual who is feeling anxious to take one of these tablets. In such cases, the tablet-taking is replacing the compulsions and will not result in a long-term reduction in anxiety. A similar action is found with alcohol, which can also be used in this manner.

Another reason why ERP may not work is that the person has a complicating additional diagnosis. Most people with moderate to severe OCD are also depressed. For the majority of people, treatment of the OCD also lifts the depression. This is not true, however, for a minority of people. Possible approaches to this are discussed in Chapter 6.

Similarly, some people have extremely high levels of anxiety and/or believe in the rationality of the obsessive thoughts. These cases, along with cases in which people have developed OCD following childhood trauma, are discussed in Chapter 6.

Finally, some people have problems controlling and tolerating their emotions. These people can find it almost impossible to engage with ERP. These individuals often have had a disrupted childhood and may be diagnosed with emotionally unstable personality disorder. It is often advisable for these people to receive help in learning how to tolerate strong emotions before embarking on ERP treatment.

Cognitive Therapy and OCD

Although it may seem logical to try to tackle OCD using cognitive therapy, there is no evidence that it offers any advantage compared to ERP. Many studies have been performed to examine any differences between the two approaches; overall, ERP generally produces similar or better results compared to any cognitive intervention. Indeed, any cognitive treatment requires an exposure element to be successful. Poorly applied cognitive therapy may make some patients with OCD worse. This is because the process of searching for evidence to confirm or refute the obsessions can become incorporated into the compulsive rituals. Cognitive therapy is also less cost-effective because it requires more training and supervision for the therapist and usually takes more time to perform. Overall, this means that more people can be helped using ERP rather than cognitive behaviour therapy (CBT).

Probably the most logical usage of CBT is that the vast majority of people with OCD can be helped with the strategy of ERP, with or without medication. For people who cannot respond or who have an additional complicating diagnosis, specific CBT strategies may be used.

Other Forms of Psychological Treatment and OCD

There is no evidence that strategies such as counselling or psychotherapy, which involve talking about the OCD problems, are useful in the treatment of OCD. Indeed, in some cases these strategies may worsen the situation as the person becomes increasingly introspective.

Family therapy can sometimes be a useful addition to ERP treatment if the family are heavily involved in either helping the person with OCD perform their compulsions or if they are unduly negative towards the individual.

KEY POINTS

- The exposure principle of treatment for OCD states that if the person exposes themselves to objects or situations which trigger the anxiety-provoking thoughts for a sufficient length of time (usually two hours) without performing anxiety-reducing compulsions, then their anxiety will reduce. This is known as exposure with self-imposed response prevention (ERP).
- ERP should be performed in a graded manner, starting with easier exposure items.
- ERP should be repeated regularly, ideally three times a day.
- Although anxiety is unpleasant, it will not lead to harm and will eventually reduce if no compulsions or avoidance behaviours are used.
- ERP can be applied to all types of OCD.
- ERP is successful in approximately 75 per cent of people who are offered the treatment.
- Sometimes ERP does not work because the individual is not yet ready to change and to give up their OCD.
- Other reasons why ERP may not work initially are that it is not being applied correctly or that a complicating additional diagnosis is preventing the anxiety from reducing.
- Cognitive behaviour therapy does not seem to add any benefit for most people with OCD above what can be achieved using ERP.
- Talking therapies in general are not helpful.
- Family therapy can be used in addition to ERP if there are specific family difficulties.

6

. . . .

Children and Adolescents with OCD

This chapter will examine the recognition and treatment of children and adolescents with OCD. Until recently, OCD was thought to be rare in children. It is now recognised to be among the most common mental disorders in childhood. There are differences between the way OCD presents in childhood and that seen in adulthood. These differences are mainly due to children's lack of maturity. This chapter will give examples, paying particular attention to recognition. Treatment for children is similar to that for adults, but there are some clear differences. First, with very young children, it is difficult to set up a rigid hierarchy and expect them to learn to be their own therapist, and so adaptation is necessary. Second, with young children, the entire family needs to be involved if the situation is not to unravel once treatment ends. Third, drug dosages are lower for children. Adolescents who present with OCD are often extremely dependent on their parents and have consequently had a very restrictive upbringing. These adolescents need help learning how to care for themselves and to engage with the world. Adolescence is a time of rebellion for many young people; for some, this means they will rebel against their treatment and fail to engage fully. Tips are given as to how to engage this group.

Finally, we will explore the idea of OCD arising acutely in childhood in some children and the possible relationship between this condition and infection. The controversial paediatric autoimmune neuropsychiatric disorders associated with streptococcal infection (PANDAS) or, more recently, paediatric/childhood acute-onset neuropsychiatric syndrome (PANS/CANS) will be discussed. These are based on the theory that some children have a very dramatic and sudden onset of OCD symptoms together with other neurological symptoms, such as extreme jerking, twitching, and loss of balance. The theory is that certain bacterial infections can trick the body to 'mistake' its own cells as being those of bacteria. In susceptible individuals, this may cause the body to attack its own cells in the brain. In a small minority of people with OCD, there is evidence that some cells in the basal ganglia (back of the brain) have been damaged in this manner. This has led to studies on the use of antibiotics in some children in the acute phase of onset.

Obsessive compulsive disorder (OCD) is one of the most common psychological problems seen in childhood. Whereas it was once thought to be rare in this age group, it is now known to be quite common, with between 1 and 3 per cent of children being affected. A recent large cross-national study of adults found that almost one in five adults with OCD gave a history of the condition starting before the age of ten years. Fortunately, childhood OCD does not necessarily continue into adulthood. OCD can be extremely difficult to diagnose in young children for two main reasons. First, young children may not be able to express their thoughts and emotions in a coherent manner or may try to hide the behaviours from others. It has been suggested that it is almost impossible to diagnose OCD in children younger than age seven years. Second, children often experience periods in which they may have obsessive symptoms which resolve spontaneously.

Bryony's Story

Bryony is a nine-year-old girl who is doing well in school, has friends, and generally appears to be a happy and healthy child. Six months ago, she was attending a local Brownie Guide meeting and discussion was held about the importance of hand hygiene. The children were shown pictures of the various types of bacteria. Bryony was very keen on watching medical dramas on television and said she wished to work in a hospital when she grew up. She was fascinated by watching the surgical staff 'scrub up' before performing operations. She started to perform the same type of washing before every meal, coming to the table with her hands in the air and wishing to repeat the wash if anyone contaminated her. Her mother had a long discussion with her and explained the reasons why this was not necessary. Bryony believed that bacteria were 'disgusting', but her mother encouraged her to also think of all the good things bacteria are capable of doing. After a few weeks, this behaviour completely subsided because Bryony found it was too time-consuming to continue, and she developed an interest in learning more about the ways in which bacteria can protect against allergies.

This story shows how, with the family treating her concerns as a normal phase of development and not taking them too seriously, the 'phase' passed, and Bryony was left with no residual symptoms. Not every situation is similar, however, and it can be difficult to diagnose the disorder in children if the content of the obsessive thoughts and compulsive rituals changes over time.

George's Story

George is an 11-year-old boy who was first noted by his parents at age eight years to be acting strangely. He would scream and become distressed if any mud landed on him or his clothing. Not wanting to play in the park, George started to complain that he had tummy pain on the days at school when students were due to play football or other outside sports. Believing this to 'be a phase', his parents asked the school to excuse him from sports. However, this extreme avoidance of mud led him to be teased and bullied at school. Suddenly, the problem seemed to stop, and he returned to playing outside again. However, his parents noticed that he would periodically stand still and blow into the air. This would last several minutes. At the same time, his school performance started to suffer, and he began to get into trouble at school for failing to hand in his work on time.

His parents became worried and took George to see his GP, who referred him to the local child and adolescent mental health service. Initially, it was difficult to find out from George what was bothering him. The family were seen together, and it was decided to also see George alone. After several sessions with the therapist, George admitted that he had extreme worries that his parents might die. These could occur at any time of the day or night, but when he had the thoughts, he had the urge to stand completely still and 'blow the thoughts away'. Unbeknown to his parents, George was waking up several times at night and quietly entering their bedroom to ensure he could still hear them breathing. This meant he was getting little sleep, and so his school performance was deteriorating.

Treatment for George consisted of a meeting with all the family to discuss the OCD – what it is and how it can be treated. George is an only child, and at the time he was very worried that his parents were older than most and so might die sooner, leaving him alone. Exposure and response prevention (ERP) consisted of George being encouraged to bring on his obsessive thoughts without performing the compulsions of repeated checking and blowing. This was extremely stressful, and he became very distressed and unable to continue. In light of this, it was decided to introduce additional treatment with sertraline. The dose of sertraline was adjusted to take into account George's age and size. He was started on a low dose of 25 mg, and this was gradually increased every week until he was on half the normal adult dose.

Once on sertraline, George appeared much brighter and was better able to engage with the ERP programme. He is currently doing well and is looking forward to moving to senior school next summer.

What Differences Need to Be Applied for Children in the ERP Programme?

Treatment of children who have OCD with ERP is identical to that for adults, except it is unreasonable to expect young children to learn the principles of the therapy and apply it themselves. For this reason, the family should normally be actively involved. Understanding OCD and the negative effect that compulsive rituals and reassurance-seeking can have on the condition is an important part of the discussion. It can be very difficult for a parent to resist offering reassurance to their distressed child, and so there needs to be a frank and full discussion in terms that the child can understand. Making a statement such as 'Mummy loves you very much and for that reason I am not going to answer your question. You remember how we talked about how answering these questions makes you more anxious?' can be helpful. It can seem to the child that a parent is being deliberatively punitive if they do refuse to answer, and so a reminder of previous discussions can be helpful. However, children are very good at 'holding their parents to ransom', and if it is late at night and everyone is tired and wants to go to bed, it can seem impossible not to give the reassurance that is required. If this happens, it is not a disaster. (It can be helpful for children to see that their parents are 'fallible'!) Of importance is that the child understands that they are loved but that part of this love is that the parent will no longer give reassurance because this will only end up making the situation worse.

In addition, with young children, it is sometimes important that the whole family be involved in treatment.

Mari's Story

Mari is an active eight-year-old who lives with her mother and two older siblings. A year after her father left the family home, when Mari was six years old, her mother moved the family to a new house that was much larger than the old one and also had white carpets and new furniture. Six months ago, Mari began to be overly concerned about keeping her room and the house tidy, and was constantly worried that she may make a mess. Mari's mother worried that she had nagged the children too much about making a mess and that this had caused Mari's problem. Due to her feelings of guilt, she would reassure Mari constantly.

Treatment involved all the family deliberately leaving some of the rooms untidy. When Mari asked for reassurance about being tidy, her mother told her that she did not mind whether the house was 'messy' or not. One final exposure programme involved all the family having a picnic in the living room on the white carpet. When they had finished, they all rolled around on the floor and ended up having a boisterous game with much laughing. Mari is now a much happier and relaxed child who is enjoying school and home life. Her mother reports that 'everyone is much happier now that I am more relaxed about the house. I have realised it is more important to have a happy rather than a perfect home'.

In the story of Mari, the entire family was able to relax and gain a better perspective and a calmer attitude towards life due to the ERP treatment. This does not mean that everyone should live in chaos and mess but, rather, that it is worthwhile to think about achieving a balance where everyone can be happy. Mari's mother also worried that she had 'caused' her daughter's OCD. In general, it is neither helpful nor possible to apportion blame in this way. Mari had experienced a number of changes in her life which may or may not have been related to the onset of her disorder. Some children with normal lives and little upset can develop OCD symptoms, whereas others who experience extreme trauma may be fine and may not develop problems. The important point in this case is that the entire family is now more settled and happier with their current situation, and there is every hope that Mari will continue to have a happy and healthy childhood.

Surely If a Child Has OCD It Is Due to Bad Parenting or to Upsetting Incidents?

The story of Mari illustrates how it is very easy for parents to blame themselves for their children's problems. The situation, however, is far more complicated than this.

We know that OCD has a tendency to run in families. Therefore, if a close family member has OCD, there is a greater chance that the children may also develop it. Again, this is far from inevitable, and more children will not develop OCD than those who do. Because people see some similarities in the behaviour of both the parent and the child in situations in which both have OCD, there is a tendency for people to blame the parent for 'causing' the condition. This is unfair. The parent can no more be held responsible for having OCD or OC traits to their personality than can the child. Both have been dealt a genetic predisposition to develop OCD, just as a parent cannot be blamed for their child having blond hair or blue eyes. In Chapter 2, we discussed resilience, which appears to be partly inherited and partly influenced by a warm, happy home environment. Despite this idea of resilience, some children brought up in a warm, loving home will still develop OCD. In other words, it is pointless to lay the blame at anyone's door for a child developing OCD. It is much more important to seek help and to start the child on the path to a happy and healthy future.

Many researchers have examined whether disruption in a child's life results in OCD. There is no conclusive evidence on this issue, with some studies linking OCD to previous life events in childhood and some finding no association.

Drug Treatment for OCD in Childhood

Most children with OCD will respond to ERP treatment and will not require drug treatment. Some children, however, will need to have a trial of medication as well.

The drug treatment of choice for children with OCD is the use of selective serotonin reuptake inhibitors (SSRIs) (see Chapter 4). The doses used in children are smaller than those used in adults and are related to children's smaller size (see **'Drugs which are commonly used for OCD in children in the UK'**). Generally, drugs for children should be prescribed according to their weight.

Drugs which are commonly used for OCD in children in the UK

Drug	Trade name	Dose range used in children (increasing with age up to ten years)
Fluoxetine	Prozac	20–60 mg/day The average is 1 mg per kg body weight per day. For example, a 40-kg child would be prescribed 40 mg/day.
Sertraline	Lustral	25–200 mg/day Generally, start at 25 mg/day and increase after one week to 50 mg/day. Any further increase depends on the age and weight of the child.
Paroxetine	Seroxat	10–60 mg/day
Fluvoxamine	Faverin	100–250 mg/day
Citalopram	Cipramil	10–40 mg/day Can increase by 5 mg per day every two weeks depending on the age and weight of the child.

Clomipramine is also sometimes prescribed to children. The reservations expressed in Chapter 4 also apply to children. Because clomipramine tends to have a greater risk of side effects compared to SSRIs, it should not be used as a first-line treatment. It should be introduced at a low dose starting at 10 mg/day and should be gradually increased to a maximum of 3 mg/kg/day or 200 mg/day (whichever is less). Clomipramine is not recommended for children younger than age ten years.

If the child has not responded to cognitive behaviour therapy involving ERP and a trial of two different SSRIs for a minimum of three months each, more specialised help is needed. Other drugs, such as dopamine blockers, can be added into the regimen, but particular care needs to be taken in using them in young people, who are more prone to side effects.

It is known that people who respond to SSRIs often relapse when these drugs are stopped. After approximately a year of treatment, it may be possible to reduce or stop the SSRI treatment. This should be done gradually over months rather than weeks and preferably under the supervision of a healthcare professional. The main risks are withdrawal side effects as well as a relapse of OCD.

People are often reluctant to allow their children to take SSRIs. It should be remembered that these drugs are not used to 'numb' or 'sedate' the child but, rather, are prescribed to try to increase the amount of serotonin in the brain, which is at a low level due to OCD.

Adolescents with OCD

Adolescence is often a tricky time. Teenagers often appear grumpy, aloof from their family, and secretive but impulsive, and they can rapidly switch from being fiercely independent to behaving like a child again. These are all a normal part of this stage of development into adulthood, as young people try to establish in their own minds who they are and what they want. This inevitably means trying to separate themselves from the family as they strive to assert their independence. In addition, adolescence is a time of changes in hormones and discovery of sexuality, along with feelings of self-doubt about appearance and attractiveness.

For a young person who also has OCD, adolescence is particularly difficult. They may struggle with wanting to go out and do the things that their friends are doing but find that their OCD prevents them from doing so. OCD often causes them to be more dependent and more in the position of a much younger child. Indeed, the fact that OCD can prevent this natural separation, individuation, and maturation from happening means that young people with OCD, even those who are well into young adulthood, can appear much younger than their years, regardless of how intellectually able they may be. In addition, normal sexual thoughts, impulses, and experimentation may be a source of huge guilt to the young person with OCD.

Those who develop OCD in adolescence might not discuss the disorder with their parents or people in authority. Adolescents very often try to hide their problems and sort them out themselves. It can be particularly difficult for parents to become aware of OCD problems because 'normal' adolescents often spend increasing amounts of time alone in their rooms and prolonged time in the bathroom as they try to come to terms with their own image as a sexually attractive adult. For parents of adolescents, the key is to leave the lines of communication between parent and offspring as open as possible. This means not talking 'down' to them but, rather, being open and honest about issues. Young people dislike being 'preached' at or 'nagged', and it is often a juggling act for a parent to maintain interest in their son or daughter without appearing overly intrusive and overbearing. Often, the young person is more relaxed in situations away from home and where they do not feel 'trapped' by the parent. The parent has to learn to listen more than they talk to the adolescent. This can be difficult to do. With younger children, the parental role is more about advice and guidance, whereas with adolescents the parent has to withdraw slightly and trust that the early lessons they have instilled in their child will stand the adolescent in good stead. While the parent is driving, for example, can be a time that the young person feels more able to talk, without direct eye contact and when the parent is preoccupied with another task and so will not react as strongly to whatever is said.

Signs that a young person may have problems with OCD, apart from clear and obvious excessive washing for no reason and checking compulsions, include the following:

- An unexpected poor performance at school
- Unauthorised absence from school
- Spending hours in the bathroom and/or toilet
- Appearing distracted

- Losing friends or struggling to make friends
- Worries that occur repeatedly
- Distress when a compulsive action is interrupted
- Getting in trouble at school for slowness or compulsions

None of these signs is exclusive to OCD. Most are seen in a range of psychological disorders as well as normal adolescence, but it is the combination of these signs together with information that can be gleaned from the adolescents themselves which may point to OCD being a problem.

Although adolescents need a degree of freedom and autonomy, they also need firm boundaries which are adhered to. These boundaries clearly need to be more liberal than with a younger child, but they still need to exist. Young people will often rebel against these boundaries, their parents, those in authority, and the system in which they live. For a young person with OCD, this can often take the form of rebelling against their treatment. Many young people with OCD who are up to 25 years of age will often rebel and refuse to participate in therapy, even though they wish to overcome their OCD. The thought of working with a structured therapy is just too overwhelming. In such cases, it is often useful to ask them what they would like their life to be like in one or two years. Where would they be living? What job/type of study would they be doing? What would their social life be like? From this, it can be determined with them what they are currently able to do. Then it must be worked out with them what skills they need to develop and what tasks they need to conquer to start edging towards their dreams. Adolescents often respond better to this type of approach rather than to a structured ERP regime. In reality, the end result is the same because by developing their skills, they generally need to perform ERP as well. The more 'problem-solving' approach can be better tolerated by some adolescents.

PANDAs, PANs, and CANs

In recent years, there has been interest in and research into the idea that an infection may be involved in a proportion of children or adolescents with

OCD (paediatric autoimmune neuropsychiatric disorders associated with streptococcal infection (PANDAS) or paediatric/childhood acute-onset neuropsychiatric syndrome). An extremely small proportion of children and adolescents seem to develop symptoms of OCD with an extremely rapid onset. This occurs in only 1 in 20 children with OCD. In these situations, the OCD is often accompanied by abnormal movements or sudden loss of coordination. These children sometimes have physical symptoms similar to those seen in a tiny proportion of children after a specific form of bacterial throat infection. The vast majority of throat infections are the result of viruses, and they cause no long-term problems. Some more severe throat infections are caused by a specific bacterium known as beta-haemolytic streptococcus group A (strep). Some weeks after a strep sore throat, susceptible individuals have been known to present with:

- abnormal movements (sometimes known as Sydenham's chorea/St Vitus dance); and
- problems with the heart and painful joints (rheumatic fever).

These problems are thought to occur as a result of an autoimmune response whereby the body tries to fight the infection. In certain susceptible individuals, the body not only 'attacks' the strep infection but also mistakenly attacks some of its own cells. In rheumatic fever, it attacks some cells in the joints and the heart, and in chorea it attacks some brain cells. Children who have such problems do get better, but there can also be long-term damage. There has been a very marked reduction in these complications of strep infections in developed countries since the early twentieth century. The reason for this reduction is not well understood, but it is thought to be due to the availability of antibiotics and the better general health and nutrition of children in the Western world. Skin rashes (scarlet fever) can also follow a strep sore throat after just a few days, but unlike the other conditions, these rashes occur earlier and are highly infectious, and they are not related to the same autoimmune diseases.

PANDAS is still a controversial concept, and not all child mental health workers are convinced it exists. It has been more widely accepted in the US than in Europe. The condition can present with an extremely rapid onset of abnormal movements associated with tics, Tourette syndrome, or OCD. In those with OCD, it appears that the symptoms generally improve over weeks or months. The children are particularly susceptible to side effects of SSRIs, and so these need to be used with care. It appears that the part of the brain known as the basal ganglia (the same area where the dopamine blockers act) is attacked by antibodies. If a child is suspected to have PANDAS, it is important to treat future sore throat episodes rapidly with antibiotics. Once the symptoms have presented, antibiotics are unlikely to give much benefit.

More recently, it has become clear that strep is not the only infection which can appear to precipitate tics or OCD in susceptible individuals. For this reason, it has been suggested that the term be altered to either PANS or CANS.

It is important to remember that the number of children affected by this type of problem is extremely small. Most children catch all kinds of infections without problems or, indeed, with the benefit of building their immunity. Thus, although interesting, in most situations OCD appears to be unrelated to infections, but future research of this type may help us better understand the development of OCD.

In reality, most children with OCD, even those with acute onset of OCD, will respond to treatment with ERP. Drug treatment may have to be used carefully because there is a suggestion that some children with this type of OCD are more likely to experience side effects. Antibiotics are only useful if the child is still showing signs of infection.

KEY POINTS

- Once thought to be rare in childhood, OCD is now known to be relatively common, affecting 1–3 per cent of children.
- OCD in childhood is similar to that seen in adults but can be difficult to diagnose due to children's lack of maturity and inability to explain their difficulties.

- ERP treatment may need to be adapted for younger patients, and family involvement is important.
- OCD medication for children is identical to that prescribed for adults except that the dose prescribed will be lower depending on the young person's age, size, and weight.
- Adolescents may also present particular challenges where the OCD can be combined with the frequent rebellion of adolescence.
- PANDAS, PANS, or CANS is the rapid onset of OCD or a tic disorder, usually with a marked and obvious onset of a movement disorder, in a young person who has recently suffered from an infection. It is believed that the bacteria 'trick' the immune system into attacking the individual's own cells. These children usually respond to cognitive behavioural therapy.

7

. . . .

Old Treatments, Modern Developments, New Research, and Potential Treatments for the Future

This chapter will examine ongoing research and the potential role this may have in the future. The chapter will first discuss physical methods of treatment. Then it will examine the role of infection and inflammation in the development of OCD. Finally, it examines potential gene modification by some hormones and how these may be harnessed to improve the outcome in OCD in the future.

First, there will be an examination of the role that neurosurgery has played for a very small number of people with OCD who have failed to respond to all other treatment approaches. This will dispel the myth that neurosurgery is the same as the 'lobotomy' performed during the early twentieth century. The reported outcomes of more specific surgery performed today will also be examined.

The chapter then discusses recent research into deep brain stimulation for people who may previously have been recommended for neurosurgery. This technique still involves wires being placed in the brain, but it does not permanently destroy brain tissue in the way neurosurgery does.

Next, the chapter will examine the more experimental transcranial magnetic stimulation as a potential alternative to more invasive procedures and possibly a technique which may be used in more routine practice in the future. This technique involves the application of powerful magnets to the outside of the head. By targeting these to act on specific areas of the brain, they can temporarily reduce OCD symptomatology. It is hoped that these may be useful in combination with exposure and response prevention (ERP) for some people unable to tolerate ERP alone.

In another area of research, it has been suggested that the glial cells in the brains of people with autism and OCD may be inflamed and unable to act typically. These cells produce glutamate, and this may tie in with recent work examining the potential use of glutamate modifiers. This theory has been taken further by some, who theorise that the normal healthy bacteria which make up an important part of our bodies may have become altered in modern life, resulting in an increase in autoimmune conditions. It has been suggested that childhood autism may also be 'autoimmune'. People with autism often have marked OCD symptoms, and so this link is also being examined.

Finally, the chapter will discuss how certain hormones may modify our genes. We know that OCD is a condition with a complex causation. Although there seems to be a genetic link, there is no clear pattern of inheritance, suggesting that other factors may be acting in a 'preventative' way to stop OCD from always appearing in its full-blown form. One theory is that oxytocin, a hormone produced when one is being nurtured or is nurturing, may bind to the gene and make it more likely to be dormant. Thus, it might be possible that good nurturing experiences in early childhood may modify or reduce OCD symptoms for some, but not all, people with OCD.

Brain Surgery

The whole concept of brain surgery is controversial and can arouse strong opinions and emotions in people. Undoubtedly, the procedures of the past were brutal and resulted in massive side effects. It must be noted that until the mid-1950s, we did not have the powerful medications which could help many people without resorting to, what seems to us today, extreme measures. Current interventions are far more targeted but still give rise to considerable controversy. In the UK today, we can assert with absolute confidence that no one would ever receive brain surgery for OCD in the NHS without first receiving all other available treatments and failing to improve with those, nor without having been fully informed of all the potential risks and benefits and subsequently consenting to the procedures. Neurosurgery is a very rare procedure for OCD, generally because ERP and drug treatment tend to work extremely well for most people. Brain surgery is, and will remain, the last resort for a very few individuals who do not benefit from less invasive procedures.

Is Brain Surgery Similar to What I Have Seen in Films?

There have been many depictions on stage and screen of brain surgery, and these generally paint a terrifying picture. In the early days of psychiatry, there were no effective drugs for psychological and psychiatric disorders. Most people with long-standing psychiatric problems were admitted to long-stay hospitals or asylums where they were kept apart from society and given food, nourishment, and a roof over their heads. Various 'treatments' which appear outlandish today were tried, including ice baths, insulin coma treatment, and sleep deprivation. Although these appear barbaric, it must be remembered that the lack of effective drugs or psychological therapies meant that there were no real therapeutic options, and so people tried methods that they hoped would improve the plight of those admitted to asylums. The 'treatment' of prefrontal leucotomy was introduced in the 1930s and was performed via two small holes in the head through which a sharp instrument was introduced which removed the connections between frontal parts and the bulk of the brain. This was introduced not as a direct treatment for mental disorder but, rather, as a way of inducing calm in the individual. This procedure was performed on hundreds of patients throughout the world before being replaced by a similar procedure which was just as crude, called prefrontal lobotomy. This procedure involved sharp implements going through the back of the eye sockets to achieve the same aim. It was developed by neurologists, Dr Freeman and Dr Watts, and because it could be performed easily, Dr Freeman claimed to have personally overseen up to 3,500 operations by the 1960s. In the mid-1950s, due to the development of both antipsychotic and antidepressant drugs, the demand for these surgical procedures rapidly declined. There was a significant mortality rate associated with the procedures. In addition, they were applied to any individual who was highly agitated and thus were used for people with schizophrenia, depression, and anxiety disorders as well as OCD.

More Modern and Precise Surgery

During the 1970s and 1980s, there was better understanding of the functions of various parts of the brain and operations were developed, mostly for intractable depression and OCD, which caused much less widespread brain damage but aimed to target specific areas of the brain. For example, a group in South West London developed a procedure known as 'limbic leucotomy' which involved small incisions or lesions being made in an area in the front of the brain. This was reported for use in people with OCD who did not respond to other treatments. It was followed by intensive ERP treatment and appeared to show good results, with 84 per cent of people with OCD showing lasting benefit with few long-lasting side effects. Overall, four types of neurosurgical operations which cause permanent lesions have been used for OCD:

- Limbic leucotomy
- Subcaudate tractotomy
- Cingulotomy
- Capsulotomy

These procedures all involve lesions within the frontal area of the brain. The widespread damage caused by earlier operations no longer occurs because of new ways in which surgeons can obtain images of the brains of individuals. Good outcomes have been reported for people with OCD. However, it must be remembered that none of these procedures has been fully investigated using the usual 'controlled trial' method of evaluation in which a 'dummy' or 'sham' procedure is compared with the treatment. This is because it is clearly unethical to submit a very unwell individual to a general anaesthetic and drill holes in the skull without performing a procedure. Currently, these procedures are limited in the UK to those who have failed to respond to repeated trials of both medication and ERP and who have profound OCD. Only a tiny handful of these operations are performed (fewer than one per year). The individual must always give informed consent, and there is also a legal procedure surrounding per-mission for surgery. These procedures depend on the country in which the person lives. In England and Wales, a second opinion appointed doctor (SOAD) and two other people appointed by the Care Quality Commission in England or the Healthcare Inspectorate Wales certify that the person has the capacity to consent and has done so. The SOAD also certifies that it is appropriate for a person to receive the treatment. In Scotland, a designated medical practitioner, appointed by the Mental

Welfare Commission, has to provide an independent opinion that the procedure will be beneficial. Two laypeople appointed by the Commission must then certify whether or not the individual has the capacity to consent and has done so. Variations of these laws exist in other European countries, in Australasia, and in the US and Canada.

Deep Brain Stimulation

A different approach to permanently destroying areas of brain tissue is the use of electrodes to stimulate differing areas of the brain to help overcome OCD symptoms. In this procedure, brain tissue is not destroyed, but electrical stimulation is used to alter the circuitry which results in OCD symptoms. This operation still requires a general anaesthetic. Small holes are then made in the skull through which thin wires are inserted and, using modern brain imaging techniques, these are moved to stimulate relevant areas in the front of the brain. A battery pack is then inserted in the chest wall to enable a small electrical current to provide electrical stimulation.

Deep brain stimulation (DBS) was first introduced as a highly successful treatment for the movement disorder Parkinson's disease. During approximately the past ten years, DBS has also been investigated for use in the treatment of severe depression, Tourette syndrome, and OCD. There have been a number of studies of DBS in OCD, but various different areas in the pathways have been stimulated, and it is sometimes difficult to compare outcomes. A study of all cases of DBS used for OCD which were reported in the medical literature from 1999 to 2014 showed that there were a total of 31 studies involving 116 people. Overall, a 45 per cent reduction in symptoms was reported by the participants. Sixty per cent of people responded to the treatment. Various different targets were used for stimulation in the studies.

A recent study in the UK examined people who had failed all other treatments and who were being considered for neurosurgery. Six people received DBS in up to four stimulation areas, and these were all compared until the best setting for each individual was found. All six patients showed marked improvements in their OCD symptoms, with more than a 35 per cent reduction in symptoms.

Overall, DBS seems to be a promising treatment for those who have the most profound OCD which does not respond to all other drug and ERP treatments.

Are There Any New and Less Invasive Treatments for People Who Do Not Respond to Drug Therapy and ERP?

A new and novel possibility is the use of transcranial magnetic stimulation (TMS). This involves applying powerful magnets to the outside of the skull. By directing these appropriately, it is possible to reduce activity in specific areas of the brain on a temporary basis. Often, this is repeated on a regular basis. Regular TMS has been shown to be useful in treating some people with severe migraine and also depression. For depression, TMS is applied daily for a period of up to six weeks.

There is evidence that TMS can improve symptoms for people with OCD which do not respond to other treatments. However, there are many different approaches to this treatment. For treatment of OCD, the magnets used with TMS must be more powerful than those used for depression, to penetrate deeper into the brain. Also, this treatment must be repeated regularly, but it is unclear how long it should be repeated for it to have a lasting benefit.

One of the differences between OCD and depression is that bouts of depression often last a few months at a time and are interspersed by periods of feeling well, whereas OCD is often, but not always, a consistent and continuous condition. It may therefore be problematic if a shorter treatment regimen is used. Research is needed to examine not only the efficacy but also the optimal way to deliver TMS to people with OCD. Furthermore, the combination of TMS with ERP is worthy of further study.

Inflammation and OCD

In Chapter 6, we discussed the way in which it appears that certain bacteria can trick the body into producing antibodies which then attack certain parts of the body instead of attacking the bacteria. These are known to cause autoimmune disorders, including conditions such as rheumatoid arthritis, coeliac disease, childhood-onset diabetes, psoriasis, and asthma. It may be that autoimmunity is implicated in a small proportion of children who develop rapid-onset movement disorders and OCD.

Another recent theory is that inflammation of the glial cells in the brain can give rise to childhood autism and possibly OCD. The work has generally been based on children with autism who also often have OCD symptoms. It has been shown that in some individuals with these conditions, the glial cells of the brain are inflamed. Glial cells were discussed in Chapter 4. These are the cells which occupy spaces between the neurones, which are the cells that transmit messages through the brain. The glial cells' function seems to be to modulate and control the transmission of messages. Glutamate is the chemical which is released by the glial cells, and it plays a role in helping control this transmission. In Chapter 4, we discussed drugs which act on the glutamate system and appear to make OCD worse or better. Some researchers have suggested that the inflammation of the glial cells upsets glutamate secretion, resulting in the OCD symptoms of autism.

These researchers also suggest that autoimmune conditions are increasing in modern society. This increase is suggested to be related to the overly clean and hygienic conditions in which children are raised. Whereas in the past, young children were exposed to a wider variety of bacteria and their immune systems learned to cope with them at a very young age, in modern society children are often kept in extremely clean environments during their very early years. This may mean that their bodies do not know how to cope with the range of bacteria they encounter later on in childhood, making them more prone to autoimmune disease. Indeed, recent research suggests that children who grow up on farms and who are exposed to a range of bacteria from a variety of animals are much less likely to develop asthma. Some researchers suggest that the restriction of bacteria in the gut, by living in ultra-clean environments and by the use of antibiotics, may lead to the development of OCD in susceptible individuals. These researchers believe that changes in the bacteria in the gut are the reason why OCD often develops during pregnancy (when hormonal changes affect the gut bacteria) or following a strep sore throat (due to treatment with antibiotics upsetting the gut bacteria). These theories are far from proven and are all highly speculative, but they do raise some interesting questions about our modern environment and the possible development of new treatments for OCD.

A recent study has found that people with OCD seem to have a more limited range of gut bacteria than a control group. The range of gut bacteria can be improved by ensuring you eat a healthy balanced diet incorporating plenty of fresh vegetables and fruit and following the type of diet outlined in Chapter 11.

Can Genes Be Modified? What Is Oxytocin?

We have already examined how although OCD tends to run in families and to have a genetic basis, this is not the whole story. Having a parent, or even two parents or close relatives, with OCD does not necessarily mean that the child will develop OCD. In Chapter 2, we examined how early life experience may modify the genetic predisposition and lead to increased resilience. Resilience to life events may be partly inherited but may also be increased by the experience of a calm, loving, stable home environment.

This does not mean that some people who have had a good home life and early life experience will not develop OCD, just that such an environment may modify the risk in those with a genetic predisposition to develop OCD. If early life experience can have an effect on resilience, how does this happen? One of many theories is that this may be related to oxytocin.

Oxytocin is a hormone which is produced by the brain in an area known as the hypothalamus. This hormone is sometimes called the 'love' hormone because it is the chemical which is produced when a mother suckles her baby, when a child or adult is being cuddled, or when we stare into the eyes of our loved one. It is thus a hormone which seems to induce caring and nurturing. It has been suggested that oxytocin may be the substance which binds to the affected genes in OCD and makes them less likely to be active. This is highly speculative and has not been fully tested.

It has also been noted that people with OCD have high levels of oxytocin in their blood and also in their brains. This has led some researchers to suggest that this might be causative in some way. High levels of oxytocin in blood seem to be correlated with more severe OCD symptoms. When given selective serotonin reuptake inhibitor or clomipramine treatment, individuals who respond show an initial decrease in oxytocin levels followed by an increase. Those who do not respond to drug treatment seem to show the opposite.

In summary, it is known that oxytocin levels are high in people with OCD. Whether this finding has any bearing on the development of OCD and whether it can be used to develop new treatments is yet to be explored.

KEY POINTS

- In the nineteenth and early twentieth centuries, surgical procedures for psychiatric conditions including OCD were crude and had high rates of mortality and morbidity.
- Modified surgical procedures developed in the 1970s and 1980s are more specific, cause less brain damage, and have a lower risk. Studies

suggest that these procedures are effective in most people who undergo them. No controlled trials have been performed.

- Deep brain stimulation (DBS) is another surgical procedure which does not cause permanent brain damage. Various sites in the brain have been investigated and have produced variable results. Overall, approximately 60 per cent of people with OCD who have previously failed to respond to other treatments improve significantly with DBS.
- Transcranial magnetic stimulation is another approach. This does not involve a surgical procedure. Powerful magnets are applied outside the skull and then temporarily interrupt the brain circuits causing OCD symptoms. This approach is still under investigation with regard to its possible role in the management of OCD.
- More speculative theories were discussed:
  - The possible role of inflammation of the glial cells was explored. Theories linking this and OCD to autoimmunity were also mentioned, as was the possible effect of gut bacteria on autoimmunity.
  - The role of oxytocin in protecting against OCD and the altered patterns of secretion in OCD were also discussed.

8

• • • • • • •

Other Conditions Which Appear Similar to OCD

This chapter examines a range of conditions which are often mistaken for OCD and which have similarities with OCD. There will be a brief mention of how these can be treated, and the evidence for both drug therapies and cognitive behavioural therapy (CBT) is also discussed. Personal stories are also presented. The conditions covered will include the following:

- *Body dysmorphic disorder* (BDD): This section on BDD will examine the similarities between OCD and BDD, but also some of the differences. It will also examine the evidence for drug treatment and how the evidence suggests that higher dosages of selective serotonin reuptake inhibitors (SSRIs) are more likely to be needed in BDD. CBT treatment usually involves exposure and response prevention (ERP), but there is also usually a greater need to examine some of the underlying beliefs and the causes of low self-esteem, which is common in people with BDD.

- *Hoarding disorder*: There has been relatively little research into the area of hoarding disorder because this condition has only recently been recognised and come to prominence. Compared to people with OCD, people with hoarding disorder are more likely to be older and to be living alone. Although little is known about hoarding disorder, research suggests that some drugs may be useful, as might CBT aimed at helping the individual to stop acquiring new items whilst discarding old items.

- *Tourette syndrome*: This condition is often accompanied by OCD symptoms. We will explore what this syndrome is and how it may be treated.
- *Hair pulling* (trichotillomania): This is a condition which has only recently been recognised as a separate psychiatric condition. There is a general lack of research in this area. Current treatment will be discussed.
- *Skin picking*: Again, this is a condition with little general recognition and little research. The severity of this condition can range from trivial to devastating and even life-endangering. Current research and treatment will be discussed.
- *Health anxiety*: Health anxiety has many similarities to OCD. There are intrusive, unwanted, worrying thoughts that the person has a serious disease. This worry causes high anxiety, and the person tries to abate this by performing a number of checks on themselves, by researching the Internet repeatedly, or by seeking reassurance from medical professionals or friends and family. Repeated trips to medical facilities can sometimes result in extreme and excessive investigation with little evidence to support any serious physical pathology.

Introduction

The fifth edition of the *Diagnostic and Statistical Manual of Mental Disorders* (DSM-5) is used widely throughout the world for classification of diseases and also for research. If a disorder is not listed in the manual, there is likely to be much less research and study on the condition. In Europe and many other countries, a different but similar type of manual is used which is produced by the World Health Organization. The *International Classification of Diseases* (ICD) covers all diseases and disorders, including those associated with mental health. The ICD has been updated to ICD-11 as of 2019, and follows a similar line as DSM-5 with respect to obsessive compulsive and related disorders.

Compared to previous versions, the DSM-5 has a number of significant changes regarding OCD and related conditions. Notably, OCD was removed from the section for anxiety disorders and placed in its own individual category of obsessive-compulsive and related disorders (see 'Disorders which have been included in the category of obsessive-compulsive and related disorders' in this chapter).

It is recognised that tic disorder, most notably Tourette syndrome, is often associated with OCD, but this is placed in the neuropsychiatric category in the DSM-5 due to the overlap of neurology and psychiatry in this condition. Another condition with many similarities to OCD, health anxiety, is included under a different classification of somatoform disorders. Both of these conditions will be discussed later.

Disorders which have been included in the category of obsessive-compulsive and related disorders

Condition	What is it?	What are the main treatments?	Other points of interest
Body dysmorphic disorder (BDD)	This condition has many similarities to OCD, but the individual is preoccupied by what they believe is a major physical defect in their appearance.	Treatments involve CBT including exposure and response prevention combined with some cognitive therapy to examine some of the core beliefs about their perceived 'abnormalities'. Drug treatment with SSRI drugs or clomipramine has been demonstrated to be useful.	Many people with BDD also have social anxiety.

(*cont.*)

Condition	What is it?	What are the main treatments?	Other points of interest
Hoarding disorder	Although some people with OCD also hoard items due to fear of disposing of items as a result of an obsessive fear such as fear of contamination or fear of loss of objects/information, this is different from pure hoarding disorder. In hoarding disorder, the individual accumulates many items until they cannot use their house in a normal fashion, being unable, for example, to sit down, sleep, or bathe without moving objects. This accumulation is not due to obsessive fear but rather to extreme emotional attachment to the items.	There is some evidence that treatment with SSRI drugs or clomipramine may be helpful to some individuals. There is also some evidence that the addition of dopamine blocking drugs can also be useful.	People with hoarding disorder are often older and more likely to live alone than people with OCD. Some individuals give a history of an unhappy childhood with either a lack of love or a lack of money. People with hoarding disorder are often hugely embarrassed and ashamed of the way in which they live.
Hair pulling disorder	This is also known as trichotillomania. The individual feels a build-up of	Treatment known as 'habit reversal' can be useful for this condition.	

(*cont.*)

Condition	What is it?	What are the main treatments?	Other points of interest
	tension and gains relief by pulling out hair. This hair pulling can involve any hair on the body but most frequently involves hair on the head, eyebrows, and eyelashes.	There are very few studies in this area. Overall, SSRI drugs or clomipramine are the most common treatment and may be helpful for some people. Dopamine blockers may also have a role. The drug *N*-acetylcysteine, which works on the glutamate system, has also been useful for some people with hair pulling disorder.	
Skin picking disorder	This is similar to hair pulling disorder because the individual usually describes a build-up of tension followed by relief when the self-harm has occurred.	In general, this has not been widely researched. Treatments are similar to those used for hair pulling disorder.	Sometimes the extent of this disorder and subsequent infection can be life-threatening.
OCD induced by drugs, illness, or another physical cause			Head injury and brain damage have been linked to this condition, as has the drug used in resistant schizophrenia, clozapine, in certain individuals.

Body Dysmorphic Disorder

Body dysmorphic disorder has many similarities to OCD. Until the 1990s, it was often either treated as OCD or, in more severe cases, considered an example of a psychotic disorder with one main symptom. In BDD, there is a preoccupation that a specific part of the body is ugly, deformed, or abnormal in some way. These thoughts cause distress, anxiety, and discomfort. In order to try to reduce these thoughts and feelings, the person with BDD may avoid a number of situations. In the most extreme cases, people with BDD may not leave their home at all or only do so under the cover of darkness. Some people will wear clothing, makeup, and accessories to try to reduce the exposure of the feature they dislike. This can often backfire, as it did with Siobhan.

Siobhan's Story

Siobhan is convinced her skin is a dreadful blotchy mess which disgusts and repulses people. In reality, there are very faint red marks on one cheek which are hardly noticeable. Because Siobhan worries so much about her skin, she always wears huge sunglasses and a scarf wrapped around her neck which also covers her cheeks. This apparel tends to cause people to look at her when she goes out on hot days. Siobhan, however, is convinced that people stare at her because they are repulsed by her skin.

People with BDD also often spend many hours gazing in the mirror. This has a tendency to increase their preoccupation and worry. If anyone stares in a mirror for a long time, they will eventually find something that they do not like about their appearance. Minor blemishes start to appear much more significant the more the person stares at them. People with BDD will also spend hours studying models and stars in magazines and on television.

BDD is a common condition, estimated to affect between 0.7 and 2.4 per cent of the population at any given time. The onset is usually in adolescence – a time when many people are preoccupied and unhappy with their appearance – but the condition mushrooms and continues from there. It is found in both men and woman, but it may be slightly more common in women. People with BDD often, but not always, have coexisting OCD. One of the problems with research on BDD is that people troubled by their appearance tend not to seek psychiatric or psychological help and instead visit dermatologists, facial surgeons, dentists, plastic surgeons, and other people whom they hope will correct their 'defect'. People with BDD are rarely happy with the outcome of such interventions, and many go on to request more and more procedures.

People with BDD often become very depressed, and there is a high rate of suicide attempts among them. First treatments of BDD focus on ERP models and encouraging the individual to face their fear without checking, mirror gazing, or other preventative measures. Typical checking and anxiety-reducing behaviours analogous to compulsive rituals include the following:

- Checking appearance in the mirror
- Camouflaging the perceived abnormality with makeup, posture, clothing, or hats
- Seeking reassurance from relatives and friends
- Skin picking to try to get rid of the flaw (consequently making the appearance much worse)
- Checking the imagined 'abnormality' by touching the affected area
- Seeking medical reassurance and cosmetic surgery by consulting dermatologists, cosmetic dentists, orthodontists, and cosmetic surgeons.

Treatment of Body Dysmorphic Disorder

Treatment for BDD is very similar to that for OCD with some minor differences. Drug treatment with SSRIs or clomipramine has been shown to be useful in BDD. The effective doses are in the higher range of those recommended. ERP treatment for BDD involves facing the fear that people will be repulsed by their appearance by taking risks and not engaging in the anxiety-reducing behaviours listed previously. Although this is still the mainstay of treatment, cognitive interventions are also often used. This treatment is illustrated in the story of Ryan.

Ryan's Story

Ryan, a 41-year-old man, was referred to the clinic by his GP, who was reluctant to refer Ryan for more surgery without a psychiatric opinion. Since his teens, Ryan has been convinced that his nose is too big. At age 35, he underwent a surgical operation to reduce the size of his nose (rhinoplasty). Initially, he felt better and gained more confidence, but then he began to worry that his nose was still rather large. He returned to the surgeon, who told Ryan that he could not recommend further operations. Ryan then went to see several doctors, all of whom told him there was nothing wrong with his nose. Due to this, Ryan became convinced that if he could afford to visit a cosmetic surgeon privately, he could obtain the 'perfect' nose. However, he had asked the GP to send him for one final opinion before he used his life's savings to have surgery. The GP refused to refer him unless Ryan agreed to a psychiatric assessment.

When he arrived for the appointment, Ryan was very unenthusiastic and did not want to engage with the therapist at all. He kept saying, 'If I just have the surgery I'll be OK'. The therapist suggested to him that he was unlikely to get further surgery and there was no evidence that the last surgery had helped. Cosmetic surgery is an imprecise science. One person's idea of a 'perfect' nose may differ greatly from another person's idea. Anyone seeking a 'perfect' nose is likely to be disappointed. Ryan believed this was wrong and that he definitely needed surgery (Figure 8.1). The therapist suggested two possible explanations for the way he was feeling:

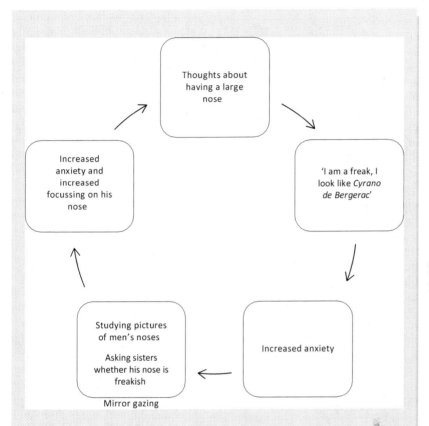

Figure 8.1 Cognitive behavioural model for Ryan's concerns regarding his nose.

- He had an extremely large nose which was ugly as he believed and was the cause of comment for everyone who saw him. The only way to rectify this situation would be for Ryan to have surgery.
- It was the way Ryan felt about his nose which caused the problem, and this fed into a vicious cycle.

Ryan listened to the therapist's theory but said he still believed that the first explanation was correct and that only surgery would correct it. He did, however, agree to have five sessions of CBT 'if only to convince my doctor that I really do need surgery'. The therapist agreed to this. Ryan appeared depressed and miserable, and the therapist was concerned about his low mood. Ryan admitted his mood had been low recently, but he believed this was purely due to the fact that he had not received surgery. Although he admitted to suicidal thoughts, he denied any plans but felt he might commit suicide if he did not ultimately get the surgery he believed he needed. The therapist suggested that his symptoms of depression may be helped by treatment with an SSRI, but Ryan was adamant that he did not need this. Ryan was asked to make a list of other men with large noses and bring it to the next session.

The following week, Ryan arrived with a list of people with large noses, including the French film actor Gerard Depardieu and other successful politicians and actors. The therapist asked Ryan what he noticed about these men. He replied, 'I know what you are going to say, yes, they all have big noses and yes, they have all had successful careers and success with women but that is different to me as my nose is much worse!' The therapist asked Ryan to bring some photographs of men he believed were attractive to the next session. For the remainder of this session, Ryan agreed to walk along the High Street with the therapist to observe how many people stared at Ryan's nose. The result of this was that contrary to Ryan's prediction, no one stared at his nose.

The next week, the therapist measured the length and breadth of Ryan's nose and also the length and breadth of his face. Ryan agreed that the nose should be in proportion with the face. From these figures was calculated the width and length ratio for his nose. Similar measurements were taken from the photographs which Ryan had brought. It was soon discovered that Ryan's nose was average in both length and width. Ryan dismissed this by saying that 'mine still looks much larger'. For homework this week, the therapist asked Ryan not to look in the mirror for more than five minutes three times a day and only to check his hair. In addition, he was asked to not telephone his sister for reassurance about his nose. Ryan did not believe that either of these requests was reasonable. A compromise was therefore reached whereby he would seek reassurance and mirror gaze as much as he liked on one day and record his anxiety throughout the day. On the second day, he was to carry out the programme as suggested by the therapist and record his anxiety. For the rest of the week, he could do whichever he believed was the most useful.

When Ryan returned the next week, his records showed that he felt better when he did not mirror gaze or seek reassurance. However, he had gone back to the mirror gazing and telephoning his sister for reassurance because he believed that by following the programme he was 'just trying to forget my problem'. The therapist proposed that Ryan walk around the hospital grounds and conduct a survey of people asking them what they thought about his nose. Ryan was fairly shy about this to begin with but did agree. Most people were complimentary about his nose, which was described as 'chiselled' and 'a fine Roman nose', and others were neither complimentary nor critical and said 'just looks normal'. After completing the survey, the therapist asked Ryan what he concluded from this exercise and he said, 'It does seem that the problem is more the thoughts about my nose rather than my nose'. From this point onwards, Ryan worked well in therapy, but he still did not wish to continue beyond five sessions. He agreed to reduce the time he spent in front of the mirror and to stop asking his sister for reassurance about his nose. He has decided to put his request to see a cosmetic surgeon 'on hold' for a while but says that although he is willing to try to 'live with my nose' for the next few months, he will seek surgery if his preoccupation with his nose increases again.

Ryan's story illustrates the use of ERP therapy for his BDD (i.e., going out in public and checking if people really stared at his nose and also asking people about his nose). This was also backed up with some cognitive work which involved testing his beliefs. So far, Ryan has resisted taking SSRI medication. However, these may help him feel better and to be able to face the challenge of treatment more readily.

Hoarding Disorder

Hoarding, or the accumulation of excessive numbers of items, is not a diagnosis by itself. Many people collect large numbers of items such as books, stamps, or ornaments. The difference between these collections and a 'hoard' is that generally a collection is organised in some way. Also, the collection does not normally threaten the individual's ability to function in the home or become a hazard.

Hoarding can be a result of many conditions. Physical illness and disability can mean that the person is unable to sort out their belongings. People with a learning disability or dementia may not be able to logically organise the items which come into their home. People who abuse substances such as alcohol or other drugs may have lost the ability to structure and control their lives. As previously discussed, hoarding may also be a feature of OCD.

Hoarding disorder refers to people who do not have any other complicating diagnosis or reason for accumulating their hoarded items. In these cases, people are frequently living in dangerous situations with risk of fire from hoarded items or even structural collapse of the property. Frequently, individuals are not referred to medical or psychiatric professions and are instead dealt with via the courts. Many are made homeless as a result of eviction due to their problems. These individuals can be very difficult to treat, and treatment can take a very long time. Unlike with OCD, drugs such as SSRIs and/or dopamine blockers may not have major beneficial effects. One of the most striking characteristics of patients with hoarding is their absolute belief that their hoards are 'valuable'. For example, an elderly woman who lived in a house which was falling down due to structural damage secondary to hoarded newspapers and letters suggested that for anyone to start throwing any of these items away was tantamount to 'committing grievous bodily harm to me'. Sufferers of pure hoarding disorder are more likely to be older than OCD sufferers (although they often give a history of the problem starting in childhood or adolescence) and to live alone, and many have a past history of childhood deprivation (either extreme poverty or emotional deprivation).

Treatment of Hoarding Disorder

It is not entirely clear whether or not SSRIs and drugs such as dopamine blockers are useful in hoarding disorder. Some studies claim that they do help, whereas others suggest they have little or no effect. One of the difficulties is that before 2013 and the publication of DSM-5, hoarding disorder was usually diagnosed as OCD. This means that many studies of people with hoarding also include people with OCD and hoarding symptoms. It is known that SSRIs and dopamine blockers can help people with OCD, but their effect on people with pure hoarding disorder is less clear.

Psychological treatment of hoarding is also based on an exposure type of model. People with hoarding disorder are often embarrassed and humiliated by their homes and the mess in which they live. They need to establish trust with their therapist and understand that this is not 'their fault' and that they are not 'lazy' or 'slovenly' but, rather, suffer from a psychological problem. Second, there needs to be an agreement that no more hoarded items must enter the house. It is pointless to start discarding items if more are being brought in. This is similar to trying to bail the water out of a sinking boat without mending the hole. Once trust has been established between patient and therapist and no further items are accumulated, it is time for the person to start discarding hoarded objects. Rules for determining whether objects should be discarded, recycled, or saved must be developed and agreed to by the patient. When making decisions about objects, the person with hoarding disorder should be encouraged to hold each object only once and not change their decision once it is made. It appears that prolonged handling of an object leads to greater attachment of the individual to that object. Once an object is discarded, the hoarder is less distressed if they do not see the discarded item again.

Albert's Story

Albert is a 65-year-old unmarried man who lives alone in a housing association flat. He previously worked as a builder but retired five years ago. Referral was made to local psychiatric services via the housing association. Although the association was keen to help Albert, his excessive hoarding was putting other residents at risk of harm because objects had spilled out of his flat into communal areas, causing a risk that someone might fall. There was concern that the weight of his hoarded items would soon put the building structure at risk, and there was fear of fire due to the excessive papers, including in kitchen areas.

For the first meeting, Albert was insistent that he should meet the therapist at the hospital. He gave a history of a deprived and difficult childhood during which he had to move several times with his unmarried mother, who had had a series of relationships with different men. When he became an adult, he was determined to work to be able to afford 'nice' things in his home. Initially, he had managed to keep a tidy and functional home. He was married from the age of 25–50 years, but unfortunately his wife died of breast cancer 15 years ago. They had not had any children. Albert was distraught after his wife died, and he had never wished to form another relationship. Initially, he worked harder, but since taking retirement five years ago, he had found himself very lonely and isolated. His hoarding problem started soon after his wife died. He would visit various house clearance shops in his area and buy a variety of objects, mostly the type of objects or furniture which he remembered from his youth. In addition, he would buy multiple books in charity shops, although he rarely found the time to read them. In the first meeting, it was immediately apparent that Albert was very embarrassed by his problem. He described himself as 'lazy' and 'greedy' for having this problem. When it was suggested that the therapist might visit his home, Albert was adamant that this could not happen.

The first stage of therapy involved the therapist gaining Albert's trust. In addition, it was important to ensure that no more items were being brought into the house. The therapist discussed with Albert the feelings he had when he found a 'nice' item or a book. Albert described his excitement and pleasure at finding the item and said it gave him a 'buzz'; however, when he returned home, he felt humiliated and despondent that his flat was so overcrowded. It was clear that Albert lived a very sad and restricted life and that buying items was his chief pleasure, even though this led to deeper despair. It was important to establish a ban on new items coming into the house but also to try to ensure that Albert had some pleasurable activities to replace the excitement that resulted from his shopping. First, a discussion was held about Albert's interests. He admitted that he was very interested in reading and books. It was agreed that Albert would not visit any of his usual shops during the next week. When he went out to buy groceries, he would only take sufficient money (and no bank cards) to do this and not to buy anything else. In addition, he would go to the local library and find out about book reading clubs as well as sign up as a member so that he could borrow books. For several weeks, Albert was resistant to the therapist visiting his home because he felt deeply ashamed about the state of his house. He was encouraged to take photographs of each room but was reluctant to do this. To start therapy, he was asked to bring a bag of items so that a decision could be made about them. Albert agreed that approximately 75 per cent of the items needed to be removed from his flat but was extremely anxious about doing so. At the next appointment, he arrived with a bag of books. Together with the therapist, he agreed that there were three categories of items:

1. Items for recycling for paper (rubbish): These were books with pages missing or which were badly torn or mouldy.
2. Items for disposal at charity shops/library: These were books in reasonably good condition but which he had read.
3. Items to keep: These were books of particular significance or value, such as first editions and family books inherited from his grandfather.

To this end, three large bags were made available for each of the three categories. Albert was then asked to take out a book and decide quickly which category it belonged in. It was important that he did not handle the item for too long because this tends to increase the attachment to an object. Also, it was negotiated that once a decision about disposal had been made, it was final. The session took two hours, and Albert found it extremely distressing and very difficult to discard items. During the session, he wept at times when discarding books and said he felt as if he was losing close friends. He was reminded of his goal of having a tidy, liveable flat with sufficient good-quality items for a comfortable life. Albert agreed to persevere, and at the end of the session, the therapist and Albert disposed of the bags in the recycling bin and at a local charity shop, leaving him with two books out of 30 which he wanted to take home. He was then given the task of continuing this process on his own until the next session.

After four weeks, Albert had progressed well and had discarded several large bags full of books. He had had one setback when he had gone back to the charity shop and said he had changed his mind, but the books had already been sent to a central sorting office. The therapist praised Albert for his progress but said the next session would have to be in Albert's home.

At the first home-based session, six weeks after starting therapy, the therapist first had to gauge the risk to both Albert and herself. There have been reported incidents in which people have been killed or seriously injured due to items falling on the hoarder. Clearly, the risk of this occurring increases once items are starting to be moved. Other risks to the therapist included health risks from extreme dirt and squalor, risk of building collapse, or risk of being trapped and fire. Any person entering such an environment, whether a professional called to help with the problem or a friend or relative, must ensure their own health and safety, as well as that of the person who hoards. In the rarest and most serious cases, if there is a serious risk to health and safety, then it may be necessary to consider legal enforcement and clearing of the property; there must also be consideration of whether the Mental Health Act is appropriate. It is often necessary for the therapist to wear protective overalls and a mask because of dust and dirt. In this case, although the hoarding was severe, there was no immediate danger, and Albert agreed not to use the cooker until the kitchen was cleared of fire hazards. First, the therapist gained Albert's permission to take photographs of the different rooms. The house was almost completely full, with piles of items covering approximately 80 per cent of all available floor space. In the kitchen, books were piled up on every work surface, and there was a risk of fire from books being piled next to the cooker. His bed was also covered, with just a small space on the edge for him to sleep. The bath was piled high with books; Albert had been unable to take a bath for several years. The living room had a small space with one chair and a television, but there was only a narrow passageway through stacks of items to reach these.

Work started on clearing the kitchen, using the same categories for items as before. Again, this was very difficult for Albert, but he began to feel encouraged as he saw the space around his cooker getting cleared and the work surfaces which he had not seen for several years started to appear.

Treating a hoarder such as Albert is a lengthy and painstaking process. Most cases will take many months, and it is not unusual for them to take a year. In these cases, it is unrealistic to expect a therapist to attend weekly for many hours to allow clearing to take place. Consideration should be given to enlisting a 'co-therapist' who may be a mental health worker, a 'befriender' from the local mental health services, or a family member or friend. The co-therapist needs to have the trust of the patient and also needs to understand the rules for the treatment:

- There is a ban on new items coming into the house.
- Each item is allocated to the 'Discard', 'Charity Shop', or 'Keep' bag.
- Each item is held for a few seconds (no more than two minutes) for a decision to be made.
- Items must only be handled once (i.e., no going back on decisions).

- Once sorted, the items are disposed of immediately following the session. In Albert's case, he began working with a befriender from his local community mental health team who agreed to visit once a week and help him discard his items. If they managed to clear as much as they had hoped, they would then go out for a coffee after having dropped items off at the charity shop. The therapist contacted them every few weeks to ensure progress and to troubleshoot any difficulties. Albert finished clearing his home 15 months after the first appointment. The local social services arranged for his flat to be 'deep-cleaned'.

Albert is now delighted with his new living situation but needs to think about relapse prevention. The therapist and Albert have developed the following plan to prevent the same situation from recurring:

- I will continue to borrow books from the library and attend the reading groups there.
- I have purchased an electronic book reader and so will no longer buy paper books.
- I will restrict my cash and bank cards when going out and only buy what I have previously decided and take money for those items only.
- If I do purchase a new item or new piece of furniture, *something of equivalent size has to be discarded.*

Albert's story demonstrates that people with hoarding disorder can often be helped but that they need to accept that they have a problem and wish to work to overcome the problem. Treatment is often lengthy, but the long-term results can be truly life-changing.

Tourette Syndrome and Tics

Tourette's syndrome is a neurological condition which starts in childhood and continues into adulthood. Many people with Tourette syndrome spontaneously get better after approximately ten years of the condition. However, approximately one-third of people have a long-term condition which does tend to get better as they age but persists for longer. The condition is characterised by a combination of involuntary noises and also movements known as tics. It can often be associated with attention deficit hyperactivity disorder, in which the individual is restless and has difficulties concentrating, and also with OCD. The tics which are seen may be vocal (sounds; e.g., coughing, grunting, or shouting out words) or physical (movements; e.g., sudden movements of the arms or legs, jerking of the head, or jumping up and down). In addition, tics may be simple (e.g., making a small jerky movement or uttering a single sound) or complex (e.g., making a series of movements or speaking a phrase).

It is thought that Tourette syndrome is due to abnormalities arising in the basal ganglia area of the brain. This is the same area that is thought to be involved in OCD.

It can often be difficult to distinguish between a complex tic and a compulsive ritual. In a complex tic, the urge to perform the tic comes on and becomes increasingly stronger until the tic is performed. Compulsive rituals are performed in response to a specific and unpleasant obsessive thought.

Tics and Tourette syndrome often result in children being teased and bullied; therefore, rapid treatment is a necessity to help these children socially develop.

Treatment of Tourette Syndrome and Tics

Some of the drugs used to treat Tourette syndrome and tics are listed in the following 'Examples of the variety of drug treatments used for Tourette syndrome'.

Examples of the variety of drug treatments used for Tourette syndrome

Type of drug	Examples (not comprehensive)	Trade names Notes
Dopamine blockers		
Haloperidol	Haldol, Dozic, Serenace	Used for many years but is one of the traditional, older dopamine blockers. Can have side effects including sedation and drowsiness, prolonged muscle contraction, stiffness, and shakiness.
Pimozide	Orap	Another traditional dopamine blocker with similar but fewer side effects compared to haloperidol.
Aripiprazole	Abilify	An atypical (newer) dopamine blocker and is often the drug used first for Tourette syndrome because it is generally well tolerated. Side effects are usually mild to moderate and often pass as the drug is continued. Common side effects include restlessness, insomnia or drowsiness, fatigue, nausea, and headaches.
Risperidone	Risperdal	Another atypical dopamine-blocking drug. This has been investigated extensively, with many studies reporting positive effects. Side effects include fatigue and somnolence, emotional disturbance, nausea, vomiting, sleep problems, and weight gain.
Alpha-2 adrenergic agonists		
Clonidine	Catapres, Dixarit	This has been prescribed for many years for the treatment of tics in childhood. Possible side effects include drowsiness, sedation, headaches, depression, dizziness, and a drop in blood pressure. People need to have their blood pressure checked before taking and whilst on clonidine.

(*cont.*)

Type of drug	Examples (not comprehensive)	Trade names Notes
Muscle relaxants		
Baclofen	Lyflex	Main side effects are drowsiness and dizziness. Adults need to avoid alcohol, and if they are affected with drowsiness and dizziness, they should not drive or operate machinery.
Clonazepam		Main side effects are drowsiness and dizziness. Adults need to avoid alcohol, and if they are affected with drowsiness and dizziness, they should not drive or operate machinery.

Psychological treatment used for tic disorder and Tourette syndrome usually involves a treatment known as habit reversal, although people with OCD will also need treatment using ERP. Habit reversal treatment has four components:

1. Awareness training
2. Competing response training
3. Habit control motivation
4. Generalisation training

Sarah's Story

Sarah, an attractive and lively 24-year-old PE teacher, was referred to the clinic with a 14-year history of unsightly and embarrassing facial tics. The onset occurred at puberty, but it was not related by Sarah to any particular life event. Throughout the years, she had received treatment with a variety of medications, including haloperidol and muscle relaxant drugs, which were partially effective.

The tic can occur at any time but is more frequent if she is anxious or bored. Close observation of the movements revealed that it commences with Sarah screwing up both eyes, followed by crinkling her nose and then making a sharp downward movement of her chin, opening her mouth.

Sarah was first asked to record the frequency of her tics over a few days. This *awareness training* is useful because many people with habit disorders are oblivious to some of the times when they perform the undesirable behaviour. Obviously, Sarah has a busy life and so the records were made as simple as possible for her to keep. She was asked to obtain a small notebook and to divide each page into columns, each representing a one-hour period. Every time she performed the tic, she was to place a mark in the appropriate column. Also, she was to record her activity at each hourly interval – for example, 'lunch with colleagues' and 'netball lesson with Lower Sixth Form'.

This diary was also useful as a baseline measure of Sarah's problem, and it was maintained throughout treatment to monitor her progress. The baseline measures showed that Sarah performed the tic an average of 300 times a day or approximately 0.5 tics per minute.

At the second session, the principle of competing response practice was explained to Sarah. The therapist said:

> One of the problems with a long-standing habit is that you have built up and strengthened the muscles of your face which are involved in the tic at the expense of the opposing muscles. What I will be asking you to do is to perform some exercises to strengthen these opposing muscles. The start of every tic begins with you screwing up both your eyes. As soon as you feel that you are going to tic, I want you to raise your eyebrows, wrinkling your forehead. You may find this easier to do if you place your thumb and index finger of one hand under each of your eyebrows. I then want you to hold this position to the count of 20 or until the urge to tic passes, whichever is the longer time. At the same time as doing this, I would like you to clench your teeth together very tightly and likewise to maintain this position.

Following this description, the therapist asked Sarah to practise the competing response in the session. The therapist then asked Sarah to list all the negative effects of having a tic and the advantages of being tic-free. She was asked to write this list down and to read it whenever she felt bored or disheartened by the treatment (habit control motivation).

Finally, ways in which Sarah could incorporate the competing response movements into her everyday life without looking conspicuous were discussed. Sarah suggested that if she were outside, she could place her hand under her eyebrows as if shielding her eyes from the sun. If she were inside and sitting at a desk or table, she could use her hand under her eyebrows to 'support' her head (generalisation training). When Sarah was seen a week later for her third session, the frequency of tics had already reduced to less than 10 per cent of the baseline level. Difficulties were discussed with her during this session and also during the following two sessions.

Six weeks after starting the treatment, Sarah was discharged from the clinic. Her tics are now occurring less than five times a day, and she believes they are controllable.

Hair Pulling Disorder (Trichotillomania)

Hair pulling disorder is sometimes known as 'trichotillomania'. People with this condition pull out the hair on their heads or sometimes eyebrows and eyelashes. Rarely does this disorder involve body hair. People with this condition often describe a pleasurable feeling of satisfaction if they have had a 'good' hair pulling session even though they are distressed about the effect of hair loss on their appearance. Some people describe being distracted and not noticing when they are hair pulling. This condition is more common in teenagers, and it tends to affect more girls than boys. Stress is a frequent precursor to the hair pulling.

Many people who have hair pulling disorder do not seek psychological help but instead may be referred to dermatologists or trichologists. Due to a feeling of shame, many do not admit to the hair pulling and thus often do not receive the help they need.

A serious and even life-threatening consequence for some people who hair pull and then swallow the hair is that the hair cannot be easily digested and can form large balls in the gut, which can lead to blockages requiring emergency surgery.

Treatment of Hair Pulling Disorder

Drug treatment for hair pulling disorder is based mostly on small trials involving small numbers of people, so it is difficult to determine the effectiveness of the treatment. The four main types of drug treatment are SSRI drugs, drugs which act as dopamine blockers, drugs which act on the 'addiction' pathways of the brain, and drugs which act on the glutamate system (see Chapter 4). None of these drug treatments, however, has been fully evaluated; thus, it is difficult to recommend them. SSRIs are likely to be useful if the person also has symptoms of OCD. Whereas some early studies suggested that SSRIs helped reduce hair pulling behaviours, more recent studies have raised doubt as to whether this is really the case. Studies on dopamine blockers (see Chapter 4) have also shown mixed results, with some studies finding them useful and others not. Hair pulling can be viewed as an 'impulse control disorder' because the act of hair pulling is usually described as pleasurable, even though the consequences are upsetting to the individual. Thus, it has been thought that it may have some similarities, in terms of brain chemistry, with a variety of conditions, including alcohol and drug abuse, addictive gambling, smoking, and kleptomania (addictive stealing). Naltrexone is a drug which is thought to block some of the pleasure centres in the brain which are activated by problematic addictive behaviours. There is some indication that naltrexone may be useful for some people with hair pulling disorder. In terms of drugs which act on the glutamate system, N-acetylcysteine has been reported to be useful for some people with hair pulling disorder. This drug was originally used for paracetamol overdose and to loosen mucous in people with cystic fibrosis or chronic lung disease. It was found to be active on the glutamate system and has been tried for several conditions related to

OCD, but is most notably used for hair pulling disorder. Despite a number of trials suggesting that it may be useful, these trials involved small numbers of patients and so it is not possible to fully endorse its use. It is generally well tolerated with few side effects and therefore may be worth trying.

Treatment to deal with the underlying stress and/or depression may be needed, as might family therapy to deal with family tensions. For many people, however, the hair pulling itself is the main cause of stress and family tension. Psychological treatment is mainly habit reversal training. This treatment was described in the section on tic disorder and Tourette syndrome. In hair pulling, it consists of the same four components:

1. Awareness training: Whereas some people with hair pulling disorder do set out to have a 'hair pulling session' to reduce stress and tension, many are unaware of their habit most of the time. Part of the treatment is to closely monitor the behaviour and also to note where they are and what they are doing when it occurs. Although many people will say there are no obvious precipitants to the behaviour, carefully recording in this way can show patterns and stressors of which they were previously unaware. Collecting and keeping all the pulled hair is also useful and, in itself, has often shocked individuals into trying to radically change their behaviour.

2. Competing response training: Forming a fist and keeping it tightly closed, or other similar activities, which are incompatible with hair pulling, may be used. Wearing a hat, or even a wig, can also form a barrier to prevent hair pulling from occurring.

3. Habit control motivation: Like any treatment, habit reversal requires motivation and commitment. Recording all the negative factors about the problem can be very useful. This list should be written on a piece of paper or recorded on a cell phone so it can be read or listened to when there is an urge to pull hair.

4. Generalisation training: Incorporating the response into everyday life can be helpful. For example, a woman who worked as a waitress decided that instead of forming a fist, she would sharply grip the tray she was carrying when she had an urge to pull her hair.

Skin Picking

Skin picking disorder is another condition described in the DSM-5 as one of the obsessive-compulsive and related disorders. Many people with the condition do not seek help from psychiatrists or psychologists, preferring to attend dermatology clinics. Diagnosis can sometimes be difficult because many people do not like to admit the condition is self-inflicted. Skin picking is a symptom and may be part of another condition, such as the following:

- Body dysmorphic disorder, where skin picking is an attempt to reduce the perceived blemish on the skin (but inevitably makes it worse).
- OCD, where the person picks at the skin to remove 'dirt'.
- Acne, where people skin pick and squeeze spots in an attempt to make them reduce (again making the situation worse).
- Either during or following withdrawal of certain illegal or prescribed stimulant drugs.
- As an accompaniment to a delusional belief that the individual is infested by parasites which they then try to remove.

These conditions all require different treatment, but skin picking can be a disorder in its own right. The severity of the disorder can range from minimal to life- threatening when an individual renders themselves prone to infections.

Treatment of Skin Picking

The studies of drug treatment for skin picking disorder have all been small, and it is difficult to give definitive advice. Studies on SSRIs for skin picking have shown mixed results, with some showing improvement and some no response. Drugs acting on the glutamatergic system have been tried, and individual case reports have suggested that N-acetylcysteine may be beneficial.

Psychological treatment for skin picking is based on habit reversal techniques (identical to those used for hair pulling and tic disorders). Again,

studies are small but seem to show that this kind of approach is beneficial. Some people have combined habit reversal techniques with some
cognitive therapy to good effect.

Health Anxiety

Health anxiety is not classified as an obsessive-compulsive and related
disorder but it does display many of the same characteristics as OCD.

Health anxiety refers to individuals who are constantly worrying about
their health. Some people focus on one particular condition, such as
cancer or heart disease. Others interpret every small change in their body
as being due to a dreadful disease. These worrying thoughts come into
the person's mind, and they may then start checking behaviours such as
checking for lumps or feeling their pulse. They may also ask for reassurance from their loved ones, or may repeatedly visit the GP or hospital for
reassurance. These checks and reassurance are identical to the situation
seen with OCD, and so they reduce the anxiety slightly, but the effect is
short-lived, and the person then seeks more reassurance. Some people
with health anxiety therefore become 'blacklisted' at their GP's office, the
local accident and emergency department, or walk-in centres. Rather like
the boy who always cried wolf, they establish the worst-case scenario for
themselves so that they find it difficult to obtain help when they really
need it.

All of us experience a range of physical symptoms every day, most of
which are not indicative of serious disease. Once someone focuses on a
symptom, however, this will generally make it worse. To test this out, try
sitting quietly and concentrate on your right big toe and imagine it is
painful. Eventually, most people will experience pain in their toe if they
concentrate in this way. In the same way, overconcentrating on any
bodily symptom will tend to increase this symptom. If individuals with
health anxiety can be taught to view their symptoms in another way, they
will often improve.

Treatment of Health Anxiety

Although only a small number of studies on drug treatment in health anxiety have been conducted, it appears that SSRIs are useful. Unfortunately, however, many people with health anxiety are very sensitive to any bodily symptoms, including side effects of drugs. It is thus best to start on lower doses and increase gradually.

Psychological treatment involves ERP combined with some cognitive interventions.

Ash's Story

Ash is a 25-year-old man who was referred for assessment by the gastroenterology team. He was extremely reluctant to see a psychiatrist but was eventually persuaded by being told that many patients benefit from seeing the psychiatrist irrespective of their diagnosis, as any emotion can have an effect on the bowel.

The history showed that Ash is the only child of quite elderly parents, who had undergone many attempts at *in vitro* fertilisation to conceive him. Consequently, he had been quite 'molly-coddled' as a young child and was always described as 'sickly', requiring considerable time away from school, although no serious pathology had ever been found.

At age 18 years, Ash moved away from home to attend university. He developed some abdominal pains and went to the student health centre. He was told that this was most likely due to his poor diet since leaving home. Ash, however, was not happy with this answer and started searching the Internet. He convinced himself that he suffered from a form of ulcerative colitis and that he would die from the complications of carcinoma unless this was dealt with. After several visits to the health centre, he was sent to the hospital to see a gastroenterologist. The consultant at the clinic performed a sigmoidoscopy on Ash and reassured him there was nothing wrong. Initially, Ash was relieved, but during the next few days he was plagued by thoughts such as the following:

- 'Doctors can get things wrong. What if he missed the pathological area?'
- 'I only had sigmoidoscopy and that can only examine the lower bowel. Maybe the upper bowl is affected.'
- 'Maybe he's only telling me there's nothing wrong because he thinks I'm really ill and the prognosis is hopeless.'

These thoughts caused Ash to ask for an urgent return visit to the clinic and eventually he was given a colonoscopy. Each new test reduced his anxiety for a while, but then the catastrophic thoughts would creep back in. Eventually, the local clinic refused to see him. By this time, Ash was so crippled by his anxieties that he was no longer attending to his studies. He returned home, where his parents were very concerned about his weight loss. Ash had started to restrict his diet to that advised for people with ulcerative colitis and so was avoiding most sources of insoluble fibre (e.g., bran, whole foods, and sweetcorn) and also any dairy produce, including milk, cheese, and cream. As well as trying to avoid physical activity in case it upset his bowel, Ash took a variety of tablets from health food shops, consisting of a range of vitamin and mineral supplements and also Chinese medicines supposed to act on the bowel. During the next few years, Ash had more investigations and saw a multiplicity of NHS and private gastroenterologists. Every time he was discharged from a clinic, his anxiety would skyrocket and he would seek out another physician and surgeon. At the time of referral to the psychiatric clinic, Ash had a body mass index of only 16, and he spent most of his days lying in bed. He was pale and unwell, and he spent his time searching the Internet for a cure for his 'ulcerative colitis'. His parents were extremely anxious and really did believe Ash had a serious medical condition. His mother said, 'Look at the state of him, he's undernourished and can barely get out of bed. There must be something seriously wrong with him that the doctors haven't found'. The family had spent more than £10,000, which they could barely afford, to try to get a diagnosis for Ash.

The case history of Ash demonstrates how medical practitioners unwittingly exacerbate the symptoms of health anxiety. Most patients will attend their GP office or hospital clinic and accept the outcome of relevant tests. However, medicine is not an exact science, and there are hardly any situations in which a doctor can honestly say he or she is 100 per cent certain. If a patient returns and becomes insistent, then the doctor, mindful of the potential for medicolegal allegations and negligence claims if a diagnosis is overlooked, will often concede to the patient's demands and order further tests. As can be seen from Ash's history, this can form a vicious cycle with a downward spiral of the patient.

In treating patients with health anxiety, the psychiatrist must first establish with the patient that there will be no more medical tests or seeking of reassurance for the duration of psychological treatment. This is easier said than done. Patients with health anxiety really believe they have a serious physical illness which may threaten their lives, and so it will seem as if the therapist is asking them to take a major risk. One way of approaching this is to present two scenarios to the patient. This can be demonstrated in the story of the treatment of Ash.

Ash's Story (Continued)

At first, Ash was very unwilling to agree to stop consulting doctors about his bowels. He believed this would be 'dangerous' and that his symptoms might progress and worsen, but the therapist said:

> I understand your concern about your bowels but if we look at this, you have been seeking a diagnosis for over seven years now. I am asking you to agree to no further investigations for the next four months whilst we start to look at alternative answers. I am going to propose to you that there are two possible explanations for your situation.
>
> Firstly, your current belief is that you have a serious bowel condition such as ulcerative colitis and that this will result in a life-threatening situation. All the doctors and specialists who have seen you have managed to miss this diagnosis, but if you keep on seeing more

specialists and having more tests, you will eventually obtain a diagnosis of inflammatory bowel disease.

My theory is that you do indeed suffer from a variety of bowel symptoms. These symptoms may well have been precipitated originally by a poor diet when you left home. However, once you became anxious that you had a serious bowel disease, your anxiety increased. Chronic and high anxiety can cause various symptoms which you describe, such as colicky pain, intermittent diarrhoea and constipation, and a feeling of nausea. Every time you go and see a specialist, you feel better for a day or two, and then start to worry they may have overlooked the diagnosis and your anxiety and symptoms get worse. In addition, your restricted diet has made you severely underweight. This diet may well be contributing to your bowel symptoms and also being malnourished means you will have low energy, lack of drive, and a feeling of malaise. This in turn leads you to spend increasing time in bed. Remaining in bed makes you weaker and also has a deleterious effect on your physical symptoms.

Ash did not agree with the therapist's theory but, persuaded by his parents, agreed to give it a try, and he also agreed that he would not consult any bowel specialists for the next six weeks. The therapist gave him a chart to take away (Figure 8.2). He also agreed to stop the Chinese medicine but decided to remain on the vitamin supplements.

In therapy, the first task was to try to modify some of Ash's beliefs about his symptoms. He was asked to search the Internet to identify some of the symptoms caused by anxiety and determine if any of those matched the ones he had. Over the next few sessions, the emphasis was placed on examining Ash's symptoms and thoughts and, by working jointly with Ash, trying to discover if there were any alternative explanations other than serious bowel disease for his symptoms. At the end of several sessions, Ash conceded that his belief that his symptoms were caused by anxiety had increased from 0 to 40 per cent. He was asked if he would be willing to try expanding the repertoire of his diet. After a long discussion, Ash agreed to include dairy produce in his diet for a week to determine if this caused his symptoms to improve or deteriorate.

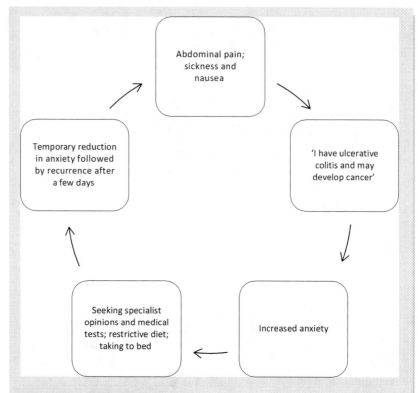

Figure 8.2 Ash's chart.

Ash managed to incorporate dairy produce without ill effect and was successfully challenging many of his thoughts concerning serious bowel disease. He was already spending less time in bed, but the therapist worked with him to consider introducing graded exercise to gradually increase his physical activity. He found that as he grew stronger and was eating a better diet, his symptoms were less prominent. After several weeks, he agreed to eat wholemeal and foods rich in fibre. Once a full and varied diet was established, he agreed to stop his vitamin and mineral supplements.

Ash started some more detailed work with the therapist examining some of his thoughts and the deeper beliefs that he held about his health and fitness.

Many of these were successfully challenged, and he stopped viewing himself as weak and sickly and began to understand that he could be a strong and healthy man. Following on from this, Ash decided to try to take up judo. He enrolled in a local class, and to his surprise, he not only enjoyed the sport but was also reasonably good at it.

Currently, Ash looks like a strong, fit, healthy, and happy young man. He no longer restricts his diet, although he does try to maintain a healthy diet, which he believes helps him perform better in judo competitions.

The case of Ash demonstrates how people with health anxiety can be helped to overcome their problems. Not everyone is as willing to try to engage in therapy as Ash and to 'take the risk' that some of their symptoms may be related to anxiety as well as to some of the behaviours they are using to try to prevent ill health. People who engage with therapy can dramatically improve and feel much better both physically and emotionally.

KEY POINTS

- Body dysmorphic disorder (BDD) has many similarities to OCD, and frequently both OCD and BDD coexist together.
- Treatment for BDD involves SSRIs as for OCD and also ERP. In addition, some cognitive techniques are often needed for BDD.
- Hoarding can be a symptom of several psychiatric and physical conditions.
- In hoarding disorder, an individual is unable to stop acquiring a huge number of possessions and is unable to dispose of the excess. This condition may be associated with a deprived upbringing (either materially or emotionally deprived).
- Hoarding disorder results in considerable shame and embarrassment, and those working with a person who has hoarding disorder need to gain the person's trust. Health and safety issues must always take precedence. The danger to the person with hoarding disorder, their

neighbours, and the public, as well as the therapist involved in helping them, must be taken into account.

- Treatment for hoarding disorder may involve SSRIs and possibly dopamine blockers.
- The mainstay of treatment for hoarding disorder is CBT involving a ban on the acquisition of any new items and a programme of controlled discarding of excess items.
- Tourette's syndrome involves vocal and/or physical tics. This condition often coexists with OCD or attention deficit hyperactivity disorder.
- Drug treatment for Tourette syndrome involves dopamine-blocking drugs such as haloperidol or the newer aripiprazole. Alpha-2 adrenergic blockers or muscle relaxants may also be useful.
- Psychological treatment for both Tourette syndrome and tic disorder involves habit reversal.
- Habit reversal consists of the following:
  - Awareness training
  - Competing response training

9

• • • • • • •

What Can Family and Carers Do to Help a Person with OCD?

This chapter will examine what family members and carers can do to help someone with OCD. In the case of the parents of a person with OCD, the natural reaction is to try to prevent their offspring from experiencing extreme anxiety and distress. This reaction means they can often get caught up being asked to participate in OCD compulsions and rituals and also to obey many of the 'rules' which people with OCD may devise to avoid setting off OCD thoughts. Despite the fact that this compliance with the OCD rituals is done by the carers with the best of intentions, it serves to actually worsen the OCD symptoms over time. It can often be useful for carers to realise that they are the people without OCD, and thus they need to set the 'ground rules' of what they will or will not tolerate and do in their own home. However, in many cases, this is easier said than done. First, old habits die hard. Second, it can be extremely difficult to resist stepping in if a loved-one is highly distressed. This will be explored in this chapter as well as possible solutions.

Throughout this chapter, it is emphasised that the safety of any children, other family members, and the person with OCD is paramount. When an individual suffers from OCD, they can become very distressed and agitated when having extreme obsessive symptoms. A minority of these people may become violent at these times. Violence is never acceptable, and family, carers, and friends have a duty to themselves and also to the person with OCD to keep themselves safe at all times. This may require families to request help from the police in extreme cases. As stated at the beginning, children are the paramount consideration. They may be harmed not only by violent actions but also by being asked to engage in OCD activities and being required to have a restricted life rather than be outside playing with friends or inviting friends to their home. This can be a difficult area for the OCD sufferer and those around them, but it is vital that the welfare of any children is always considered first and foremost.

Introduction

As demonstrated in previous chapters and through the personal stories of OCD sufferers, OCD is a problem which has a huge impact on the whole family. Severe OCD can result in a delay of normal maturation, with a young person living at home dependent on their parents and siblings for decades. On the other hand, many people with severe OCD are unable to work and unable to form long-lasting relationships. Many live alone and lead isolated and restricted lives, which can also cause worry and concern to friends and relatives.

One of the main problems of living with a person with OCD is knowing how to deal with their obsessions and compulsions. Family members may be asked for constant reassurance, asked to carry out activities which the person with OCD finds difficult, and often asked to carry out compulsive rituals. These requests and demands can cause major problems in families. Family members do not wish to see a loved one disturbed and upset and will understandably try to do everything they can to reduce the distress. As previously discussed, the problem is that reassurance-seeking or the completion of compulsive rituals may temporarily reduce the discomfort and anxiety, but this effect is short-lived and very soon more requests and demands are made. Similarly, it can often seem easier for family members to take on tasks and chores to help the person with OCD, but this can also escalate. A question I am often asked by relatives of people with OCD is how they should work with the person with OCD to prevent themselves from being dragged into the 'OCD quagmire'.

It is very important that family members do not blame themselves for trying to help their loved one. This is a normal and natural reaction, and any caring person would do whatever they could to try to prevent the distress caused by OCD. It can be heart-breaking to witness the emotional turmoil being experienced by a loved-one. It would not be helpful or prudent for someone who has been providing reassurance and help to suddenly stop doing so. Full and frank discussions need to be held both with the person who has OCD and with other family members. First, the other family members need to establish in their own minds what is 'reasonable'. This may take some time to work out. OCD can often creep up gradually, and suddenly people find themselves living very restrictive lives with their relative with OCD. What has become 'normal' is far from normal in fact. However, it can be difficult to realise this when living with someone with OCD, and so it is worthwhile taking time to think through what is and what is not acceptable. If available, it can be useful to discuss this with another person who is outside the family, such as a GP or a counsellor, who can help establish some ideas for the family. If a family member has OCD and is under the care of mental health services, their relatives can ask for a 'carer's assessment', in which their own problems and needs are assessed and help such as counselling can be offered.

Some relatives may find the obsessive fears so difficult to understand or so exaggerated that they are tempted to ridicule or belittle the fears. It is extremely important, however, to recognise that these thoughts are profoundly disturbing to the individual with OCD and are therefore extremely serious in their mind. Although they may realise their thoughts are either irrational or exaggerated, the fear accompanying these thoughts is very real and they are unable to 'snap out of it'. Instead, family and friends need to listen and try to understand what their loved one is experiencing.

A discussion must be held with the person who has OCD and their family members to ensure everyone involved understands OCD and that reassurance and compulsive rituals only temporarily help the symptoms of OCD and serve to increase symptoms in the long term. It is essential that everyone is open and clear about this as otherwise, if reassurance and help with compulsions are suddenly withdrawn, it can feel like punishment to the person with OCD. It must also be clear that the ultimate responsibility for overcoming OCD lies with the person who has it. Other family members need to care for themselves and their own health and wellbeing. Although they will be supportive to their relative, they cannot take responsibility for their relative's treatment. Of course, the situation is different with a child who has OCD, in which case the parent has to assume much more responsibility in helping the child overcome OCD (see Chapter 6).

Once the ground rules have been established within the family, it is then time to try to implement them. This is unlikely to be a smooth ride. First, old habits die hard, and it is very easy for all family members to slip back into old routines. Second, the person with OCD may temporarily become more distressed, and this can make it very difficult to resist. It is vital that there be no violence or threats from anyone. Violence and similar behaviours are fully discussed later in this chapter.

Violet's Story

Violet, a 30-year-old woman, lives with her parents, who are both in their sixties, in a house in a small market town. She was a much-wanted child who was born after her parents had been told that they were unlikely to ever have children. Consequently, she was always rather 'spoiled' and was used to getting her own way.

At the age of 11, she developed a fear of dirt and germs. This led to excessive washing and cleaning behaviours. In order to prevent distress to her daughter, Violet's mother did everything Violet asked her to do.

At the time she was first seen in the clinic, Violet ruled her entire house. Her father had taken early retirement to care for Violet, and her mother had not worked since Violet was born. Most of their time was spent indoors, and her mother had a list of daily cleaning which Violet expected her to perform. If Violet did not believe this cleaning was performed 'properly', then she would demand her mother repeat the entire process. Occasionally, Violet's demands resulted in her mother cleaning for eight hours a day.

Feeling unable to wash and care for herself, Violet also insisted that her mother wash her. She would stand in the shower whilst her mother cleaned her with antibacterial shower gel. Again, if Violet believed this was not performed 'properly', she would demand that her mother repeat it until she felt 'right'. Going to the toilet would take Violet up to an hour to urinate and four hours to defaecate. She performed these activities alone, but she demanded absolute silence in the house when this occurred. The slightest noise would result in her repeating her compulsions again and taking even longer. Her father was only allowed to leave the house when Violet gave 'permission', and when he returned with shopping or other items, a strict 'decontamination' procedure of all items was demanded by Violet. The family rarely left the house, but every year spent two weeks in a holiday camp in July, which they had done for more than 20 years. Whilst away, there was little evidence of Violet's OCD, but it would return as soon as she came home.

Violet's story demonstrates the absolute control that a person with OCD can inflict on a household. Both parents were keen to 'do what was right' for their daughter, but in trying to avoid upsetting her, they had made the situation worse. The story also shows another interesting observation for some people with OCD: their symptoms can sometimes 'disappear' in a new environment. Unfortunately, they will return the longer the person remains in this different environment. In other words, if Violet's family had remained in the holiday camp environment, her OCD would have gradually returned over the next weeks.

In this case, it is likely to be hopeless to work with just Violet. Her parents have adapted their whole lifestyle around her OCD. Indeed, in a case such as this in which the situation has developed over decades, it is often necessary to move those like Violet into a new environment away from her parents to work on her OCD treatment. Meanwhile, her parents would receive help to try to re-establish their own 'normal' life.

Violet's Story (Continued)

A trial of inpatient treatment was offered to Violet. She was insistent that she would not move away from home. When her parents urged her to accept the treatment, pointing out that they were not going to be around forever to do everything for her, Violet responded saying, 'Well, I will then get myself a maid'. Because Violet refused to engage in any therapy, the therapist started to work with the family and to encourage the parents to establish 'ground rules' of what they would and would not tolerate.

First, her mother said she was uncomfortable washing a 30-year-old woman. This was explained to Violet. The first time her mother refused to wash her and Violet was told to just stand in the shower if she could not wash herself, Violet screamed and cried for two hours. Her parents did not respond, and she eventually left the shower unassisted. This situation was extremely difficult for Violet's mother, Doris, who found herself unable to resist Violet's demands because she did not wish to see her daughter in a distressed state. Violet's care coordinator therefore arranged for her mother to have a carer's assessment, to identify the support she needed. For the carer's assessment, Doris was offered an appointment at the community health team. She was seen by a member of the team, and it was agreed that whilst she was going through such a stressful period, she would need counselling so that she could discuss her feelings.

The next area that was agreed to be tackled was the household cleaning. Initially it was agreed that Violet's mother would clean the house for a maximum of 30 minutes daily. Again, Violet screamed and cried, which her parents found very distressing but managed by supporting each other to resist the demands to repeat the clean.

After several weeks, Violet realised that her parents were not going to 'give in'. She agreed to accept treatment and to come to the hospital. Despite agreeing, she was extremely angry with her parents, who she believed were 'unreasonable' and that 'they ought to do what I tell them'. During her treatment, a new behaviour emerged whereby Violet would telephone her parents and demand that they tell her that 'all is OK and you won't catch an infection'. Obviously, this reassurance-seeking was not helpful in her programme. A meeting was held with the family, and it was agreed that when such requests were made, the parent would reply, 'Violet, I love you very much but answering these questions is not helpful to you. I have been asked by the hospital not to answer these questions'.

After several weeks in the hospital, Violet was still insistent that she would not engage in an exposure and response prevention (ERP) programme, which she believed was 'disgusting and unreasonable'. She was still telephoning her parents both to seek reassurance and to beg them to take her home. This was an extremely difficult time for her parents as they felt guilty even though they also knew they were acting in Violet's best interests. Violet was started on a selective serotonin reuptake inhibitor, which she was happy to take, and this reduced some of her fears and worries. Still unwilling to embark on an ERP programme, a family meeting was held to discuss her future. With the support of their counsellor, Violet's parents told her that they were not willing to take her back home. Violet became very angry and abusive, and both parents were distraught. The counsellor reminded them that they were doing this for Violet's best interests. At a second meeting, Violet was calmer. Her parents explained that they would visit her and that she could come home, initially for daytime visits, but that they could no longer have her living at home. A discussion was then held as to where Violet should live. Her local social worker agreed to look for local supported accommodation.

Violet is currently settled in a hostel which is a few miles from her parents' home. Her parents visit once a week, and Violet goes home on Sunday

> afternoons. Her parents look more relaxed and happier. Violet is still unwilling
> to engage in ERP treatment but has improved in her symptoms due to the
> medication and also the change in environment. It is hoped she may accept
> ERP treatment in the future.

Violet's case is interesting because Violet herself is not keen to receive
therapy. Her parents realise that for the benefit of everyone, she needs to
change. It is neither ethical nor practical to 'force' Violet to accept
treatment. From her point of view, she says she would be happy to
remain at home and with her parents waiting on her and agreeing to
her demands. This is not reasonable for her parents, who also need to live
their lives. By altering what they will do in the home, Violet started to
understand that life at home was changing and that she needed to think
about accepting help and treatment.

Throughout the years, I have seen many people who are not willing to
accept treatment with ERP at first. This can be because, at present, the
treatment seems worse than the condition. Fear of the unknown is
another major factor. People generally are fearful of change, and OCD
can seem to be a 'reliable, good friend' rather than the life-destroying
monster it appears to everyone else. It is not possible to 'do' ERP to
anyone; they need to want to do it and to lead the process. The best
thing to do in these cases is to leave the individual until they are ready
and willing to accept treatment. This may take months, years, or even
decades. Some people never decide to accept treatment. The key is to
ensure they understand the treatment and to leave the door open for their
return to therapy if they chose to do so.

Risk to Children When a Parent Has OCD

Children are the most vulnerable people in a family because they do not
have the choices open to adults. When a parent has OCD, this can lead to a
range of problems for the children. Parents who spend hours engaged in
compulsive rituals may neglect their children, and occasionally in these

cases, they might need to be taken into care. More frequently, there are less severe problems but still issues that need to be addressed and prevented.

Some parents with OCD incorporate their children in their compulsive rituals. This could involve extensive washing and cleaning compulsions. Indeed, I have seen children whose skin has been rubbed raw by an overzealous parent trying to 'decontaminate' them. This is unacceptable, and no child should be subjected to such treatment. If alerted to this, the children's welfare should be assessed by a qualified professional.

Parents may also demand children perform actions in a certain fashion guided by OCD, or they may restrict their children's ability to play outside or with friends and to bring friends home. Again, this is unacceptable. Children must be free to experience a 'normal' childhood, irrespective of the problems of their parents. In such situations, the children's welfare must always be the prime consideration. Again, the children need to be assessed by a qualified professional. The parent needs to stop placing these restrictions and demands on the children. This is easier said than done, but it is non-negotiable for the welfare of the children.

How Involved in Care and Treatment Should Families Be?

Assuming that the person with OCD is an adult, the level of involvement of the family and friends in the person's treatment will vary. Treatment with ERP or medication requires the person with OCD to want to engage in the treatment to try to overcome the problem. If the person with OCD wants friends and family to help with treatment, then it is best for that person to define how they can help. Similarly, the person with OCD will be able to say whether or not they would like family and friends to attend any appointments with them. It can be very difficult to see a loved one undergoing treatment and not to be asked to help, but in fact, this may be the way in which the individual is learning to take a step forward and to overcome OCD themselves. It is usually best for family and friends to ask if they can help and to leave it to the individual to decide one way or another. Sometimes an individual with OCD is reluctant to express their fears openly, and it can take careful and sympathetic listening and support to understand the obsessions. Indeed, if there is a high degree of shame and embarrassment concerning the obsessive thoughts, they may be unwilling to discuss these with those who are closest to them. In such situations, it is important that some ground rules are still set to keep everyone in the family on 'an even keel'.

Sometimes it can be difficult for families to withhold reassurance and not provide help with compulsions because it seems as if they do not care. It is important to demonstrate care in ways which are more 'healthy' and productive. Depending on the nature of the OCD and the stage of the individual in their 'OCD journey', care may be demonstrated by going for a walk with the loved one or having family dinners and discussions on non-OCD topics.

Violence and OCD

Violence, threats, and abusive behaviour are never acceptable. Sometimes, people with OCD may 'lash out' if a relative interrupts their compulsive rituals either on purpose or accidentally. Whatever the situation, violence is always unacceptable. Family members are often reluctant to report violence to the authorities. Although this is understandable, it may not be helpful. Although violence may be 'out of character' for the individual, there is still conscious control in OCD. Ignoring and 'brushing violent episodes under the carpet' can lead to an escalation of violence. Not only is this dangerous for the person who is the victim of this violence but also it is damaging to the person with OCD. If they learn to 'lash out' whenever their compulsions are interrupted or when someone does not meet their demands, they may some day commit a very serious violent act. The rule for those who are threatened with violence is simple: they must protect themselves. This may mean leaving the situation or contacting the police. Acting in this way is to the benefit of other family members and the person with OCD. It can be difficult because families do not wish to inflict further distress on their loved one, but it is in the best interest of everyone involved that it is crystal clear that violence in any form is unacceptable.

KEY POINTS

- Family members need to establish 'ground rules' about what is and what is not acceptable and what they will tolerate.
- Giving reassurance to a person with OCD offers temporary relief, but then the anxiety returns.
- Giving reassurance or taking over jobs and performing compulsions for the person with OCD makes the situation worse in the long term.
- It is difficult to stop engaging in behaviours such as reassurance-seeking or helping with compulsive rituals because it can cause extreme distress to the OCD sufferer. A frank discussion needs to be held with them before implementing the change.
- The person with OCD needs to be willing to engage in ERP; it is not a treatment that can be 'done' to them.
- People with OCD have to determine their own 'rock bottom' point and when they will accept treatment. Family members must try to ensure that their own lives are as unimpaired by their relative's OCD as possible.
- Sometimes it is necessary to make difficult decisions, such as refusing to allow a son or daughter to remain living in the house, in order to help those with OCD start to change.
- If the person with OCD is a parent, the needs of the children are paramount. Children should be free to develop, grow, explore, and form friendships, free of any OCD restrictions imposed by others. If this is not the case, then the child's wellbeing needs to be assessed by a child health professional.
- Violence and threats are never acceptable. Family members must always protect themselves. There should be consideration about calling the police after any violence has occurred.

10

. . . .

What Can You Do to Help Cope with Your OCD?

These final chapters will examine how someone with OCD can help themselves and seek treatment. Advice will be given on setting up a self-treatment grade exposure with response prevention programme (ERP), as well as resources and organisations which can be helpful in achieving this. The advice will be given as a step-by-step guide for developing a personal ERP programme to tackle OCD.

It will also examine what to do if an individual is finding difficulty accessing help and will give useful contacts and organisations as well as written material.

OK, I Have OCD but How Do I Get Help?

This next section is geared to people living in the UK but may also be applicable to other countries. OCD (and body dysmorphic disorder (BDD)) have official guidance produced by the National Institute for

Health and Care Excellence (NICE). This body declares the treatment you should receive within the NHS and is produced for England and Wales. In Scotland, NICE guidance is adopted by the Scottish Intercollegiate Guidelines Network (SIGN) which adopts and monitors the application of NICE guidance as well as producing some of its own guidance. In Northern Ireland the body is NICE in Northern Ireland which adopts and monitors the NICE guidance. The original guidance for OCD came out in 2005 but has been regularly updated. The current guidance is lengthy but can be found at:

www.nice.org.uk/guidance/cg31/chapter/1-Guidance

It can also be obtained from HMSO as clinical guideline 31 [CG31], and is available from:

National Institute for Health and Clinical Excellence,
MidCity Place,
71 High Holborn
London, WC1V 6NA

This guidance states that everyone with OCD should have access to special-ised OCD treatment. This includes psychological therapy involving exposure and self-imposed response prevention (ERP). The intensity of treatment offered varies with the severity of the condition, but ranges from low inten-sity (usually ten hours) therapy from local Psychological Services in Primary Care, through to intensive specialised services funded nationally. In add-ition, the guidance recommends treatment with selective serotonin reuptake inhibitors (SSRIs, e.g. sertraline, fluoxetine, paroxetine, fluvoxamine, citalo-pram or excitaloprame; see Chapter 4) or clomipramine, and advises that those people who do not respond to these or to ERP should additionally be offered a dopamine blocking agent (as discussed in Chapter 3).

In short, everyone in the UK should be able to receive appropriate treat-ment for OCD. The first thing that someone needs to do to seek help is to visit their GP and ask to be referred for psychological therapy for OCD, or ask to be prescribed an SSRI. If there is any difficulty with this, it is worthwhile referring to the NICE clinical guideline 31 [CG31] (2005). All

GPs should have access to Psychological Treatment in Primary Care Teams (sometime known as IAPT or Increasing Access for Psychological Therapy). Many of these Psychological Services will also accept direct referrals from patients themselves, which can be useful if you do not feel able to discuss your worries with your GP. Every region should have such services, but the waiting lists can vary from days, to in some cases, months.

In some situations your GP may refer you directly to other mental health services which will then decide with you the best course of action to take in your particular circumstances.

Once referred or receiving an appointment, most people with OCD should be offered graded exposure with self-imposed response prevention (ERP; see Chapter 5 for further details). Occasionally, other treatments may be offered if there are complicating diagnoses. For example, people with emotional instability may need to be seen by a specialised team for treatment of this first, or people who have experienced extreme trauma may need to address that first. Sometimes people with OCD are offered anxiety management training. Where this can be helpful to address some of the symptoms of anxiety, it is not generally helpful for OCD. If worried you are not receiving the correct help, then you should raise this with your therapist.

If the treatment in the Primary Care Service does not help, you should be moved into secondary care services and eventually should be sent to a specialist team who specialise in OCD. Some parts of the country have specialised regional treatment centres for OCD, although unfortunately this is not true of every region. In addition, there is a shortage of therapists specialising in the treatment and management of OCD. However, it is usually possible to find someone locally.

If an individual has not responded to treatment locally and has been offered the treatments listed above, then they may need to be referred to a National Treatment Centre for OCD. For England and Wales, people who fail to respond to a range of treatments locally can be referred to a Highly Specialist Team for OCD and BDD via the provision of NHS England Highly Specialist Services for OCD and BDD. Details can be found here:

www.england.nhs.uk/wp-content/uploads/2013/06/c09-sev-ocd-boy-dysm.pdf
www.swlstg-tr.nhs.uk/documents/related-documents/our-services/336-
national-service-referral-criteria/file

People with OCD and BDD who live in Scotland, Wales, or Northern Ireland can also be referred to these services via their local services.

What Can I Do to Help Myself?

Some people with OCD may decide to try and tackle the OCD themselves. This may be because they have a mild problem and do not wish to, or are unable to, take time from work or other commitments that therapy may entail. Others may have tried therapy before and found that the pace was too fast and they had difficulty in complying. Others still may just want to try and overcome the difficulties themselves. Whatever the reason, you should remember that overcoming OCD does involve commitment and bravery and can be hard to do on your own. Even if you do not wish to seek professional help immediately, it may be worthwhile contacting one of the self-help groups listed at the end of this chapter.

If you still decide to go ahead on your own, then the following chapters are designed to help guide you through this process. Remember this is not going to be easy and that, inevitably, you will fail and slip back at times. Just treat every slip up as a learning experience which makes you stronger for the future. The next two chapters examine general issues to bear in mind and how to tackle OCD. The successive chapters then concentrate on special considerations in the treatment of different types of OCD.

Are There Any Organisations Which Offer Help and Support?

There are a variety of self-help and support organisations for people with OCD and their families. Many regions have several organisations and the list below is geared to the UK.

Name of Organisation	Website	What they offer	Notes
OCD Action	www .ocdaction .org.uk/	Helpline; website containing information on OCD; books available online; local support; conferences for people with OCD and their families; lobby government and others about OCD matters.	UK's largest OCD charity
OCD UK	http:// ocduk.org	Helpline; website containing information on OCD; books available online; local support; conferences for people with OCD and their families; lobby government and others about OCD matters.	
TOP UK (Triumph Over Phobia)	www .topuk .org/	Offers local treatment groups in some areas; website containing information; lobbying of Government and others about issues relating to OCD and phobic disorders.	Offers its own treatment groups for those with mild to moderate OCD or who do not wish to go through the NHS
MIND	www .mind.org .uk/	Mental health charity which provides information on a variety of mental health issues; lobbying of Government and others on mental health issues.	MIND media awards are prestigious awards given for informative and sensitive portrayal or information on mental health issues.

(*cont.*)

Name of Organisation	Website	What they offer	Notes
International OCD Foundation	https://iocdf.org/	Website containing information for people with OCD and healthcare professionals; training courses available for professionals.	This organisation has arisen from the US-based OCD Foundation which seeks to inform the public, educate professionals, and raise awareness of OCD.

KEY POINTS

- There are various ways in which you can access treatment.
- In the UK, all regions should have access to psychological therapies in primary care.
- In the UK, the National Institute for Care and Health Care Excellence (NICE) has published guidance on the treatments people with OCD and BDD should receive. These are published in England but accepted by other parts of the UK.
- Treatments that may be offered may include medication and psychological therapy.
- For psychological therapy, the key component is ERP, but this may be combined with other treatments.
- There are several charities dealing with OCD who can offer you assistance, support, information, and in some cases help to start therapy.
- If treatment in local services is not useful, do not give up as you should then be referred to more specialist services.

11
· · · · · · ·

General Principles
of Treatment

In this chapter the general principles of treatment are set out with examples. More detailed examples and advice for self-help treatment are given in later chapters for each of the different types of OCD thoughts, but it is best to read this chapter first. This chapter outlines the basic principles of graded exposure treatment combined with response prevention (ERP).

Questionnaires and diary records to record your progress are given in Chapter 19.

Introduction

Before embarking on a self-guided therapy programme or any therapy programme at all, it is wise to try to be as physically fit and healthy as you can be, to help you feel in the best situation to tackle the programme. This means ensuring that you drink sufficient fluids, eat regular healthy meals, and try to get plenty of sleep and some exercise. Some information about this is given in Chapter 12.

Next, it is important to remember that you are not 'going mad' but have a problem with unpleasant, anxiety-provoking thoughts, images, or ideas. In order to cope with these thoughts, you have undoubtedly developed a number of strategies to reduce the discomfort caused by the thoughts. These strategies have been fully described in Chapter 3, and may include compulsive thoughts or behaviours which reduce the anxiety, such as checking and washing compulsions, as well as seeking reassurance from others or taking some precautions and avoiding situations where the obsessional thoughts are triggered. Unfortunately, these strategies have the effect of fuelling the problem and making the situation worse. Treatment will involve stopping these behaviours and learning to face the fear without these. Some people use alcohol or drugs in an attempt to block out the anxiety. If this is the case for you, then it is important to obtain some help first to overcome these problems before embarking on an exposure programme which is likely to initially increase anxiety levels and therefore may mean that there is a greater tendency to resort to temporary relief from drugs or alcohol.

Finally, do try and discuss options with your GP and read up about the treatment options available in general and in your local area.

How Should I Set About Starting Treatment for Myself?

The first thing to do if you want to start working on your OCD is to fully assess the problem yourself. Imagine you had a magic wand and could make all your OCD symptoms go away. What would your life look like? Where would you be living? What job would you be doing? What would your social life look like?

After this, the next thing is to assess what you would need to do to achieve this. Would you need to go back to college to gain some qualifications?

What would be necessary for you to learn to be more independent, etc. This list may appear daunting but, bear in mind, there is no rush and every step in the right direction is a step nearer your goal.

You may like to keep these goals somewhere nearby to remind yourself of your dreams when treatment is tough. Some people stick a reminder of where they are aiming for next to their bed, or keep it written on a card to look at when they become disheartened.

Example of a Life Goals Chart

In Chapter 13, the case history of a young woman, Grace, who has contamination fears, is given. When she decided to start treatment, she first thought about what her life would be like if she could overcome her OCD. She decided on the following:

Working life	I would be working normal hours and not going in early and staying late to clean areas I had touched.
	I may apply for a promotion as I have remained at the same grade for over 6 years due to my OCD taking up my time.
Home life	I would start looking for a place of my own, near to my parents but not living with them so that they and I can have our personal freedom and space.
Social life	I would go out with my friends without constantly making excuses.
	I would start socialising with work colleagues.
	I will start going on walks again with friends and try to get fitter.
Relationships	My final goal of treatment is to take my parents out for a meal and a drink without any OCD precautions.
	Once I am comfortable going out with friends and family, I may try dating again.
Personal leisure time	I will have time to read and to play computer games.
	Also, I will start going for country walks both alone and with others.

Grace pinned these goals onto the side of her bedroom cabinet so that she could remind herself of where she was heading as she started treatment. They therefore served as a reminder of her overall goals of treatment whenever she felt down or that she was getting nowhere.

What Next?

Think about your problems and write them down. This may be something like 'Fear of dirt and germs and worry that I may become ill and spread the infection to other people'; 'Fear I may contract HIV'; 'Fear I may be a paedophile and may act on this'; 'Fear that unless I perform everything perfectly I will be rejected'; 'Fear that unless I check doors, windows, gas, and electrical appliances, a disaster will occur'; 'Fear that unless I perform tasks in a set way I won't feel "just right" and will be anxious and uncomfortable'. These are just a few of the possibilities. It can be difficult to identify exactly what the fear is, but it is worth spending time to try and pin it down. Many people may have more than one major fear or 'theme' of their obsessions. Identifying the fear in this way not only makes it easier to perform the next step in the ERP but it also makes the OCD seem more manageable. People with OCD are often overwhelmed by their problems and feel they 'cannot see the wood for the trees'. By isolating a few 'themes' in this way, it can make you realise that the problem is, indeed, containable.

How Do I Develop My Goals of Treatment?

Looking at the fears you have identified, consider what task you would be able to do to demonstrate to yourself and others that you have overcome this. So, for example, for a fear of contamination it may be to 'Visit a public toilet, sit on the toilet seat without using disinfectant, use the toilet and leave with a 30 second hand wash'. For fear of paedophilia it may be 'Sit in a place full of children without checking'. For fear of disaster occurring in the house it could be 'Leave the house without checking'.

For perfectionistic fears it could be 'Deliberately leave the house without checking my hair and clothes'.

Although this stage is not essential, it can help with devising the hierarchy.

Set Out a 'Ladder or Hierarchy of Fears'

The next stage is to identify the stages on the way to facing up to the fear **without performing any anxiety-reducing compulsive rituals or reassurance seeking**. It is important to remember that these tasks need to be performed without the compulsions, and the anxiety needs to be scored (explained in the following) in this way. For some compulsions such as 'hand washing', there will still be a ban on the compulsions and a whole 'new' way of hand washing will be introduced. Once you have identified the stages in this way, score the anxiety/discomfort you think you will feel whilst engaging in them. A useful scoring system is to score as follows:

0 = no anxiety
2 = mild anxiety
4= moderate Anxiety
6 = severe anxiety
8 = extreme anxiety/cannot be higher/panic

The following is the kind of hierarchy someone may have who has fear of dirt and germs for fear of contracting and spreading an illness:

Task (all to be peformed without washing rituals)	Anxiety rating (0 to 8)
Touch door handles in home (apart from toilet handles)	3
Get dressed and undressed without hand washing in between every item	4
Touch the outside of my trousers without washing my hands	4

(*cont.*)

Task (all to be peformed without washing rituals)	Anxiety rating (0 to 8)
Touch toilet door handles in home	5
Touch shop door handles, pelican crossing buttons outside	5
Bring shopping home from supermarket without washing outside packaging	5
Prepare food without first washing hands repeatedly	6
Use utensils straight from the drawer without rewashing	6
Use plates and cups without rewashing	6
Drink or eat something bought outside the home	7
Sit on a public bench in the park without placing newspaper on the seat (and without showering as soon as arriving home)	7
Travel on train sitting on the seats and holding on to handrails	7
Travel on crowded bus holding on to handrail	8
Touch public toilet door handle	8
Use public toilet	8

The hierarchy may contain many more items than the one above. It is also important to remember that the exposure tasks should be performed **without performing compulsive rituals**. With something like hand washing, clearly everyone needs to wash their hands during the day, but the key here is the extent and way in which this is done. Most people with 'decontamination rituals' perform them in set ways. For example, they may always wash in running water and may wash beyond their wrists. The hand wash may take several minutes. In the exposure programme, all hand washing should be banned apart from before meals or food preparation. Hand washing should involve putting some water in the basin and then washing to the wrist only for about 20 seconds (or the time it takes to sing 'Happy birthday to you' in your head twice). Programmes should not be performed immediately before preparing meals, but would best be performed after eating to prolong exposure time.

How Should I Perform My Exposure Tasks?

Exposure tasks need to be performed consistently and regularly. You need to start at the bottom of the hierarchy and not mix them up. Stick with one or two items and conquer those before moving on.

Some people try to 'jump around' the hierarchy and suddenly perform a much more difficult item. This is not a good idea. People who do this end up disappointed and disillusioned. Remember that you need to learn to walk before you can run! It takes time but the gradual approach is best. Sometimes life can suddenly mean you find yourself facing a more difficult task. If you manage to achieve these then, congratulations. If, however, you find them too difficult, do not get too disheartened, and remember to get back to the items you were doing before and continue in a slow and steady manner. It could be that a special event is due to occur, and this could mean facing up to challenges and fears that you have not yet practised. In such cases, it is worth spending some time deciding what you would feel able to tackle e.g., if a family outing involved eating away from home and you have not tackled this fear then you need to decide what you are able to do or not do and see if you can compromise or make things easier for yourself. In such cases and if appropriate, discussion with a sympathetic family member or friend, if available, could help. You may even need to take your own food for example, until you are ready to tackle this exposure.

The exposure must also be performed regularly, ideally three times a day, but at least daily if you are to experience benefit. Record your anxiety during each exposure task (using the same 0–8 scale discussed above). Many people find it useful to record the anxiety more frequently than once, and it may be that it is helpful if you record the anxiety just before you start the exposure task, during the exposure task, and then afterwards. If you record it three times, it is easier to see that often thinking about performing the exposure task is worse than actually doing it. You will find that initially your anxiety will last for two to three hours, but the more you practise, the shorter amount of time the anxiety will last, as well as the anxiety not reaching such high levels.

You may find yourself performing compulsive rituals before you really realise it. This is normal and natural. If you do perform the compulsions, then just go back and re-expose yourself to the fear again. With decontamination compulsions, after touching the item, it can be useful to touch your body, clothes, and hair, and, if possible, lick your hands, as this is much more difficult to 'undo'. Also, it is important not to 'decontaminate' yourself too quickly. For example, it is better to do a contamination task **after you** have eaten or gone to the toilet, as otherwise the hand washing may 'undo' the exposure. If you do need to wash your hands before two hours have passed since your 'contamination', then you should touch the same item on your hierarchy again.

Compulsive thoughts are much more difficult to control, and for this reason, it is often best to make a recording of the obsessive fear-provoking thought and listen to this on repeat on your mobile phone or similar portable device whilst performing exposure. It is difficult to always 'undo' the exposure if the exposure is repeated!

Once the items at the bottom of your hierarchy are causing little or no anxiety, it is time to step up to the items causing moderate anxiety. You will probably find that, having done the groundwork with easier items, these more difficult items are now easier than you expected and may only cause mild anxiety.

Once you have conquered the items causing moderate anxiety, move up to the more difficult items.

At the end, when you have performed all the items on the programme, take stock of where you are with respect to your initial therapy goals. Think about your lifegoals and whether now is the time to move forward by taking on a training course or other challenge. Remember that obsessions can expand to fill a vacuum in your life, and so keeping busy can be useful in the battle to overcome OCD.

Example of a First-Week Programme for a Person with Contamination Fears

Programmes for week commencing: 12 July

1. Touch door handles in home (apart from toilet handles)
2. Get dressed and undressed without hand washing in between every item
3. Touch the outside of my trousers without washing my hands

	Programme No. 1			Programme No. 2			Programme No. 3		
	Before	During	After	Before	During	After	Before	During	After
Monday									
AM	6	5	2	5	4	3	6	5	2
Lunch	6	4	2	5	5	3	5	4	3
PM	6	4	3	5	4	2	6	5	2
Before Bed	6	4	2	5	4	3	6	4	2
Tuesday									
AM	6	5	2	5	4	3	6	5	2
Lunch	6	5	2	5	4	3	6	5	2
PM	6	5	2	5	4	3	6	5	2
Before Bed	6	4	2	5	4	3	6	4	2
Wednesday									
AM	6	5	2	5	4	3	6	5	2
Lunch	6	5	2	5	4	3	6	5	2
PM	6	5	2	5	4	3	6	5	2
Before Bed	6	4	2	5	4	3	6	4	2

WORKSHEET

	Programme No. 1			Programme No. 2			Programme No. 3		
	Before	During	After	Before	During	After	Before	During	After
Thursday									
AM	4	4	1	5	4	2	4	3	2
Lunch	4	3	1	4	4	2	5	3	2
PM	4	3	1	5	4	2	4	4	2
Before Bed	4	4	1	4	3	2	4	3	2
Friday									
AM	4	4	3	4	4	2	4	3	2
Lunch	4	3	1	4	4	2	5	3	2
PM	4	3	1	5	4	2	4	4	2
Before Bed	2	3	1	4	2	2	3	2	1
Saturday									
AM	2	2	1	2	3	2	2	2	1
Lunch	2	1	1	2	2	1	2	3	2
PM	1	3	1	1	2	1	1	2	1
Before Bed	1	3	1	1	2	2	2	2	1
Sunday									
AM	1	2	1	2	2	2	2	2	1
Lunch	2	1	1	2	2	1	2	2	2
PM	1	1	1	1	2	1	1	2	1
Before Bed	1	2	1	1	2	2	2	2	1

As you can see from this example, every day the overall anxiety levels reduced. This was not always the case as sometimes there were days or times which were somewhat more difficult, but the overall trend was that items which had previously caused moderate anxiety were now only causing mild levels of anxiety.

It would therefore be reasonable to introduce one of two more difficult items on to the programme for the next week. Items which are only causing mild anxiety can then be dropped from recording, although in this case, as they are everyday actions, they should be continued in daily life.

Occasionally people find they have attempted to move on too quickly. In such situations, you should then drop back down the hierarchy and maybe start to find a progression that is not as difficult as the one you have just tried.

What If I Cannot Sort Out a Hierarchy Because Everything Is Causing Maximal Anxiety/Distress?

For a few people, everything seems too frightening, and it seems impossible to arrange items in a hierarchy in this way. If this is the case, then you can start with a programme based on your daily activities. It is generally best to start with the first thing when you get up. This may be getting up, getting ready, dressing, and getting ready to face the day. If, for example, you have a fear of doing something incorrectly and being criticised for it, then you could start by not checking your clothing and taking the risk of doing this imperfectly. It would then be important not to check throughout the day. You can then continue to work through the day when you have succeeded in your first task.

Taking Things to Extremes and Risk Assessment

In 'normal' life, most people do not touch toilet seats without wash their hands or walk out of the front door without checking that it is closed. Nor would you deliberately wish harm on a loved one. However, in ERP treatment, you are often asked to go to 'extremes'. It is important to note that whereas these things may be extreme, they should never be frankly dangerous. Therefore, if you had a fear of HIV, at the end of treatment you may decide to go into a clinic dealing with HIV and eat a sandwich in there without washing your hands, but you would not inject yourself with HIV-positive blood! If you have a fear of asbestos, you may decide to enter a building known to contain undisturbed asbestos and touch the wall, but no one would ever expect you to handle asbestos itself, which could be risky. If you have a fear of being a paedophile, you may decide to write 'I am a paedophile' on a piece of paper and throw it in a bin. It would not be safe to, for example, shout out loud in a street that you are a paedophile, due to the potential reactions of others. In all of the examples, it is necessary to weigh up the real risk with the obsessive fear of risk.

Everything in life has some risk. For example, most of us will drive a car, walk along the road, and cross a road, even though road accidents account for the most deaths worldwide among children and young people under 30 years. Even if you decide to stay at home, it is far from safe, with 6,000 deaths/year recorded in the UK as a result of home accidents (www.rospa.com/Home-Safety/Advice/General/Facts-and-Figures; www.rospa.com). By touching money and other items and then not washing your hands before eating, there is a very slight chance you might catch an illness. However, millions of banking employees, cleaners, and hospital workers around the world have lived to tell the tale.

The real issue is always trying to weigh up the 'risk' of exposure against the horror of OCD which can leave you trapped and can make you prone to many other physical and mental diseases. When phrased in that way, the small 'risk' of, for example, shaking many people's hands or facing up to your fear of acting inappropriately seems small when compared to the reality of living with OCD.

The reason why some of the exposure tasks can appear extreme can be explained by the pendulum theory. With therapy, the aim is to make someone 'swing' from being trapped by OCD over towards 'normal'. 'Normal' is always difficult to define but we will say it is what the majority of the population would be happy doing. If in ERP you get as far as this 'normal', then all appears fine and good. There are however two pitfalls to this. Firstly, after you finish ERP, you may find yourself slipping back a small amount. Whereas this may be fine for a few people, it does run the risk that you are on a slippery slope to return to OCD. Secondly, and probably most important, is that you have not really tested your OCD 'beliefs'. OCD thoughts may constantly be asking you whether this is safe or not. If you do something that seems 'extreme', then you can always remind yourself of the exposure when the doubts creep in! I must repeat, however, that these more 'extreme' exposures must not be frankly dangerous but just 'extreme' in your own mind.

The following figure demonstrates the Treatment Pendulum. Instead of sticking with your OCD, you will need to go somewhat beyond the normal towards the opposite end of the spectrum (labelled extreme risk-taking in the figure).

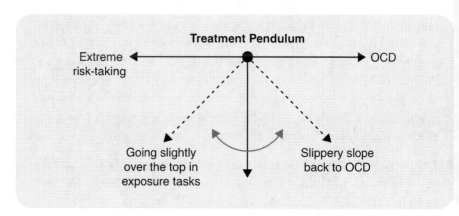

Taking Responsibility

Any therapist who has worked a while with people with OCD will be familiar with the issue of 'shifting responsibility'. This is where the patient will do really well and go rapidly through the hierarchy with little anxiety during the sessions when accompanied by the therapist, but is completely unable to complete the same programmes on their own. The person with OCD feels that they are not responsible for any of the dreaded dire consequences that they fear may occur if they expose themselves to the fear without 'putting it right'. Just by being there, the therapist can be a form of reassurance. It is therefore vital that such an individual with OCD creates their own hierarchy and chooses where to start without the 'approval' of others.

If you are in doubt, then ask yourself whether you will be able to perform a similar exposure whether or not you are with others or due to see a therapist and take the risk that you are doing it 'correctly'.

What If I Have a Set-Back?

Life has its ups and downs. Bad and good things happen. These can disrupt an exposure programme. Sometimes things can happen and your OCD will try and tell you it is because of the exposure programme itself. At such times, you need to stop and try and think rationally about the situation. For example, in Chapter 13, Grace, who has a fear of dirt and germs, had a slight blip in her programme when her mother developed a chest infection. In the following chapters you will find other examples of this type. At such times it is necessary to engage your rational brain and ignore the OCD thoughts suggesting it is your fault. This is not easy but is an important part of therapy.

Troubleshooting

Therapy does not always work as perfectly as it does in books and there are certain things you need to be aware of before starting.

Firstly, the obsessions will still persist for a long time, even after you have faced up to them. The important thing is not to give in to the compulsions. Eventually, over time, the obsessions will fade.

In addition, sometimes as you start to tackle one obsession, another even worse obsession develops. Do not get distracted by this. Remind yourself that, however unpleasant, it is just an obsession and once you have dealt with one obsession, you can move on to dealing with the next one. Do not get disheartened, this is all normal and will just take time. Remember, you will overcome the difficulties at the end.

Also, when you first start ERP, you can feel worse for a little while. This can be because you have carefully restricted your life to control your obsessions. Breaking down these safety behaviours and facing your fears can make you feel worse for a while until you start to see the benefits. In short, there is light at the end of the tunnel!

What If the Anxiety Is Not Coming Down?

Have you exposed yourself for long enough without performing compulsions? Remember it will take two to three hours often before the anxiety comes down. The other issue is whether you have performed the exposure three times a day? Although it does not have to always be three times a day, it must be at least once or twice a day if you are to see good results. Three times a day usually leads to the quickest results. Have you been honest about your compulsions? Are you still getting some reassurance or performing other compulsions which will serve to maintain your anxiety? However tempting it can be to engage in compulsions, they really do help to maintain anxiety.

If you are sure about all of the above, then it may be worthwhile considering either trying a course of SSRIs or trying some professional help, in which case, it is recommended that you speak to your GP.

Reward and Praise Yourself

Finally, remember that ERP is far from easy. You have needed to be very brave to face up to your fears. Once you have truly faced your fears you need to reward yourself. Take pride in what you have achieved. Remember that true heroes experience anxiety but face up to it. That is what you have been doing so you deserve to be kind to yourself. OCD is not a weakness nor a character flaw but a very real illness, just as any physical illness is not a character flaw or weakness! Praise yourself for what you are doing and remind yourself of where you are heading. Do not get discouraged if progress seems slow; it is much better to have a slow but effective programme than a 'miracle cure' which collapses within a short time.

Set yourself little rewards after completing your programmes with whatever you enjoy that does not break the bank cost-wise. Maybe a relaxing soak in a bath (assuming you do not have washing compulsions!). Perhaps a walk in the park or a favourite meal? Just try and pamper yourself a little!

Good luck and remember, even people who do not succeed the first time, often succeed when they try again. Be kind to yourself and keep your sense of humour!

Steps to Setting Up a Self-Exposure Programme

- Start writing down what you want to do with your life if you were free of OCD. It is often helpful to divide this into the following headings (see **'Grace's Story'** in Chapter 13 for an example):
  - Work
  - Home
  - Relationships
  - Private leisure time
  - Social leisure time
- Define the problem in simple terms, e.g. fear of dirt and germs leading to avoidance of touching things that other people have touched; fear of contracting HIV leading to avoidance of red marks anywhere, public toilets, and medical procedures; fear that I may cause a disaster to happen by not checking household appliances, windows, and doors; fear that I may inadvertently sexually abuse a child leading to avoidance of children; fear that if I am not perfect I may be criticised and ridiculed; horrible violent images coming into my mind leading to me having the urge to perform compulsions to prevent these events happening.

- Define what you would like to do at the end of treatment that would demonstrate to yourself and others that you have conquered your OCD. This should be a specific behaviour and not just 'feel better'.

  Some examples could be: 'to be able to go out of my house to visit my sister in her home and play with her children'; 'to go to a restaurant and eat a meal without cleaning'; 'to complete a written assignment on time without checking'.

- Develop a hierarchy of fears (see above). **Remember the idea is to face up gradually, reliably and predictably to the things that you fear and to stop taking the 'precautions' to undo this!**

- Pick an item on the hierarchy which causes you some fear but that you can tolerate without performing compulsions. Then perform this at least daily (ideally three times a day).

- As your anxiety or discomfort comes under control move up the hierarchy.

- Reward yourself for your progress.

Once completed, make sure you have a relapse prevention plan. This means writing down signs that signify you are relapsing and plan what you will do and how you will act in such a situation. Keep this somewhere safe! Look at if you find yourself slipping back.

12

• • • • • • •

How to Better Manage Your Symptoms Before and During Treatment

Many people with OCD have neglected themselves for a considerable amount of time. This can have an adverse effect on your physical as well as mental health. In addition, some people try to overcome OCD by using substances, or restricting their diet or fluid intake, as an attempt to control their OCD or because 'the OCD tells them to' do certain things. By nature, many people with OCD tend to have an 'all or nothing' approach to life and this in itself can lead to periods of feast or famine which can have an effect on general health and wellbeing. It can therefore be helpful to try to improve your general physical health either before or during treatment.

Wellbeing and OCD

Many people with psychological problems have associated health problems, which may have gone unnoticed due to the severity of other difficulties. Indeed, some of these, such as restrictions in fluid intake or severe dietary restrictions can have really dangerous health consequences and need to be tackled as a matter of urgency. For most though, it is just the opportunity to have a good health 'MOT' in the knowledge that the better your general health is, the better you will feel and the stronger you will be in tackling your mental health problems.

Improving general health and looking after physical and mental health is particularly important for people with OCD, for a number of reasons. Firstly, many people with OCD neglect themselves and their physical wellbeing due to various factors, including that they are too busy performing their obsessive-compulsive rituals to look after themselves; they have become depressed alongside their OCD and this makes self-care more difficult or because the obsessive-compulsive thoughts encourage them to do things which are detrimental to their health. Secondly, treatments such as ERP are in themselves stressful, and it is important that an individual puts themselves in the best position to tackle their OCD, and this includes feeling as well as possible. Thirdly, we know that people with long histories of mental health difficulties often have poorer physical health than the general population, as they are often reluctant to seek help from their GPs and other professionals.

The important steps to ensuring better health and wellbeing include:

- Drinking sufficient fluids (preferably water or non-sugary drinks)
- Having a well-balanced regular diet
- Regular exercise
- Avoiding alcohol and alcohol excess; stopping smoking and avoiding non-prescribed drugs
- Sleep hygiene
- Balancing everyday life with activities to give a sense of achievement as well as pleasure

Fluid Intake

Everyone needs to drink sufficient fluids to keep themselves healthy and feeling well. Many adults in the UK do not drink sufficient fluid. This is even more prominent in some patients with mental health problems who may try and restrict fluids. This can have potentially serious or even fatal consequences.

People often talk about 'giving their kidneys a rest' by not drinking much fluid. This could not be further from the truth. Kidneys have to work harder if they have little fluid. They work best when the person is well-hydrated and drinking plenty.

To combat losses via urine and sweat in normal temperatures (i.e., not on a hot day in summer) and with a person involved in normal exercise (i.e., not doing any sports or gym sessions) then an individual needs to aim for **2 litres (4.4 pints) of fluid a day**. This needs to be increased in very hot weather or if the person has been active.

Symptoms from dehydration may be thirst and a dry mouth but with people that are chronically drinking too little, these may not be apparent. Other symptoms which can occur include:

- Headache
- Feeling flushed and hot
- Breathless on exercise
- Increased anxiety symptoms

Remember there are 1,000 mls or 100 cls in a litre. A normal cup contains about 150 mls of fluid and a large mug, 200 mls.

Recommended intake advice is:

- 2 litres (4.4 pints) of fluid a day
- More in hot weather
- More after exercise
- Drink at least one mug of fluid every hour between the hours of 8:00 a.m. and 6:00 p.m. (to avoid waking at night)

Some people with OCD do drink too much fluid and this can be extremely dangerous. It is important that you keep hydrated without drinking too much. Two litres is a good guide for most situations. In very hot weather or when engaged in strenuous exercise, you will need to drink a bit more but this should not be more than 3 litres in almost every situation, unless running a marathon when you may need a little more.

Many people with mental health problems can vary their weight dramatically by having periods of 'feast and famine'. This is very bad for your general health and ability to withstand problems like infection. The fitter you are and the better you feel, the easier it will be to stick to your treatment programme.

To add to the difficulty, some drugs used to treat mental illnesses can have a profound effect on your weight. If this is causing you a problem, you should always discuss this with your care coordinator or consultant psychiatrist, who will be able to advise what is best for you.

When starting treatment, it is often clinical practice to record your height and weight (if this doesn't happen to you, you can always ask your practitioner to do this). From these figures your **Body Mass Index or BMI** can be calculated:

- **Healthy BMIs are between 18 and 25**.
- 25–30 means overweight
- 30+ is seriously obese
- Under 18 indicates underweight
- A BMI of 15 or under usually indicates a serious and potentially life-threatening starvation
- However, weight can vary by a few kilograms every day and week to week, so does not need to be monitored too closely

Sometimes people claim they have 'heavy bones'. This is not true as there is very little variation between the weight of the skeleton of individuals of similar height. Extremely athletic individuals (such as some Olympic athletes or members of the British Lions Rugby Teams) have BMIs in the 'overweight' range. This is because muscle is heavier than fat and these individuals have an extremely high percentage of muscle. This is extremely unlikely to be the case for most patients entering treatment.

Healthy Eating

This guidance is based on a Western European diet and some details may vary in certain cultures. If in doubt, then ask your Team to refer you to a dietician for advice.

Sustaining a healthy diet full of vitamins and minerals is essential to maintaining your health both now and in the long term. This diet will help protect you from illnesses such as infections and also illnesses related to being overweight or even underweight. A healthy diet is also important for keeping a variety of 'good' bacteria in your gut. This range of 'good' bacteria can help ward off infection and there is increasing evidence it may affect your mood and psychological symptoms as well. There is some evidence that people with OCD are more likely to have a limited range of 'good' bacteria in their gut which can worsen the situation. The best way to overcome this is to eat a well-balanced diet with a range of vegetables, fruit, natural yoghurts, blue cheeses, seeds, and nuts. There is also some evidence for fermented or pickled food being helpful. However, rather than getting overly caught up about this, the best way forward is to eat a well-balanced diet such as the one described here.

The most important factor is to reduce or cut out processed food wherever possible and replace either with foods you cook yourself or raw foods. There are some basic rules that everyone should try to follow:

- Eat at least **five portions of different fruits and vegetables every day** – try and make sure they are of **different colours** (as these are more likely to contain a variety of vitamins and minerals). Replacing desserts with fresh fruit or having fruit juice with cereal for breakfast are all easy ways to try and achieve this. There is evidence that having ten small portions of vegetables and fruit has the best health outcomes, but this is a big step for many people and therefore we advise starting at five a day and increasing once you are used to that.
- **Avoid high calorie, low nutrition items** that do not add to your overall health e.g., cut out **sweets, cakes, fizzy drinks**.

- **Vary your protein sources** to include vegetable proteins such as seeds, nuts, beans, and pulses. If you eat meat, try and vary these types as well and try to have lower fat meats frequently.
- **Eat at least two portions** (approximately the size of the palm of your hand) **of oily fish per week** (e.g., mackerel, salmon, and tuna).
- **Eat at least three eggs per week**.
- **Limit meat to one portion a day** of less than six ounces (to approximately cover the palm of your hand). Replace with alternative protein sources which will vary your diet, providing a greater range of nutrition and proving kind to your pocket.
- **Most calories** will come from **carbohydrate-rich foods essential for energy**, e.g., potatoes, pasta, rice, couscous, bread, cereals. **Eat at least three portions of differing carbohydrate-rich foods a day – each portion should be approximately one cup.**
- Try and eat as many of your carbohydrate-rich foods in the least refined versions as possible e.g., try **wholegrain pasta, bread, and rice**.
- Try to have potatoes with skins and try to boil or mash rather than fry. Limit chips to a maximum of one mug-full once a week.
- **Drink at least one pint of semi-skimmed/skimmed milk a day** – particularly important for women and anyone who has severely restricted their diet in the past, or replace some of this with natural yoghurt.

If you find this too daunting, then start by introducing five portions of fruit and vegetables a day and try to cut out artificially sweetened or high-calorie fizzy drinks and then gradually work through the list.

Exercise

Exercise is known to improve mood. It has been shown to be useful for a range of psychological problems but particularly anxiety and low mood.

Even if you have been unable to do much exercise before, you should start increasing your activity. This must be introduced gradually, particularly if you are aged over 40 years and/or have done little exercise before. Luckily, with regular practice, you will increase your fitness levels rapidly.

Anyone, no matter how inactive and whatever age, can improve their fitness levels with a little effort.

There is plenty of reliable information which support you in this (listed at the end of this chapter). Also, it can be useful to try a local group which specialises in an area which interests you. You may feel sports clubs are only for those who are 'good at sports', but they are mostly organised by enthusiastic amateurs who would be very happy to welcome you, help, and advise! (Some suggestions are at the end of this chapter.)

If you have not exercised much before, start with a gentle walk for **20 minutes** and try to repeat this **at least three times a week**. As this becomes easier, try to increase your speed and also the time spent walking.

In some areas, your GP can refer you to a gym for little or no cost to yourself if you fall within certain risk categories. An assessment from a personal trainer at a gym can help you to set out goals and safely increase your fitness.

Try and chart your progress and see if you can add a little every week. **Do not try and do a prolonged workout and then nothing** – this will inevitably result in muscle pain (often 48 hours after the exercise which can last for several days and restrict your exercise again) – try and do little and often. Your exercise should make you very slightly breathless but so that you can still talk easily. Try and maintain this level of activity for 20 minutes, which will help to improve the efficiency of your heart.

Exercise will really help you maintain fitness and a healthy weight as well as helping in other areas such as sleep. **The feeling of wellbeing which you will experience with exercise will help you to stick to your mental health treatment programme**. However, like everything, it must be done in moderation!

Alcohol, Smoking, Caffeine, and Non-Prescribed Drugs

For your general health, it is always best to take as little alcohol as possible and to have a zero-tolerance policy towards illicit drugs. This is because alcohol and drugs, even in modest quantities, can interfere with treatment.

If you have had a serious alcohol or drug problem, this needs to be addressed by the appropriate service. You will have already been given advice and help about your future relationship with such substances and relapse prevention.

If, however, you are like the majority of our patients and like to have an occasional social drink, you may wonder why we might worry about this in your own home environment.

Alcohol is a sedative drug and reduces anxiety. Thus, for anyone with an anxiety disorder, it appears to have a short-lived beneficial effect. The problem is this is not a true change and is unlikely to make it easier for you to face your fears at other times. Secondly, when alcohol is being broken down after consumption, it can cause an increase in anxiety levels which can make your condition worse. The same is true of drugs called benzodiazepines (e.g. 'Valium', 'Librium') or street drugs such as cannabis.

Of course, one of the most addictive drugs which will have a profound impact on your health is nicotine. There is no doubt about it, most people who smoke will die of conditions related to their smoking. Stopping smoking is the single most important thing anyone can do to improve their health. Nicotine is actually a stimulant and can increase anxiety. People think they need a cigarette to 'calm down', but in reality this is purely due to the physical craving and addictive properties of nicotine. However, it is not easy to give up such a powerfully addictive drug and it is usually necessary to seek some help. You can be prescribed nicotine replacement by your GP and there is an NHS app which can give you help, support, and advice. Details of organisations which can help are listed at the end of this chapter.

The most important thing about drinking is to ensure you drink sufficient fluid. However, too much caffeine (found mostly in strong coffee but also to a lesser extent in tea and some fizzy drinks) can increase symptoms of anxiety. Side effects of too much caffeine are shaking, difficulty in getting off to sleep, heart pounding, and other symptoms found in anxiety. It is therefore a good idea to try and **reduce caffeine intake** and particularly to stop drinking any caffeine containing drinks in the **late afternoon** and **evening** when they can **interfere with sleep**. It is not a good idea to stop all caffeine-containing drinks immediately as this can cause unpleasant side effects. The best way is to reduce them gradually.

The following steps may help:

- Firstly, stop drinking coffee after 4:00 p.m. and replace this instead with weak tea, fruit juice, or water.
- If you are a heavy coffee drinker, try replacing every second cup with tea, decaffeinated coffee, or even better, fruit juice or water. After a few days, you could try and halve the amount of coffee again and so on.
- Try to stop all caffeine-containing fizzy drinks and replace them with fruit juice, water, or even fruit-flavoured fizzy waters.

The advice overall for alcohol and other drugs is:

- No alcohol is preferable; otherwise, very minimal alcohol throughout your treatment, and you may even discover you enjoy feeling healthier once you have overcome your OCD!
- No illicit drugs ever.
- If you have had a problem with alcohol addiction or dependency in the past, then it is advisable not to return to drinking at all.
- If you have **not** had an alcohol problem and wish to return to social drinking, you should not go over 14 units of alcohol a week; should have at least two alcohol free days a week; and should reduce the recommended upper limit of 14 units to 7 if you are over 60 years old. (Units of alcohol are often listed on the side of bottles or cans but 1 unit is approximately half a pint of normal strength beer or lager.)
- The most important step any smoker can make to better health and longer life is to stop smoking.

Sleep Hygiene

Individuals need a varying amount of sleep. Overall, this is approximately eight hours, but many people manage on far less than this. Many sufferers of psychological or mental health problems have got into the habit of going to bed very late and getting up late in the morning or even early afternoon. This is bad for your health in a number of ways, for example:

- You do not get the exposure to natural light which helps to balance your sleep-wake cycle
- You will have difficulty finding any employment
- You will have difficulty engaging in a social life, which is important for general wellbeing

Some people find it difficult to fall asleep as they have got out of the habit of falling asleep at 'normal' times. Sleeping pills are not the answer and often compound the problem. It may however be possible to adjust your normal medication to try and improve the situation. Other things which may help are:

- **Ensure you take some exercise** – preferably in the **open air and natural light** during the day but do not do this after your evening meal as this will tend to energise you and make you less sleepy!
- **Do not read** or engage in any other activity **in your bed/bed space**. Your body needs to learn to associate going to bed with sleep.
- **Restrict your intake of tea, coffee, and caffeine**-containing drinks and **never** have these **after 6:00 p.m**.

If these measures do not work after you have tried them for several days, try to speak to your GP or health worker who will give you more detailed sleep hygiene rules to follow.

Balancing Mastery and Pleasure Activities

To have a happy and fulfilled life and feel good about ourselves we need to have a selection of activities which give us feelings of both mastery or achievement and also pleasure. This is similar to the adage 'all work and no play makes Jack a dull boy', but on the other hand, carrying out only pleasurable activities with no sense of achievement is also not good for your health.

People who have psychological and mental health problems often spend so much of their time thinking about their symptoms that they have little time for anything else. You may find, therefore, that you need to give this some consideration and intentionally introduce these activities into your life; and remember, there must **always be a balance between mastery and pleasure**.

Although it may sound odd to some, many people have extreme difficulty in accepting praise and enjoying themselves, as they feel 'they are not worthy'. It is vital that these people learn to accept themselves and appreciate their own worth as seen by others.

Examples of Items You May Introduce for Mastery

Try and achieve only two or three of the following suggestions a week. When you are feeling 'down' it is often difficult to feel like doing anything, so do not be hard on yourself and limit yourself to a couple of these suggestions every week.

- Sticking to your Treatment Programme
- Getting up and going to bed on time
- Making drinks or cooking for others
- Sticking to your healthy eating programme
- Sticking to a gradually increasing exercise regime

Examples of Items You May Introduce for Pleasure

- Accepting praise
- Engaging in an enjoyable activity such as going for a walk, going to the gym, or for some, reading a book
- Talking with friends/family
- Engaging in a hobby you enjoy
- Watching a programme which interests you on television

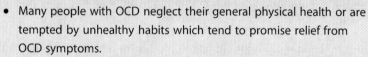

KEY POINTS

- Many people with OCD neglect their general physical health or are tempted by unhealthy habits which tend to promise relief from OCD symptoms.
- Being healthy and well will make it easier to undertake OCD treatment.
- Drinking sufficient fluid, preferably water, is vital for health. You should aim to drink one to two litres a day or slightly more if the weather is hot or you are exercising.
- Drinking too much water is dangerous. You should not drink more than three litres except in hot weather or extreme exercise (such as marathon running).
- Eating a well-balanced diet will improve the bacteria in your gut, which in turn may help with general wellbeing, weight stabilisation, low mood, and possibly OCD symptoms.
- Regular exercise is important for general health as well as beneficial for mood.
- Alcohol is unhelpful for OCD as it only reduces the anxiety for a while and drinking can get out of hand. Alcohol can worsen your physical and mental health.
- Non-prescribed drugs are not useful for OCD. Stick to the medication advised by your healthcare practitioner.
- Smoking does not 'calm you down'. Instead, it is the fact that you are withdrawing from an addictive substance which makes it feel that way.
- Sleep is important and can be improved using the sleep hygiene methods described in this chapter.
- It is also important to balance activities which are fun and give joy alongside activities which give you a sense of achievement.

Self-help resources and other organisations offering support and advice

Problem	Organisation	Contact	Comments
Healthy eating	NHS	www.nhs.uk/live-well/eat-well	
Exercise	NHS	www.nhs.uk/live-well/exercise	
Exercise	NHS	www.nhs.uk/live-well/exercise/couch-to-5k-week-by-week	Nine-week plan to get individuals increasing from no exercise to running 5k
Exercise	Parkrun	www.parkrun.org.uk www.parkrun.com/countries	Free weekly 5k walks or runs in local parks. Initially started in the UK but has now spread to around the globe
Exercise	Silver Fit Charity	https://www.silverfit.org.uk/	Sessions run by older adults for older adults to improve fitness as we age.
Alcohol	Alcoholics Anonymous UK	www.alcoholics-anonymous.org.uk	Help and advice for anyone who feels they have a problem with alcohol or wishes to reduce their drinking
Alcohol	Alcoholics Anonymous around the world	https://aa.org	International AA
Alcohol	Drinkline	Contact their free helpline on 0300 123 1110 (weekdays 9:00 a.m. to 8:00 p.m., weekends 11:00 a.m. to 4:00 p.m.).	Advice to those worried about their own, or a loved one's, alcohol use.

(cont.)

Problem	Organisation	Contact	Comments
Drugs	NHS	www.nhs.uk/live-well/healthy-body/drug-addiction-getting-help	List of other organisations which can help in the UK
Smoking	NHS	www.nhs.uk/live-well/quit-smoking	Help and advice to stop smoking

13

. . . .

Overcoming Fears
of Contamination

Treatment for all types of OCD is essentially the same and features prolonged graded exposure in real life to the feared situation combined with self-imposed response prevention. The necessary steps to set about doing this have been fully explained in Chapter 11. This chapter will address additional factors and difficulties which may arise with contamination fears. The chapter will describe what constitutes contamination fears, and look at fear of dirt, germs, and illness as well as the idea of 'mental contamination', when an individual fears becoming 'contaminated' by an abstract agent such as 'evil' or 'bad thoughts'. Risks and dangers of both OCD with contamination fears and risks of any treatment itself will be explored. Issues such as how the pandemic impacts on successful treatment and what should be done in such circumstances are also discussed. Personal stories will be used as a guide to help you plan your treatment.

Introduction

Fears that you may in some way become contaminated are some of the most common presentations of OCD. Although most people may experience this as anxiety, many also describe the feeling of disgust. Whereas this chapter uses the terms 'anxiety' and 'fear', these can be replaced by the idea of disgust and the horrible feeling associated with this. Some people fear dirt and germs as they worry they may become ill and pass on the 'contamination' to others, resulting in illness for them, whereas for some the 'contamination' is more tied in with ideas such as 'perfectionism', whereby they feel that by becoming 'contaminated' they are making themselves less perfect and should attempt to correct this. Fear of contamination by dirt or germs may be general or may be more specific, such as fear of contracting HIV or germs from animals such as dogs and cats. For others, they may be anxious about their own bodily functions and may spend a long time in the toilet ensuring they have passed all faeces or urine, and then feel the need to spend a prolonged time ensuring that both themselves and their surroundings have no trace of any of the feared 'contaminant'. The emergence of the novel coronavirus, SARS-CoV-2, or COVID-19 in 2019, spreading to Europe and the Americas in 2020 as a pandemic, has presented further contamination worries for many people, as so many of the population have been urged to take precautions against 'contamination' which would previously have been considered wildly excessive, such as frequent prolonged hand-washing, using alcohol gel, and avoidance of close proximity to other people. At any point, when conducting an exposure programme, it is important to comply with current national guidance in a pandemic. This means sticking to the rules and not taking them further than the advice. Other people may fear contamination by things such as radiation, or even rays that may be thought to exude from the television. For some people, the 'contamination' is more obscure and is a fear of being 'infected' with an idea or a character trait of others. Another common contamination fear is a fear of chemicals such as rat poison, weed killers, petrochemicals, or even medication. These are just some of the variations that are commonly seen in patients with OCD.

The most common compulsions seen in people with contamination fears are 'decontamination' washing compulsions. These can vary from feeling the need to remove all clothes and have extensive showers or baths to frequent and excessive handwashing. Some people use soap which can, if used excessively, destroy the body's natural barrier to infection, while others can progress onto more dangerous chemicals which can cause severe chemical burns. Other people may have different ways of 'decontaminating' without resorting to physical washing and may have developed certain thought patterns and behaviours which seem to 'undo' the contamination.

Avoidance is a very common feature of contamination fears. This may be avoidance of other people so that the individual physically distances themselves from normal accepted contact from others. People with fears of contamination by dog faeces may avoid walking on grass, visiting parks and other places frequented by dogs. Those with fears related to more mental contamination may avoid places associated with bad memories or specific areas of the country which have become associated in their minds with 'bad things'.

Seeking reassurance from others is also common in those with contamination fears. People may either ask family or friends to check that something is clean, or they may ask others to perform 'decontamination' activities themselves as an extra precaution. Some will spend a considerable amount of time researching different diseases, germs, or sources of contamination on the Internet by way of reassurance. Just like compulsions, reassurance only helps reduce anxiety for a short while and becomes almost 'addictive', where more and more reassurance eventually is needed.

Dangers of Contamination Fears

These have already been discussed in full in Chapter 3, but are important to remember as you embark on therapy.

One of the most common dangers of extensive washing rituals is the damage this can do to an individual's skin. Our skin is a very effective barrier in preventing infection. On the surface of the skin are many millions of 'good' bacteria which help to prevent more 'dangerous' bacteria from being able to penetrate into the body and cause harm. The skin also has natural oils which similarly help to form a barrier. Extensive washing and scrubbing of the skin will break down these barriers to infection and can lead to an infection being able to gain a hold. Obviously, corrosive chemicals and household cleaning agents used on the skin have an even more dramatic effect.

Some people are so preoccupied with totally emptying their bowels that they can get a prolapse of their rectum requiring surgery. Others may have a restricted diet to avoid going to the toilet. Restriction of drinking sufficient fluid to avoid needing to pass water is a common issue for people with contamination fears and as many as 20 per cent of people with profound OCD have renal damage due to drinking insufficient fluid.

Dangers of ERP Treatment

Mood and Anxiety

Some people may find that their mood drops and their anxiety rises with ERP. A temporary increase in anxiety is completely normal, as is a drop in mood, but the key is that these should be temporary and not place you at increased risk of issues such as self-harm. If you feel your mood is spiralling out of control, then it is important to stop the treatment and seek further help.

Many people are very hard on themselves and try to progress far too quickly and much faster than a trained therapist would advise. Remember this is a slow and gradual therapy; you will experience anxiety and even a slight drop in mood, but these should be bearable and short-lived.

Difficulties During a Pandemic

In recent years we have seen a number of new viruses infect humans with the potential to spread and cause serious illness or even death. Severe Acute Respiratory Syndrome (SARS), which caused epidemics in mostly South East Asian countries, with some cases exported to Canada in 2002–2003, is now under control. Others include Middle Eastern Respiratory Syndrome (MERS), which arose in 2012 in the Middle East and also registered a few cases in the US. Ebola, which exists in Sub-Saharan Africa and has occasionally been exported elsewhere, was first recognised in 1976, but an epidemic in Africa lasted from 2013 to 2016. All of the above pose absolutely no threat to anyone embarking on ERP treatment for contamination fears, unless they are in highly unlikely and unusual circumstances. Human immunodeficiency virus (HIV), which can cause acquired autoimmune deficiency syndrome (AIDS), is another disease which is thought to have arisen in West Africa, but was first reported amongst the gay male population in New York in 1981. HIV/AIDS is a frequent concern of people with contamination fears (see **'Marie's Story'** in Chapter 3.) In reality, HIV infection occurs mainly through sexual contact, receiving contaminated blood, ingesting infected breast milk, or coming into sexually intimate situations with semen or vaginal secretions. Anyone who is not engaging in risky behaviours such as having unprotected sex with multiple partners, intravenous drug abuse, or living in an area in Africa with a high rate of infection, is extremely unlikely to catch HIV. Even for healthcare workers that accidentally prick themselves with an infected needle, the risk has been estimated to be less than 1 in 200. Therefore, it can be seen that ERP tasks such as performing normal activities of daily living, touching items in the bathroom and toilet, using public toilets, and travelling on public transport, will not result in HIV infection.

However, in 2020, after the identification of a new disease in China, a pandemic was declared due to the spread of a novel coronavirus known as SARS-CoV-2, which causes COVID-19. Unlike other viruses, very little was known about this illness which swept across the globe, resulting in various countries implementing lockdowns for their citizens. The World Health Organization (WHO) issued guidance which included:

- Washing hands with soap and warm water for a minimum of 20 seconds and doing so frequently whenever an individual returns home.
- Using alcohol-based hand gel when soap and water is not available.
- Using facial coverings over the mouth and nose when in close proximity to others who are not in a person's immediate family.
- Maintaining a 'social distance' between individuals. This distance was applied differently in various countries but was usually between 1.5 to 2 metres unless mitigating measures (such as facial coverings) were used. This meant avoidance of hand-shaking, touching, or hugging friends and acquaintances.

These measures seem to be at variance with ERP for contamination fears. Indeed, the International College for Obsessive Compulsive Spectrum Disorders (ICOCS) issued the following guidance during the pandemic:

- Medication for OCD was not contraindicated and may be the best treatment at these stressful times.
- People with OCD should be advised to strictly adhere to government guidance during the pandemic but not to carry this out more scrupulously or more intensely than the recommendations, e.g. to wash hands for 20 seconds or the time taken to sing 'Happy birthday' twice and not substantially longer than this.
- It is important to maintain mood during the pandemic and so ERP may reduce mood and may be contraindicated at that time.
- ERP should generally not take place but individuals with OCD should be encouraged to schedule daily activities to keep themselves occupied and maintain their mood.
- Any ERP should be approached cautiously, be within the limits of government guidance, and would be best carried out in a centre specialising in OCD.
- Activity scheduling (as discussed in Chapter 11) can be particularly useful in coping with anxiety and depressive symptoms during stressful times such as the pandemic.

Mental Contamination

The principles of dealing with fear of more abstract forms of contamination are exactly the same as those described for individuals dealing with other forms of contamination. In mental contamination you may fear 'catching' a personality trait from either a specific person or more generally from others. This may lead you to avoid certain situations and places. Other people may have had a specific thought in a certain place and thereafter feel that the place and anything associated with it is 'contaminated'. Whatever the form of your contamination fear, the way to tackle it is the same as any other obsessive fear, i.e., face up to the fear without performing anxiety-reducing activities such as compulsions and seeking reassurance from others.

How the Body Protects Us from Infection

The human body has several defence mechanisms to protect us from dangerous infections. Ironically, in OCD, an individual can place themselves at greater risk of infection by breaking down these barriers in an attempt to be 'clean'. The body protects itself in several ways:

- An external barrier to infection
- Chemicals which 'fight' the infection
- Blood cells which form an 'army' to remove and kill alien invaders such as bacteria and viruses.

The first line of defence to many infections is the skin. The skin consists of several layers. The top layer is waterproof (covered in natural oils), and this prevents many germs getting through the skin. In addition to the barrier of the skin itself, it is also covered by millions of bacteria which are not harmful, and which themselves form a barrier to other dangerous bacteria. At the University of Sydney, they performed an experiment whereby they examined the normal bacteria on people's hands. They then asked the same people to go out and touch areas often considered to be contaminated, such as toilet door handles, stroking animals, and shaking hands with vagrants sleeping in the park. After the study, when the participants had touched these 'contaminants', the bacteria on their hands were examined again. The findings were that the bacteria on their hands remained unchanged! This demonstrated that on healthy skin, normal bacteria could help to prevent any 'dangerous bacteria' remaining on the skin. Now, I am not advocating that we all stop washing our hands completely, but I think it is worthwhile remembering what we are trying to achieve when we wash hands.

Other barriers to infection other than the skin include the mouth, eyes, and nose, which all have antiseptic properties, and then, of course, the stomach, where acid helps to destroy most bacteria.

Once a bacteria or virus has penetrated into the body then there are two main defences. First, there are antibodies, which are chemicals produced by the body specifically to fight that type of bacteria or virus. These act more quickly if the body has encountered this germ before. Second, there are white blood cells which attack and kill germs. Again, they work best if the body has encountered them before.

How to Help the Body Cope with Infection

The first most obvious answer is that over-washing or washing in strong chemicals makes a person more vulnerable to infection, as the natural barriers of the skin are broken down. Washing should generally be restricted to 20 seconds and only after using the toilet, before handling food, and before meals. On each occasion, the hands should be washed once and you need to resist the urge to repeat this.

Many people in the UK do not get sufficient exposure to sunlight to produce adequate vitamin D stores. Vitamin D helps to support an effective immune system. It is advised that most people in the UK may require vitamin D supplements during the winter months. For people with OCD, this can be exacerbated, as they may avoid going outside and so may require vitamin D supplementation throughout the year.

Good levels of health and wellbeing can also help protect the body from infection. This has been discussed fully in Chapter 12. Attention to a well-balanced diet, regular moderate exercise, good sleep hygiene, avoidance or drinking little alcohol, and avoidance of smoking and other non-prescribed drugs all help the body to fight infection.

Children have traditionally played in 'dirty' environments. In the past they would have had early exposure to a range of animals, played in mud, and generally been 'unclean'. Today, there has been a tendency to protect children and to try and keep them in a clean and almost sterile environment. The rise of autoimmune disorders such as asthma has been thought by some researchers to be due to a lack of exposure to a wide variety of dirt and germs. Similarly, it is felt that exposure improves a child's ability to withstand infection. Obviously, young babies need to have clean food but as they grow, they need to be able to explore without having every area sanitised and sterilised for them. Exposure to everyday dirt may build up the number and types of bacteria in the gut. The range of bacteria in the gut is known as the 'microbiome'. Throughout our life cycle, a good healthy range of bacteria in the gut is maintained by a diet high in fibre and consisting of a wide range of vegetables and fruit. There is evidence that a healthy microbiome consisting of a wide range of 'friendly' bacteria may help to ward off infections.

Setting Up a Treatment Programme for Contamination Fears

In order to set up your own programme of treatment for OCD with contamination fears, firstly you need to follow the steps outlined in Chapter 11. These are:

1. Define the problem.
2. Set out the overall goals.
3. Develop a hierarchy of practical tasks which you can perform up to three times a day without carrying out any 'putting it right' compulsions or

reassurance-seeking (three times daily is ideal but try to ensure you do them at least daily).

4. Rate the anxiety each of these tasks is likely to cause you using a 9-point scale (from 0 to 8).

5. Choose an item on the hierarchy which causes you mild to moderate anxiety and start to practise doing this regularly every day. Your anxiety will fluctuate but generally, if you are exposing for long enough and are not engaging in activities which 'put right' the exposure, then your anxiety should come down after several days of regular practice.

6. Reward yourself for your success and bravery. Remember that this process is not easy and that you are being very brave to tackle your fears. Maybe also reward yourself in some other way, such as setting aside some time to read a book with a cup of tea/coffee for an hour on the days you have successfully completed your exposure.

7. Once you have shown that your anxiety has reduced, then move up to the next item on the hierarchy.

8. Finally, once you have completed all the items on your hierarchy and have successfully overcome your OCD, you need to be extremely proud of yourself. You have stood up to your worst fears, which takes courage and persistence.

9. Now work out how you are going to maintain your gains in everyday life. This means ensuring that you are not slipping back into avoidance behaviours etc.

10. Many people find it useful to write out a 'relapse-prevention' plan. This means writing down all the things that you know are 'warning signs' that OCD may be starting to re-emerge. Then write down the steps you need to take if this happens. Keep this paper safe and remind yourself of it whenever you feel tempted to slip back into OCD behaviours.

Personal Stories of Treatment of Contamination Fears

Here are examples of two people who tackled their OCD contamination fears. Neither of them is likely to be exactly the same as your OCD fears but they may serve as an example on how to tackle the fears in practice.

Contamination fears could be fear of dirt and germs, specific illnesses such as HIV infection, fear of radiation or asbestos as well as fear of a more obscure type, such as contamination by 'evil' or by 'bad thoughts'. There are multiple types of 'contamination fears' but all can be tackled in the same way by gradually facing up to your fears without any of the 'putting it right' behaviours such as washing, performing other 'decontamination' behaviours, asking for reassurance from family members, or seeking reassurance from the Internet.

Grace's Story

Grace is a 30-year-old woman who developed a fear of dirt and germs at the age of 11 years old. Initially she began to express the fear after she had been shown pictures of bacteria at school, where the children had been encouraged to practise hand hygiene. Instead of just taking the advice on board, Grace began to stress and worry that she may have passed dangerous germs onto her friends and family. Over the years these symptoms grew, but at the time of starting treatment, Grace was washing her hands 10–20 times a day and was trying to avoid touching other people. This problem had caused her to have dry, flaky skin on her hands. She often avoided going out with friends to avoid the fear that she may 'pass on her contamination' to them.

When at university, Grace had managed by being more scrupulous than others about cleanliness and hand hygiene, and friends at that time had teased her that she was 'a bit OCD'. Over the intervening years, she had started to work in an office as an accounts manager. She would arrive at the office early and immediately clean her workstation before her colleagues arrived. Her packed lunch was prepared by herself, and she was considered aloof as she refused to join in the office practice of bringing in home-made cakes and biscuits, for fear of spreading infection. She was also seen to be always making excuses to avoid office outings and parties. Being unable to shake hands, touch, or have physical contact with others, including her parents and family members, was affecting her work and social life, as well as her relationships with others.

Two years earlier, Grace had moved back to living at home with her parents, having split up from her boyfriend following arguments about her OCD. Her symptoms were causing some friction in the house as she attempted to make her parents adhere to her 'OCD rules', and also because her nightly 'decon-tamination' shower was taking over an hour and restricting access that others had to the bathroom. Similarly, going to the toilet would always take 15–30 minutes, as Grace had to make sure she was completely clean and that she had cleaned all the surfaces with antibacterial wipes. Grace fully accepted that her fears were unreasonable and, as she put it, 'over the top', but she found it difficult to stop herself.

In order to address this problem, Grace set up the following hierarchy of items she felt she needed to tackle.

Problem	Fear of spreading contamination of dirt and germs from myself or others by not being careful of hygiene and that this may result in illness or harm to others.
Target	To go out for a meal and drink with my parents to thank them for looking after me recently. During this I will not check everything is 'clean' and I will not perform any washing and bathing 'rituals'.

Item on hierarchy (starting with easiest and all to be performed without washing/ cleaning compulsions)	Anxiety rating	How often to be performed (3x/day is ideal)
Touch door handles in home (apart from toilet handles)	3	3 x/day
Get dressed without handwashing in between	3	Once a day
Use utensils from kitchen without washing	3	3x/day
Touch shop door handles, pelican crossing buttons outside	4	2x/day
Bring shopping home from supermarket without washing outside packaging	5	Once/day

(cont.)

Touch toilet door handles at home	5	3x/day
Prepare food without first washing hands repeatedly	6	3x/day
Eat food purchased outside the home and without checking and cleaning it first	6	Once/day
Use the toilet within 5 minutes and without extensive self-cleaning and cleaning of surfaces	7	3+ times/day
Have no more than one shower or bath a day and to complete this within 20 minutes without repeatedly washing myself and without washing all areas afterwards	7	Daily
Touch public toilet door handle	8	3x/day
Use public toilet, touching the flush etc.	8	Once/day
Bringing in a cake I have made to share with work colleagues	8	Once/day
Going out with friends/work colleagues to a pub or restaurant	8	Once a week
Final Goal: To go out for a meal and drink with my parents and be able to appropriately touch them and others without cleaning rituals being performed	8	Once and repeat as often as wished

To commence her treatment programme, Grace decided to start by touching door handles around the home, and to get dressed without repeated handwashing. Although she did not want to give up all her handwashing, she agreed that she would not wash her hands immediately after touching the door handles. As she was at work during the day, she therefore decided to wash her hands before breakfast and then to touch all the door handles at home before going out. She then repeated this when she returned home from work, after her supper, and last thing at night, so that she went to bed with 'dirty hands'. Although she initially felt anxious about this, once she had done it, Grace found it surprisingly easy. Her anxiety would be 3–4/8 to start with but subsided over the next hour. The handwashing that she now did was very different to her extensive handwashing OCD rituals. She placed the plug in the wash basin and used the water in this way rather than placing her hands under running water.

Similarly, to break the habit of excessive washing and repeating, Grace decided to only use the shower once a day and to stand under the shower without washing and without using soap or shower gel.

Over the course of a week, she found that these were easy tasks and so moved on to touching toilet doors at home and touching shop door handles and pedestrian crossing buttons. Once again, this was difficult at the outset but became easier as the week progressed. Unfortunately, towards the end of the second week, her mother developed a chest infection. This immediately made Grace panic as she felt she could have been responsible for this. Deep down, she knew this was false and that it was much more likely that her mother had either caught this on the bus or at her work as a GP receptionist. Her anxiety got worse, but Grace realised that she had to continue with the programme. Due to this set-back she didn't move up the hierarchy for another ten days.

Once she started the more difficult items on her treatment plan, Grace found she needed to move more slowly. She would still repeat the items three times daily when possible but found that items such as preparing food for herself and her parents without first washing her hands repeatedly was very difficult. Her parents encouraged her, but she became very anxious and panicky when they started to eat the food and Grace could eat only a few mouthfuls on the first occasion. To her surprise her anxiety did start to come down after an hour and she started to feel better as she saw her parents carrying on as usual.

After 12 weeks, Grace was able to complete her final goal of therapy and treated her parents to a meal out. Although the anxiety of performing the programme had been stressful and caused her to have periods of panic and low mood, overall, she could recognise the benefits. She was now starting to make friends at work for the first time in her working career, had been out with older friends, and was generally able to enjoy life.

It was now time for Grace to introduce her relapse-prevention plan. She started by writing out all the benefits of not having OCD and put them visibly on her wall. She gradually introduced more 'normal' washing in the shower on the understanding with herself that if she found herself taking longer again, she would revert to using water only.

Currently Grace does find that occasionally when she is feeling stressed or unwell, or if a bad event happens, her obsessions and compulsions start to increase. She recognises these for what they are and so starts to tackle them one by one before they get 'out of hand'.

Patrick's Story

Patrick is a 38-year-old single man who trained as a carpenter. When he was 18 years old, his parents separated, which Patrick found extremely upsetting. One evening around this time he went out with friends on the train to Bradford city centre to see the horror film 'American Psycho'. The plot of the film concerns a man called Patrick Bateman, who is jealous of the success of his acquaintances and goes on to murder and abuse various people. After the film, Patrick's friends started to tease him about having the same name as the main character in the film and suggested that there were similarities in the way they both looked. They started giving him the nickname 'Psycho'.

To begin with, Patrick played along with the joke, pretending that he was dreaming up evil plots. After a few weeks, however, Patrick began to worry that he may become tainted and contaminated by 'evil'. He started to wash his hands repeatedly whenever he had been outside, in case he had been contaminated by passers-by. He started avoiding travelling anywhere near the cinema where he had seen the film. As his fear developed, he began avoiding anything and anyone who had been to or come from Bradford. Patrick lived with his mother and younger siblings at this time, but his father worked in Bradford. Whereas Patrick had always been close to his father, he started to avoid him and eventually cut off all contact with him. Despite his problems, Patrick was able to work in his local area provided there was no connection that he could see to Bradford.

Patrick decided that he needed to tackle these problems by facing up to his fear of contamination and his fear that he had become evil. He recognised that he would never deliberately harm anyone and that his OCD was the cause of his problem. Patrick's notes on self-therapy are shown in here. These items were all to be performed without any excessive washing or handwashing. Patrick decided to have one shower a day lasting no more than 20 minutes in total and to only wash his hands after the toilet or before meals.

Problem	Fear of contamination by evil arising from the film 'American Psycho' and leading to me avoiding anything or anyone who has been to Bradford
Final Goal	To watch the film 'American Psycho' in Bradford

Hierarchy	Anxiety Level (0–8)	Number of times per day to perform
To walk past Morrison's supermarket* and return home without washing (*Morrison's head office is in Bradford)	4	3
To walk along Bradford Road and sit on the bench until the anxiety subsides	5	2

(cont.)

To go into Morrison's supermarket and buy an item of food and to eat this without washing	6	2
To write an email to my dad and explain what I am doing to overcome my problem, and not to 'decontaminate' myself when he replies	6	To perform once but to retain email
To allow a letter from my dad to come to the house, touch it, and touch all my possessions afterwards	7	To 'recontaminate' all possessions 2–3 times per day
To meet my dad at a cafe near my home	7	Once but not to 'decontaminate' afterwards
To visit my dad in Bradford	8	Once a week but without 'decontaminating'
To watch the film 'American Psycho' at home	8	Daily
To watch the film 'American Psycho' at my dad's house	8	Once but not to 'decontaminate' afterwards

In order to assist with focussing on the programme, Patrick would try and concentrate and repeat to himself that he was a 'Psycho'. When he eventually watched the film with his dad, Patrick realised that it had dark humour and he actually managed to laugh at some of the film.

KEY POINTS

- The skin and the body have good defences against infection.
- Compulsive cleaning activity can reduce the effectiveness of the body's natural defences against infection.
- General wellbeing with a good diet, moderate exercise, and adequate exposure to natural light can help the body's defences against infection and also help to make ERP treatment easier.
- Some special care and modification of ERP programmes are necessary during a global pandemic.

14

· · · · · ·

Fear of Harm to Self or Others Due to Failure to Act

This chapter examines the common obsession regarding fearing something bad will happen due to failure to complete things safely, or tring to obtain the 'just right' feeling before being confident, or the fear that your memory is unreliable. These commonly involve checking compulsions. Sometimes it can also involve performing an action until it feels 'just right'. This is a frequent feeling in people with various types of OCD. The issue of habitual behaviours and why people with OCD often feel they may have a poor memory is also discussed.

Introduction

Most of us have a quick check around the house or before going on holiday that the windows are shut, the gas, lights, and appropriate electrical appliances are switched off, and that the doors are closed. However, for people with obsessive fears of harm occurring to them, their family, or their property, such a cursory look is not sufficient. Instead, they can develop multiple elaborate rituals involving repeated checking and finally vigorous pulling on the front door.

Other people may feel the need to check that everything is safe and well within their neighbourhood (see **'Mohammed's Story'** in Chapter 3). This can result in the person becoming a 'nuisance' in their neighbourhood. Others may feel the need to check everything is safe in the workplace.

In this type of OCD, people will often feel unable to cope and so try and get others to 'take responsibility' for the behaviour. So, they may ask a partner to check the house before leaving rather than do it themselves or they may seek reassurance that all is safe and well from others (see Chapter 10). Indeed, in therapy, some people feel so overwhelmed that they prefer it if the therapist asks them to perform a particular task rather than performing it themselves. This is because they may then feel that the therapist is responsible should any disaster ensue!

Other types of obsessions which can fall in this category are thoughts or often images of something terrible happening to a loved one, friend, family, or even a stranger, and the 'belief' that because you've had this thought it makes it more likely to occur. Self-help for this type of problem is covered in Chapter 15.

Habitual Behaviours and Memory

One of the things which is often reported by people living with OCD is that they have a poor memory. They will say that they feel the need to check safety because they cannot remember whether or not they have performed the action. In reality, much of what we do in everyday life is habitual and we do not remember it unless something 'remarkable' occurs. For example, I may ride my bike into work. When I get there, I am unlikely to remember every moment along the way. I may remember specific things that took my attention, such as a car which cut in a bit too close to me, or the flowers which had grown up in a particular part of the park, but it is likely that I will not remember every detail of my journey. This same loss of memory of specific details is seen when we are all doing activities of daily living. Therefore, we may not specifically remember locking the front door or switching off the light, but we know that we do this every day, and so unless we were distracted by an unusual event (in which case we are likely to remember it) it is most likely that we switched the light off or locked the door as usual.

Another reason why people with OCD find it difficult to recall details is that they are usually anxious most of the time. Anxiety can make it more difficult to note issues and remember them. Depression is also very common in people with moderate to severe OCD, and again this can impair the memory.

All in all, it is unlikely that your need to check is due to a deficient memory and is much more likely to be purely due to OCD.

Kate's Story

Kate is a 40-year-old woman who has always been careful and meticulous. She lives at home with her husband and two children aged 15 and 13 years. Since the birth of her eldest child, Kate had started to be overly careful about safety around the house. Before going to bed at night, she would go around the house checking that every door and window was closed and locked. After doing this, she would check every light switch and appliance was switched off at the mains. She said she felt the need to keep on turning items on and off and pulling on doors and windows until she convinced herself they felt 'just right'. Initially this took her five to ten minutes, but over the years it had increased so that she was spending over an hour every evening repeatedly checking everything was 'safe'. Even after this, she sometimes got up in the night to repeat the checks. Because it took so long for her to get out of the house due to her checks, she had reduced her trips outside. On occasions, she had asked her husband to check for her, but he was unhappy to do it and felt this was 'stupid' and so she did not trust him to perform her compulsions for her.

Realising that the best way to tackle this was to go to bed without checking, Kate tried this but never managed to stay in bed for more than 30 minutes before she would get up and check everything in the house. In order to help herself, Kate devised the following programme:

Problem	Fear that harm will occur to my home or family via an intruder entering my house or by a fire caused by my leaving the electricity or gas switched on
Final Goal	To go out and to go to bed without checking.

Hierarchy	Anxiety Level (0–8)	Number of times per day to perform
To switch the light off in the living room once and to not return to this room before going to bed or going out for at least 1 hour	4	3x/day
To switch off the other lights in the house once and not to return to check before going out or going to bed	5	3x/day
To switch off the gas cooker after cooking and not to return to check	6	2–3x/day
To only switch off electrical appliances after using them and not to check at other times at all	7	Make sure I use at least three electrical items every day
To stop checking windows at night or before going out.	8	To go out twice a day for at least 1 hour without checking and no night checking.
To pull the front door shut and turn the key in the lock without checking. Similarly at night to shut and lock the door once and then go to bed.	8	3x/day (leaving the house for at least 1 hour)

The above programme worked well for Kate. Initially she found it difficult to sleep but then found that she did sleep better than when she had been checking constantly. Some people find this strategy extremely nerve racking, and in such cases it can be a good idea to, for example, switch on all the lights and go out for one to two hours to see if anything bad happens. Obviously, this cannot happen with gas taps which need to be switched off once (but not rechecked thereafter). Similarly, it is possible to leave electrical appliances switched on at the mains but with the appliance switched off and leave the house.

KEY POINTS

- Fear of harm occurring due to failure to act is a common OCD symptom and often results in checking and repeating compulsions.
- People with OCD often claim to have poor memory. This can be a result of anxiety and depression but also most of us do not recall specific details of actions or behaviours we perform regularly, e.g. our journey into work, unless something unusual happens. Similarly, most of us do not remember switching off appliances, closing windows, or locking doors, which we may do regularly.
- Performing an action until it feels 'just right' can also occur in these types of obsessions. Just as in all types of OCD, the way to confront this is to just perform the action once, without repeating and without waiting for it to feel 'right'.

15

· · · · · · ·

Fear of Harm to Self or Others Due to Your Own Actions (or Thoughts)

This chapter will examine the obsessive fear that a person may commit an act they do not wish to do. This includes people who have images of themselves performing violent acts, people who worry that they may shout out something inappropriate or detrimental, as well as a variety of other behaviours. One example of a very distressing type of obsession is people who have images of themselves harming others by knocking people over in the road or even starting to wonder if they have committed an awful crime which they may have heard about via the media. People with this type of obsessive thoughts have been known to 'confess' to the police and in severe cases may be arrested for wasting police time.

The idea of 'thought-action fusion' is the idea that having a thought is as bad as performing the act or that thinking of an event makes it more likely to happen.

Fear of shouting out something inappropriate or obscene is also discussed and the distinction between this and Tourette syndrome.

Taboo obsessions involving fear of paedophilia are often in this category but because of the extreme distress and misunderstanding these obsessions can cause, they will be discussed in a separate chapter.

Introduction

Almost everyone has experienced a minor version of this in their life. A common example would be standing on a train platform and suddenly having the thought that you are going to throw yourself onto the track. You do not want to do this and so may feel anxious and take a step back. Another almost universal experience is the part of a Western wedding when the wedding guests are asked if they 'know of any cause or just impediment why these people should not be joined together in matrimony' and are asked to declare it. Most people have the thought they may shout out at that time and their heart beats a little faster in the process! Obsessive-compulsive fears that you may commit a horrible act are much worse than the above examples and can lead to extreme depression and thoughts of self-harm. One feature which can compound the issue is the idea of thought-action fusion. Not everyone with obsessive fears of acting inappropriately has thought-action fusion, but it is still worth discussing this first.

Thought-Action Fusion

Thought-action fusion is the idea that having a thought is morally equivalent to performing the act. So that, for example, having an image of hitting someone come into your mind is equivalent to actually hitting someone. Sometimes a person feels that having a thought of a particular event makes it more likely that the event will occur, for example, having an image of a loved one having an accident makes it more likely that such an accident will happen. Of course, here is a clear counterpoint to these arguments: if thinking about an event made it more likely to happen, then we would have all won the lottery by now!

Having a thought is also not the moral equivalent of doing the deed, as these are unwanted thoughts which come into your mind. The more appalled or scared you are by the thoughts, the more you are likely to try and push them out of your mind and make an effort not to have the thoughts again. The more effort you apply to not having the thoughts, the more likely these thoughts are to pop into your mind. This was discussed in Chapter 3 when it was suggested that if you sit still and think of anything you like but, under no circumstances should you think about a pink hippopotamus, most people immediately have an image of a pink hippopotamus.

An example of believing that the thought is equivalent to the deed is shown by Pip. Pip is a 40-year-old man who had thoughts and images of himself punching people. In reality, Pip had never been aggressive in his life. Due to these thoughts, he felt constantly guilty and believed he was a totally bad and evil person. Of course, all of us have unpleasant, abhorrent, horrible thoughts from time to time. Most of us just accept this. However, if you believe this to be evidence that you are bad or evil, then you will try very hard to push these thoughts away. Putting so much energy into trying not to have thoughts will make the thoughts much more likely to occur. Treatment therefore involves facing up to the fear. For his treatment, Pip recorded himself saying 'I'd like to punch that person in the face'. He would then travel around playing this on continuous loop on his mobile phone via an earpiece when he travelled into and out of work. After a few weeks, Pip became bored with the recording and his anxiety went down.

Worrying that having a thought about a horrible event happening makes it more likely to occur can be very frightening and scary. One thing I have often done in therapy is to ask people to give me some numbers and we would put these numbers on a National Lottery entry and then I would ask them to think about these numbers as often as possible. Needless to say, none of us have become millionaires, or even ever had a small win this way! Sometimes people say that only bad (and not good) things happen if you think hard enough about them. For this, it may be easier to think about a bad event that would cause inconvenience rather than disaster for the first step. Examples could be willing the cooker or the refrigerator to break down by repeatedly thinking about it. In therapy, we will often ask a patient to think of something bad happening to the therapist, such as them having a car accident on the way in to work. The patient would then be asked to wish this would happen and to write to the therapist saying something like 'I hope you have a horrible life-changing car accident on the way in to work'. This is usually much easier than thinking about harm occurring to a loved one. Once the intermediate steps have been taken, then it may be easier to 'wish' harm or disaster to befall loved ones. Once again, and as in previous examples, sometimes a recording in your own voice describing the awful scene can be useful. Although very stressful to listen to at first, with repeated one-hour sessions three times a day, the distress and anxiety reduce.

Violent Thoughts

Violent thoughts can take the form of either believing you may act in a violent way, such as stabbing a loved family member or deliberately harming your child. These thoughts are horrible and abhorrent and the individual is scared that they may act in this way. The individuals that have these obsessive thoughts are non-violent and hate the thought of the act.

Other individuals may have obsessive images or thoughts of some terrible event happening to a family member, friend, or even strangers, or on a world-wide basis. They then fear that having this thought makes it more likely to occur or that by having this thought it means that they wish it would occur, or even that having the thought is as bad as actually performing the violent or heinous act.

Everyone has experienced violent thoughts which are totally out of character and lead to a feeling of anxiety. This is a normal human experience. The way to cope with this is to accept the thoughts for what they are, 'just thoughts', and not to let them interfere with your normal relationships and everyday life. Of course, this statement is easier said than done, and many people plagued with these thoughts isolate themselves from their loved ones in an attempt to 'protect them'. The principles of treatment are almost exactly the same as for those with paedophilic thoughts discussed earlier in this chapter.

Theresa's Story

Theresa is a 20-year-old supermarket worker. At school, Theresa had witnessed that several of her classmates carried knives. At the age of 15 years old, she heard about a boy being stabbed outside the school gates. She was understandably upset and shocked by this incident. After this, she began to be increasingly worried that if she were in the presence of a sharp knife, she may inadvertently lash out and stab someone. Whenever she saw a knife, she would have an image of herself stabbing anyone that was nearby. This was particularly concerning when at home with her parents and siblings.

She started avoiding sharp knives, which meant she asked to be moved (at her workplace) to work in the clothing section where she was away from the knives used in food preparation and also the knives in the household section. At home, she would ask her parents to remove all sharp knives from the kitchen area and would only cook if this had occurred. She had to ask her mother to chop vegetables or meat before she could cook it. She would refuse to eat using a sharp 'steak' knife and would only use more blunt knives to eat. Even with blunt knives, she would use them and handle them to the minimum. This problem interfered with her social life as she was careful not to go to places where there were people eating with sharp knives. She had refused a promotion to supervisor at work as this would have required her moving across the entire store, including areas where there were knives. Eventually spurred on by feeling that she was missing out on life, Theresa decided to tackle the problem.

Problem	Fear that I may pick up a knife and stab someone
Final Goal	To work and socialise in the vicinity of sharp knives and to be able to use them to cook

Hierarchy	Anxiety Level (0–8)	Number of times per day to perform
To handle a butter or similar blunt knife and carry it about in my pocket all day	4	Throughout the day
To hold a butter knife in a 'threatening position'* whilst watching TV with the family	5	Every evening when at home
To handle a sharp knife and to walk around the home with it	6	Whenever in the home environment
To start cooking my own meals and use a sharp knife at least once during each cooking episode, but ask mum to remove the sharp knife when I'm not using it	6	2–3x/day depending on shift patterns at work
To go out with friends to a steak house	7	Whenever possible
To sit holding a sharp knife in a 'threatening position'* whilst watching TV with the family	7	Every evening at home
To work in an area at work close to sharp knives	8	Speak with supervisor to arrange every day
To cook, prepare meals and drinks, leaving all the knives in the kitchen	8	At least 3x/day

* This involved Theresa holding the knife by the handle and pointing it away from herself.

In Theresa's situation the above programme worked. Some people may benefit from adding in a recorded tape with their obsessive thoughts.

Fear of Shouting Out Something Inappropriate and the Distinction between This and Tourette Syndrome

Many of us have had the fear of shouting out something inappropriate which may lead to catastrophic consequences or social humiliation, as with the example in the wedding service given at the beginning of the chapter. Overcoming these kinds of thoughts is exactly the same as any other type of obsessive thoughts, or in other words it involves 'taking the risk' and not avoiding certain situations. People with pure OCD will not shout out anything inappropriate but will need to prove this to themselves in order for the anxiety to reduce.

One condition which often can present with OCD features is Tourette syndrome. This involves people having facial or other parts of the body involved in a twitch or grimace which may be accompanied by coughing, throat clearing, grunting or making of another type of noise. These movements or noises are called 'tics'. The tics which are seen may be vocal (sounds; e.g., coughing, grunting, or shouting out words) or physical (movements; e.g., sudden movements of the arms or legs, jerking of the head, or jumping up and down). In addition, tics may be simple (e.g., making a small jerky movement or uttering a single sound) or complex (e.g., making a series of movements or speaking a phrase). Tourette syndrome has been discussed alongside a case description of a young woman treated for this disorder in Chapter 8. Most people with Tourette syndrome have symptoms which have been described before. A small number (fewer than one in five men and fewer than one in six women with clinically diagnosed Tourette syndrome) will present with a history of shouting swear words and other obscenities or inappropriate sexual touching without being able to control this. Of course, it is the poor individuals who have this form of the condition who are the most likely to be shown in the press and on TV due to the dramatic nature of the condition. Treatment of Tourette syndrome with both drugs and psychological treatment involving habit reversal is discussed in Chapter 8. Many people with Tourette syndrome may also have OCD; indeed it has been suggested that up to 60 per cent of people with Tourette syndrome also have obsessive-compulsive symptoms. However, Tourette syndrome usually appears between the ages of 2 and eleven years and any inappropriate shouting, swearing, or touching approximately five years later. Suffice it to say that, if you are an adult and have never shouted out obscenities, swear words, or touched people inappropriately, then the fear you may do this is obsessive rather than due to Tourette syndrome.

Lucy's Story

Lucy is a 29-year-old mother of two children who lives with her partner Rory. Following the birth of her first child, when she was 25 years old, Lucy began to have concerns that she may 'contaminate' the baby by not sterilising objects sufficiently well. With the help of Rory, her family, and a self-help group for maternal OCD, Lucy overcame this problem.

However, two years ago, her second child was born. Lucy coped well with the pregnancy but once again developed obsessive thoughts following the birth. This time the thoughts took the form of believing that she would shout out that she had performed a sexual act with the baby. Lucy knew she had not done anything inappropriate but was still fearful of shouting this out. She found this problem so embarrassing that she told no-one of her difficulties. Indeed, she did not dare to tell Rory because he had once read in the local paper about a man who had been convicted of possessing child pornography and had made the comment that 'someone who did that should be beaten up'. Lucy began to worry that she would shout or say out loud that she was a paedophile. Consequently, she avoided all mother and baby events and started being more aloof with Rory, often making excuses to sit in another room from him. At night she would go to sleep after Rory was asleep and wake up early in case she said something in her sleep. Her relationship with Rory was deteriorating and she could not think how to put this right.

Luckily, she remembered that someone in her maternal OCD group had had a similar problem. She had now moved away from where she previously lived and would not be able to attend any groups, but she called the group leader and managed (after much hesitation) to discuss it with her. Her group leader urged Lucy to discuss this issue with Rory and suggested some written material about obsessive urges which she should also show to Rory.

That evening, Lucy was extremely scared and anxious when Rory came home from work. She told him she needed to talk to him. After they had put the children to bed, they sat down together. Rory looked worried and anxious himself. Lucy said, 'Do you remember when, after the birth of Pearl, that I had OCD?' Rory agreed that he remembered it well. She then went on to explain that, as well as contamination fears, people with OCD sometimes had thoughts they would do something that they didn't want to. Rory said he had understood this. Lucy then explained her fear that she was going to blurt or shout out something inappropriate. Rory accepted that and asked what it was Lucy was afraid of. She then told him. Rory was relieved and hugged her explaining that he thought she was getting bored with him and that was the reason for her aloofness. He said he would read the papers that she had found on this type of OCD and together they could work on this problem.

Problem	Fear of shouting out inappropriate comments such as 'I am a paedophile', leading to avoidance of social situations or places where there are other people
Problem	Fear of shouting out inappropriate comments such as 'I am a paedophile', leading to avoidance of social situations or places where there are other people

Hierarchy	Anxiety Level (0–8)	Number of times per day to perform
To tell Rory about my problem	Initially 8 but fell to 1 very rapidly after I saw his response	Once
To go for a walk for an hour in the local area with Rory and the children after he returns from work	5	Once a day

(cont.)

To go for a walk to the local park with the children	6	2x/day
To meet my sister for coffee with our children	6	2x/week
To go to the local shops with the children and talk with the shop assistants who may know me (and where I live)	7	1x/day
To go to parent and toddler group and stay there for at least one hour	8	3 x/week
To go to a film on my own and sit through the whole thing	8	1x/week

The case history of Lucy demonstrates how her fears were exaggerated when around people who knew her as she worried they would be in a better position to report her to the authorities and to take her away from her children. If you have difficulties in having a conversation of this type with a loved one, then it could be helpful to get a third party to meet with you. This must be someone who understands your OCD, so could be a therapist, a volunteer working with an OCD charity, your GP, or even a trusted family member or friend.

Fear of Having Already Committed a Heinous Crime or Dangerous Act

Some people have obsessive thoughts about having done something without meaning to. For example, they may worry they've pushed someone over, been sexually inappropriate, knocked someone over whilst driving, or committed a crime. Once they have had this obsessive thought, they will then perform compulsions to counteract this thought. This may take the form of going back to the area to look for any evidence of the 'deed' or 'confession' to someone else or just reliving every movement they made in their mind. Of course, as with all compulsions, these reduce the anxiety but only by a small amount and for a short time before the anxiety rises again and the urge to perform another check or compulsion.

Treatment involves allowing these thoughts to flow freely but not performing the compulsions.

KEY POINTS

- The term 'thought-action fusion' refers to the idea or belief that a thought is morally equivalent to performing the act or that thinking a thought makes the event more likely to occur. This is very common in people with unpleasant obsessive thoughts.
- People with obsessive thoughts of violence towards others will not act on their thoughts but, in fact, are so concerned by the thoughts that they go to great lengths to prevent themselves acting in this way.
- People with Tourette syndrome have a build-up of tension and then an involuntary movement which may take the form of a facial tic, a bodily movement, and an utterance such as a noise or throat clearing etc. Rarely, this can also involve shouting out obscenities or swearing without the desire to do so.
- Many people with Tourette syndrome also have OCD, but this does not mean that many people with OCD have Tourette syndrome. About 15 per cent of children with OCD have a history of a tic disorder. Tourette syndrome and OCD are thought to be genetically linked.
- Some people with OCD have a fear that they may have done something dreadful and not noticed it. A typical example is people repeatedly checking whether they have been in a car accident by repeatedly driving back and forth. Another example is people confessing to 'crimes' just in case they have committed them.

- Treatment of worrying thoughts or images involves facing up to the fear in a structured way. Each episode of exposure should last between one to two hours or until the anxiety has reliably reduced by at least half, e.g. something initially causing extreme anxiety is now reduced to moderate anxiety.

16

• • • • • • •

Overcoming 'Taboo' Obsessive Thoughts

This chapter examines the treatment of 'taboo' obsessions. People with these kinds of obsessions often have very distressing images, thoughts, or even impulses which are against everything they believe in. These types of thoughts can be amongst the most distressing for an individual. Occasionally they are misunderstood by society or even healthcare professionals. Treatment involves accepting these distressing obsessions as thoughts rather than an active desire to commit abhorrent acts and allowing the thoughts to come without trying to push them away or 'put them right'.

Introduction

One of the most distressing types of obsessive-compulsive disorder is having severely distressing taboo thoughts. These can often be misinterpreted by the person who has them and also by other people including healthcare professionals. Common examples of these type of obsessions are:

- **Paedophilic obsessions**. Thoughts that you may be a paedophile or may have abused children, or images of yourself doing this.
- **Violent obsessions**. Thoughts or images of yourself committing an act of violence or doubting whether you have done this. Often these thoughts of violence are towards people that you love.
- **Blasphemous obsessions**. These are thoughts which go against an individual's fundamental beliefs about religion.
- Other obsessions include thoughts that you may have an alternative sexuality or that you may not truly love the people who are closest to you.

Paedophilic Thoughts

Since the early part of this century there has been increasing publicity about various people in the public eye who have been accused, and sometimes convicted of, sexual offences against children and under-age girls and boys. This has led to a greater awareness of paedophiles in the general population. A person who is a paedophile is someone who acts in an illegal way either by engaging in sexual activity with an underage person or by watching such activity online. A paedophile will therefore generally go out of their way to spend time with young people.

In terms of sexual attraction, most people find some younger people sexually attractive. For example, many men will admit to finding school-girls sexually appealing. The sexual desirability is generally less with younger children and increases as the young person goes through puberty. Despite finding these young people attractive, the vast majority of the public does not act on this desire.

People with paedophilic obsessions are appalled by any feelings of sexual attraction to a young person and will go to great lengths to ensure they cannot possibly act this out. Having an understandable disgust for people who act out their sexual desires with young people, someone with paedophilic obsessions may become extremely distressed and depressed by their thoughts. Unlike some other obsessive thoughts, it is often difficult to explain the nature of the thoughts to others including family and friends. This feeling of isolation can lead to the individual becoming increasingly depressed and isolated.

People with paedophilic obsessive thoughts are extremely unlikely to act on these thoughts. This is because they find the thoughts abhorrent and have no desire to act on them. A true paedophile, in contrast, will normally seek opportunities to be with children and young people, may 'groom' his or her victims, and will find thoughts of sexual behaviour with children exciting rather than abhorrent.

Many people who have obsessive fears that they may sexually attack children, spend considerable time checking whether or not they are becoming sexually excited. This can take many forms. Some people may have originally developed the obsessive thought because they were aroused already and then came into contact with a child and that lead to the fear that it was the presence of the child which had caused the excitement. Others may feel the urge to check whether or not they are aroused when near to children. In the case of a man, this could, for example, take the form of putting a hand in a trouser pocket to check whether or not the penis is engorged. This activity itself, especially when repeated frequently as a 'check', can lead to enlargement of the penis. In addition, excitement, fear, and anxiety can sometimes have a mild arousing effect, and all of these could lead to the misinterpretation that the individual is truly a paedophile.

Whereas it is important to watch out for any dips in mood during any form of exposure treatment for any form of OCD, this can be particularly pertinent for this type of obsession, as shame often means it is not discussed and shared with others. Also, there is the fear that it may not be understood by others if it were to be discussed.

Indeed, if people with these thoughts do discuss them with others, there is always the fear that they may be misunderstood and misinterpreted by family members and friends but also by some healthcare professionals. In such cases, it may be helpful to show them written material such as that found in this book or information such as that produced by the International OCD Federation or, in the UK, charities such as Mind (links at the end of this section).

It is important to remember that these sexual urges can occur in both men and women. **'Ethan's Story'** in the following section gives an example of a man with such thoughts, but it could equally have been a woman.

Ethan's Story

Ethan is a 30-year-old man who works as a primary school teacher. Following university, Ethan started at teacher training college. Whist in his final year at college he was sent on placement for six weeks and was allocated a class of 10–11-year-olds. Although he had done short trials of teaching supervised by other teachers, this was the first time he had taught a group himself for a prolonged period.

Initially all went well, and he was enjoying the experience. Half-way into the placement, there was a story in the media about a primary teacher who had been sexually abusing some of the children in his class. Ethan was appalled by this story and felt shocked, sickened, and couldn't understand how anyone could do such a thing. Whilst this event was being discussed in the news, he was out with friends one night and they began to tease him that maybe he 'fancied' some of the pupils in his class.

Initially he laughed this off, but it began to prey on his mind. The thought that he may be a paedophile came increasingly into Ethan's mind over the next few days. These thoughts made him anxious, and he began going over in his mind every action he made. He started avoiding standing near any of the children. This was noticed by the children, with one girl asking him 'Don't you like us any more, Sir?' He also started wrapping tissue paper around his penis in order to reassure himself that he had not acted inappropriately.

Ethan took time off sick to avoid the situation and worries. In addition, Ethan began avoiding other places where he may bump into children such as roads with schools where he may be in close contact with children. His sister had three daughters aged 6–12 years, and whereas Ethan had always been a very devoted uncle, he started to avoid visiting them and refused to baby sit when asked (an event he had previously looked forward to). He spoke with his GP who offered him treatment with Sertraline or to refer him locally. On balance, Ethan decided to try and tackle this first without any additional help. He reassured the GP that if his mood did start to significantly dip then he would make an appointment and consider his offer again.

Problem	Fear that I may have inadvertently sexually abused children
Final Goal	To take my nieces on a day out to a theme park without taking any 'precautions' To go on a field trip with my class at the end of term without taking any 'precautions'

Hierarchy All of the items below to be performed without wrapping my penis in tissue paper	Anxiety level (0–8)	Number of times per day to perform
To record the statement 'I am a paedophile' on my mobile phone in my own voice and to listen to it on continuous play via headphones for an hour	4	3x/day
To listen to the 'I am a paedophile' tape for an hour whilst looking at photographs of school children (e.g., school prospectus brochures)	5	3x/day
To watch the film 'Bugsy Malone'	6	Once a day

(cont.)

To watch the film 'Bugsy Malone' whilst listening to the 'I am a paedophile' on continuous play	6	
To walk around the streets near the local schools whilst listening to the 'I am a paedophile' recording	7	Twice a day in the morning and evening. At weekends to walk in parks where children are; 3x/day
To visit my sister and play my usual rough and tumble games with my nieces	7	Once a week
To go into school and teach class	7	Next placement to discuss starting by teaching for two hours alone only; daily

(GP to write asking for a phased return to work and advising no more than two hours a day initially for one week and increasing thereafter) |
To go out on a day trip with my sister and nieces and interact with them as normal	7	At the weekend
To take my nieces to a theme park on my own	8	Once
To take my class, along with other teachers, on the end of term trip to the activity centre and stay overnight with the other teachers	8	Once

Ethan presented with fairly mild paedophilic OCD. Others may be much more distressed as well as embarrassed and may not have a supportive family and work. If the worries are more extreme, it may be better seeking professional help. One of the issues of exposure by going to places where there are children whilst looking anxious could lead to the individual being stopped as parents and others may report this to the police. For this reason, it is best to start with techniques such as the continuous tape and looking at pictures and videos before going out on the street.

Here are some other helpful links concerning paedophilic obsessive thoughts:

- https://iocdf.org/expert-opinions/am-i-a-monster-an-overview-of-common-features-typical-course-shame-and-treatment-of-pedophilia-ocd-pocd/
- www.mind.org.uk/information-support/types-of-mental-health-problems/obsessive-compulsive-disorder-ocd/symptoms-of-ocd/

Blasphemous Thoughts

Many people will have blasphemous thoughts. Once again, the more a person tries not to have these thoughts, the more they come into their mind. Treatment involves deliberately bringing on these thoughts by repeatedly writing them down or by listening to a recording of them in your own voice. The personal story of Ali shows how this can be treated.

Ali's Story

Ali is a 30-year-old Muslim man who lives at home with his parents and siblings and works as a solicitor in the family firm. He had always been a meticulous and scrupulous young man who attended to detail. In the past he had had some contamination fears which he had overcome with the help of his own programme.

However, at the age of 29 years he began to have abusive and obscene intrusive thoughts about God. These were extremely upsetting to him and at first he was embarrassed to discuss them with anyone. Instead, he started praying repeatedly to try and 'undo' the thoughts. This began to take over his life and he was taking on fewer and fewer duties at work and spending most of his time praying.

His father spoke to him, and Ali expressed the fear that he had been overtaken by evil spirits. His father did not believe this to be true but urged Ali to go and talk to the local Imam. Luckily, the Imam had met other people with similar obsessive thoughts and advised Ali to research OCD. The Imam also reassured Ali that, although it would normally not be acceptable to have blasphemous thoughts or material when entering a mosque to pray, the Quran does say that Muslims should do whatever is necessary to be mentally, as well as physically, well.

Ali researched OCD and came up with the following programme. He checked this with the Imam before proceeding.

Problem	*Abhorrent blasphemous thoughts*
Final Goal	*To be able to enter a mosque and attend prayers as normal and to adhere to the praying times expected of a Muslim but not to pray outside of these times*

Hierarchy	Anxiety level (0–8)	Number of times per day to perform
To write down my blasphemous thoughts on a piece of paper and walk around with it in my pocket	5	All the time but read 3x/day after prayers*
To put the piece of paper up on the side of my bedside cabinet	6	Once but to look at it before going to sleep

(cont.)

To record the thoughts on my mobile phone and listen to it on continuous loop for an hour	7	3x/day after prayers*
To walk past the mosque whilst listening to the recording of blasphemous thoughts on my mobile phone	8	3x/day after prayers*
To enter the mosque at a quiet time whilst listening to the tape of blasphemous thoughts on my phone	8	2x/day**
To attend a Friday service with the paper with blasphemous thoughts in my pocket	8	Every week***

* This was after prayers, as if performed before prayers, then the prayers may 'undo' the exposure to the blasphemous thoughts.
** This was at a quiet time as other worshippers may be offended by his listening to his mobile phone.
*** Having the paper in his pocket was instead of the mobile phone recording to avoid offence to others.

KEY POINTS

- Many people have horrible, abhorrent obsessive thoughts concerning issues such as paedophilia, violence, or thoughts that are contrary to a person's religion or standards.
- People who have paedophilic obsessive thoughts are very different to paedophiles. In people with OCD paedophilic thoughts, these thoughts

are extremely distressing. These people will normally avoid children or avoid feared situations with children.

- People who are paedophiles enjoy thoughts of sexual activity with children and seek to get opportunities to be in close contact with children.

- Blasphemous obsessive thoughts can occur in people with OCD who belong to any or even no religion at all.

- Sometimes it can be helpful to discuss with a trusted local Imam, priest, vicar, rabbi, or minister etc. Of course, whether or not they will be helpful will depend on how much they themselves understand about OCD and the nature of obsessive thoughts.

17

......

Loss of Something (Objects or Part of 'Self')

Fear of loss of an object or even fear of losing part of your body is a fairly common obsessive fear. Other people fear inadvertently divulging personal or other information and will go to great lengths of checking to ensure this does not occur. Treatment as always involves taking the risk and facing up to the fear. Also, in this chapter, we will examine hoarding, both as a symptom of OCD and also as a standalone condition.

Introduction

Most of us are careful when we leave a public place that something has not fallen out of our pocket or bag. For people with obsessive fear of loss of an object, they may take a very long time to check, often returning repeatedly. Sometimes the fear is of losing part of the body or even losing the mind or soul, even though the individual realises this is not logical.

Sometimes the fear is that the person may inadvertently drop something with important information on it and that would result in harm or some catastrophe.

Fear of Losing an Important Item

Fear of loss of an item usually means that the individual takes a number of precautions before venturing outside. This usually means ensuring that all pockets and bags are firmly secured and checking this throughout their journey. If they stop or sit anywhere, there may be an elaborate ritual to check they have not left anything behind, often excessively checking areas of the floor and all surrounding areas to make sure they have not dropped any item. Frequently, there may be the urge to return and check the area repeatedly. Treatment involves facing up to the fear without putting it right. In other words, picking up personal items and placing them in your pocket or bag without checking repeatedly that they are secure. The programme would also involve sitting or staying in a public area without checking for lost items and certainly not returning repeatedly. The key elements of a possible exposure programme for such fears are outlined below.

Myfanwy's Story

Myfanwy is a 28-year-old woman who lives with her partner and their two children aged five and seven years old. Two years ago, her grandfather died. Having been extremely close to her grandfather, Myfanwy found it very difficult to come to terms with this loss.

Over time, she found that she gradually began to be concerned about losing items when she left the house. Her children were checked by her when they went to school to ensure their pockets were all fastened securely, but the major issue was her fear that she would lose something herself. Gradually, she stopped taking a handbag when she went out and reduced what she carried to a minimum, putting one credit card in a case which contained her mobile and her key. She would repeatedly check her pockets to ensure they were empty before leaving the house and had stopped wearing gloves, even on the coldest of days, for fear she would lose them. Her partner repeatedly told her that losing a glove or other item was no big deal. Myfanwy knew this but felt compelled not to lose anything as she felt this meant she was 'out of control' and may then lose other people in the way she lost her grandfather.

Myfanwy had been to bereavement counselling which had helped her overcome her grief, but this had not reduced the OCD about loss of objects. If she stopped or sat in any area, she would spend up to ten minutes looking around her and ensuring she had not lost anything or left anything behind. Performing these compulsions at a children's playground, when with her daughter, had caused other children to comment on her behaviour, and so they had started asking her not to take them to the playground.

After Myfanwy had left an area, she often felt compelled to return to ensure she had not lost anything, even though she knew she had all her possessions with her. Going out for a meal or a drink was impossible for her, as she feared she would be so long checking everywhere when she left and would then have the urge to go back repeatedly. She felt this was having an effect on her children and so she decided to set up a treatment programme for herself, as per the following.

Problem	*Fear of losing objects due to the worry that I will 'lose control' of myself.*
Target	*To leave the house with the children, visit a playground, sit on a bench, and eat at the cafe, without constantly checking that I have everything*

Item on hierarchy (starting with easiest)	Anxiety rating	How often to be performed (3x/ day is ideal)
To place some money (coins) in my pocket and go out for a walk with the pocket undone	4	3x/day
To carry items in a handbag and go out carrying this	5	3x/day

(cont.)

To allow my daughters to go to school without checking their belongings are secure and recording what they have taken with them	6	Once a day
To let my daughters go and play immediately after school without checking that their items are safe	6	Once a day
Walk along the High Street go into two shops to look around, and not retrace my steps despite carrying a handbag and loose change in my pocket	6	Once a day
To buy an item of clothing with pockets that do not have a fastening and keep some paper in this pocket at all times	7	To wear the item all day
To have a cup of coffee with friends in the park or on my own in the park or cafe	7	Once a day
To go to the swing park or playground with my daughters and sit on a bench without checking when I leave	8	Once a day after school
To go to the cinema and leave before the lights come on and without checking	8	Once a week
To go to the Social Club with Dave (partner), have a drink, and leave without checking	8	Once a week

> Myfanwy completed this programme over eight weeks, starting with the less anxiety-provoking items and repeating them daily, until she felt her anxiety had reduced significantly, when she would move on to more difficult items.

Fear of Losing Important Information

This fear is not substantially different from the fear of losing items. The main difference can be that there is fear of losing more items. This can go to extremes so that people can fear inadvertently writing information on unlikely items and losing them, or even fear that their DNA will be found and used against them. For example, a person with this fear may avoid touching any item for fear that it may lead to someone obtaining information about them for manipulative or criminal reasons. As well as being overly careful about their possessions, they may also check items such as paper on the ground dropped by others or even leaves, in case these are items they themselves have touched. In extreme cases, I have seen people who have hoarded many bags of rubbish collected outside for these reasons.

Mairead's Story

Mairead is a 30-year-old woman who works as a legal secretary. When she started her job some years earlier, she had signed a declaration that she would not divulge any details of clients to anyone. Over the years she took this very seriously. However, a few years ago, she said to her husband that she had met a person that he had mentioned when they were talking. She instantly became worried, as this person was a client of her legal firm. Although she had not given her husband any details at all, she felt she had betrayed the trust of the firm. She confessed this to the senior partner, who was unconcerned.

Following on from this, however, she began to worry that she may inadvertently release confidential information and she would spend 30 minutes at the end of the day ensuring that she had no work documents on her person. She always left her personal ID badge, and even her 'work shoes' at work, for fear these may hold confidential information in some way. In addition, she felt the urge to constantly check with her boss if any information had been leaked. Her boss was understanding initially but had begun to be irritable and dismiss her very rapidly. He suggested that she seek help to conquer this problem. Her increasingly long working hours were also having an effect on her marital and social life. Mairead therefore created the following hierarchy to work on:

Problem	Fear of accidently and inadvertently disclosing confidential information
Target	To go into work and complete a day without checking, leave on time, and take my ID card home with me

Item on hierarchy (starting with the easiest) All items to be performed without 'confessing' to my boss	Anxiety rating	How often to be performed (3x/day is ideal)
To take my ID pass home in my pocket	5	Daily
To take my 'work shoes' home with me and wear different pairs of shoes into the office	5	Daily
To take a blank piece of paper from the office notepad and drop it in a litter bin outside the office without checking what is on it	6	Lunchtime and evening
To write my office phone number on a piece of paper and deposit it in a litter bin outside	7	Lunchtime and evening
To write either my email address OR my password on a piece of paper (not both and alternate) and deposit in a litter bin outside	8	Lunchtime and evening

Mairead completed this programme over 12 weeks. Initially she found it extremely anxiety provoking but this settled as she progressed.

This fear can sometimes overlap with the fear of losing part of one's body, which is described next.

Fear of Losing Part of One's Body or Mind

Fear of losing part of your body is a relatively common fear in people with OCD. Obvious fears may be fear of hair loss, which can lead to excessive checking of brushes and combs and counting lost hairs; taking photographs of the suspected hair loss repeatedly; and gazing in the mirror. Treatment is, in this case, to take the risk and to stop the checking and reassurance-giving activities whilst facing up to the fear-provoking situations such as hair washing or even, in some cases, going out on windy days for fear of losing hair.

On the other hand, fear of losing part of the body is often worrying to the individual, who will usually realise this fear is irrational. They may fear that a limb, a finger, or a facial feature may be lost and will avoid situations which they feel may put them in danger. This could be avoiding going out in wet, stormy, or windy weather for fear of losing a body part or else other places, situations, and activities which they fear are 'dangerous' in this way. Compulsions often involve checking the areas by touch, in a mirror, by photographs, or by seeking reassurance from others.

Some people are so concerned about losing part of themselves that they may even store waste material produced by the body, such as urine and faeces, thereby creating a major health hazard to themselves and others. Others may be fearful of depositing their DNA on objects and that this may be used against them.

Seth's Story

Seth is a 25-year-old gardener. As a teenager, at a difficult time when his parents were going through an acrimonious divorce, Seth had been in trouble with the police for stealing items from the local park and shops. He was caught, arrested, and cautioned, and had no subsequent offences. However, he had found the experience of being arrested, and all his neighbours and friends knowing about this, embarrassing and humiliating.

After leaving school, he had started working at the local parks department as a gardener. Initially, he was teased about how he now had a better opportunity for 'thieving'. Seth found this embarrassing. He worried a little about inadvertently taking items and being arrested again, but this soon became a bigger fear that he may lose part of his body, which may lead to him being implicated in a bigger crime.

To combat this fear, he wore long leggings and a long sleeve top underneath his jeans and shirt, even on the hottest days in summer. He always wore gloves and also a hat or cap. At first, he did not worry about dropping hairs, but then this fear grew, and he started shaving his head to prevent this happening. Eventually he would have difficulty speaking in public without covering his mouth with a handkerchief in case he spat and distributed his DNA on items. At this point he decided to tackle the problem and face up to his fear.

Problem	Fear of losing part of myself outside the home which will lead to my being convicted of a crime I did not commit
Target	To go into work wearing shorts and T-shirt in the summer and without wearing gloves and a hat

Item on hierarchy (starting with the easiest)	Anxiety rating	How often to be performed (3x/day is ideal)
I will stop shaving my head immediately		
Walk around for an hour without wearing a hat	4	3x/day

(cont.)

Remove gloves and touch the items I am using at work	4	3x/day
Remove a hair and drop it as I am walking along outside	5	3x/day
Keep my finger- and toenails and cut into smaller pieces. Deliberately drop a piece outside the house	5	
Go out without gloves and touch my work tools etc.	6	All day
Go out without gloves and touch door handles of shops and public buildings (such as library) and public toilets	6	3x/day
Stop wearing leggings and long sleeve top under my clothing and continue a normal day at work	7	All day
Wear shorts and T-shirt to work	8	All day

The fear of losing part of your mind or that your mind may be sucked into an 'alternative universe' is another form of fear of loss of objects. This fear may lead people to avoid certain activities that they think will result in them losing their minds and then give themselves specific tests as a compulsion to ensure that their mind is intact.

Reuben's Story

Reuben is a 19-year-old man who was hoping to go to university to study dentistry. During his final year at school, he would play video games to relax from studying. At this time, he found that he often felt completely taken over by the games and would almost feel as if he was part of the action on screen.

He then started to worry that he may not be able to get his mind back into his body. He realised that this was not true, but it still started to worry him.

After this he began to avoid his video games, and gradually this escalated so that he would avoid watching TV for fear he may become 'trapped in the screen action'. Eventually, Reuben avoided reading anything for fear he may become 'stuck' in the book. He also became worried that water going down plugholes or flushing toilets may also take part of his mind with them. If he inadvertently saw a screen and watched some TV etc., he would mentally test himself by reciting the names of his favourite games in his mind, to convince himself that his mind was still 'intact'. This issue meant he would avoid emptying the bath, sink, or toilet, which caused considerable friction in his family. Being aware that this problem would mean he would not manage to go to university or realise his dream of becoming a dentist, Reuben set out the following programme for himself:

Problem	Fear of losing all or part of my mind into a 'black hole'
Target	To be able to go to Malachi's house, use his toilet and flush it, wash my hands under running water, and play video games with him

Item on hierarchy (starting with easiest) All to be performed without 'mental checks'	Anxiety rating	How often to be performed (3x/day is ideal)
Read for 60 minutes (newspaper/book etc.)	4	3x/day
Wash hands in flowing water	4	3x/day
Flush toilet	5	3+x/day
Stay in room whilst bath empties	6	Once a day

(cont.)		
Watch programme on TV	6	Twice a day
Take a shower	7	Twice a day
Play video games for one hour	7	3x/day

Reuben completed this hierarchy over eight weeks and is currently at university studying to become a dentist.

Hoarding

Hoarding or the collection of a large number of objects which interferes with your ability to function can be found in many conditions. In order not to hoard items to their detriment, a person needs to be able to:

- Identify items which need to be kept, discarded, or thrown away
- Sort items into these categories
- Successfully discard items outside of the living space

People with difficulty seeing may have problems identifying objects for example. Some people have difficulty in sorting items such as people with cognitive difficulties or severe addiction problems. Others with restricted mobility may hoard because they are unable to physically discard items.

Many people with OCD have difficulty discarding items. This could be due to fear of contamination, either fear they will contaminate themselves from the bin or else fear that they may contaminate others by discarding 'contaminated' material. Other people with OCD may have difficulty in discarding items for fear of losing something, either throwing away something important or something that they fear may be incriminating. These people often check their rubbish bags repeatedly. Treatment for OCD hoarding is identical to all treatment for OCD; in other words facing up to the fear and taking the risk without checking.

Hoarding disorder is a standalone condition which is categorised as one of the obsessive-compulsive disorders but has some differences from OCD. In hoarding disorder, the individual does not have horrible obsessive thoughts leading to the hoarding nor do they perform compulsions to reduce their discomfort. In pure hoarding disorder the individual forms a very strong attachment to the items they hoard and it is highly emotional for them to discard these items.

Sometimes relatives will complain that someone is a 'hoarder', whereas the collection does not restrict anyone or cause any danger. It is interesting to consider the difference between a collection and a hoard. In a collection, the individual knows exactly what they have and has arranged it so that an item can be found. An example of a collection is someone who has a large number of books on shelves or in cupboards, but these do not encroach on areas where they sleep, eat, cook, or relax. A hoard of books would be books everywhere in huge piles, encroaching into inappropriate spaces, and where the owner would have difficulty in locating a specific book. So, a person with a collection would normally have them classified in some way, would be able to locate individual items, and would not have them encroaching into their ability to perform activities of daily living.

Hoarding disorder is a serious condition and can result in death. There have been many examples in local papers of people who have been crushed to death by their hoard. Many more may have been involved in house fires due to paper and flammable material being in proximity to cooking areas. Trips and falls over the hoard are a particular and frequent hazard.

People with hoarding disorder are frequently extremely ashamed and embarrassed by the condition and will go to great lengths to avoid having other people in their homes. This shame and embarrassment means they do not often seek help from healthcare professionals.

Another problem with hoarding disorder is that it was only recognised as a real psychological problem in 2013, with the publication of the *Diagnostic and Statistical Manual of Mental Disorders,* volume 5, by the American Psychiatric Association. This text lists all psychiatric and psychological conditions and defines what they are. As hoarding disorder is a relatively recent addition, there has been less research into this condition compared to other diagnoses such as OCD, although this is rapidly improving. Also, many people have encountered difficulty accessing help, as many health-care workers may not be familiar with hoarding disorder and its treatment.

Treatment of hoarding disorder is slightly different from the ERP model that has mostly been described in this book. The treatment involves two strands. Firstly, it is important not to allow more items that can potentially be sorted into the home. It is pointless trying to discard items if more are coming in all the time to replace them. Next, items need to be sorted and discarded appropriately. The key components in tackling hoarding disorder are:

1. A ban on bringing any new items into the house.
2. Choose one room or area of your home. This allows you to see real change, whereas flitting from room to room can be disheartening and makes it difficult to assess your progress.
3. Start to sort items into two piles:
   a. Keep
   b. Discard
4. Try the OHIO method. This stands for Only Handle It Once (this was described in a book by Tolin, Frost, and Steketee in 2013, which you will find listed in the References). The longer people hold objects, the more attached they become to them; therefore, it is important to make a rapid decision to keep or discard. If you are having problems thinking about this, there are some questions you can ask yourself which are:
   a. Is it valuable?
   b. Is it of important sentimental value and is this value worth more than the advantage of having a tidier home? E.g., keep photographs of family members but it may be less important to hang on to items of clothing of deceased relatives.

   c. When did I last use it? If the answer is more than a year or so ago, then it can probably be discarded.

   d. Is it likely I will use it again in the next six months?

   e. If I did discard it and then needed a similar object in the future, how would I manage this?

   f. In the case of books or magazines from which you have intended to cut out articles, if this hasn't been done immediately, then it is unlikely to happen, and so these should be discarded. The content is also likely to be online.

5. The period of sorting should be fairly short. No more than an hour at a time, as otherwise attention can wander. Sometimes this can be an hour twice a day, but this should not be when unduly tired. Although it can appear a mammoth task when you start, it is surprising how soon you will see dramatic improvements.

6. Once a decision has been made about the fate of a particular item, it is important to remove it fairly quickly from the home as otherwise, if left in the home, it is often tempting to take it back.

7. Once an article is discarded it is gone and should not be retrieved!

8. Some people have great difficulty deciding what to do with an item. If this applies to you it can be very useful to have a trusted and patient friend or relative who can help and encourage the discarding process. Please note that I said the person should be patient and guided by you. Having an impatient person who brusquely decides for you is counter-productive and likely to end in an argument.

9. It can also be helpful to have contact with others who have similar problems. A list of organisations that deliver such help is given at the end of this book.

Online Resources: Help for Hoarders

www.helpforhoarders.co.uk is a website giving practical advice.

www.mind.org.uk/information-support/types-of-mental-health-problems/hoarding/about-hoarding/ is another website offering helpful advice for hoarders.

https://hoardingdisordersuk.org/ is a UK-based organisation which offers advice on hoarding and also runs some self-help groups in certain areas of the UK.

www.hoardinguk.org/ is a UK-based charity offering advice, helplines, and local support groups for hoarders.

www.ocdaction.org.uk/search/node/hoarding is a UK-based charity offering advice, helplines, conferences, and leaflets about various aspects of OCD, including hoarding disorder.

www.ocduk.org/ is a UK-based charity offering advice, helplines, conferences, and leaflets about various aspects of OCD, including hoarding disorder.

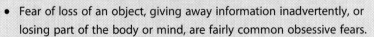

KEY POINTS

- Fear of loss of an object, giving away information inadvertently, or losing part of the body or mind, are fairly common obsessive fears.
- The feared consequences may be the perceived concern about the loss itself or the idea the individual may be implicated in something untoward.
- Treatment involves giving up the precautions, taking the risk, and facing the fear.
- Many people with OCD may hoard objects, due to either a fear of losing something, contamination fears, or for another OCD reason.
- Hoarding disorder is related to OCD but in these cases the items are hoarded due to a sentimental attachment to them as well as excessive acquisition of objects.
- Some people have OCD as well as hoarding disorder and, in these cases, both need to be treated using a separate approach.
- People with hoarding disorder are often ashamed of their condition and go to great lengths to hide it.
- Treatment for hoarding disorder involves making a commitment not to bring fresh items into the home.
- Items can be sorted for a maximum of one hour or until the attention starts to wander (many people can only manage 15 minutes). Items are kept or discarded; those items that are going should be removed from the home immediately after the sorting session. Items should be held once and for as short a period as possible, in order to avoid strengthening emotional bonds with the object.

18

• • • • • • • •

Overcoming Obsessive-Compulsive Slowness, Perfectionism and Symmetry

This chapter will examine the idea of obsessive-compulsive slowness and how to tackle this problem, as well as examining perfectionism, the need to perform actions until they feel 'just right', and symmetry obsessions. Ideas such as 'Lucky Dip' and 'Chance' programmes will be described.

The overlap between autism and OCD will also be examined, as well as consideration about the role of other diagnoses in symmetry obsessions.

Obsessional Slowness

Some people with OCD present as being very slowed down and find that everything takes much longer than usual. In these situations, one of the most common causes is that the person is trying very hard to be absolutely perfect. Of course, perfection is rare and most of us strive to be 'good enough', because striving to be always perfect often means that very little gets done. These people usually fear that if they do anything which is not perfect then they will be a 'failure' or will be criticised or less 'loved' in some way. Another group of people with obsessive slowness are just slow because they doubt that they are doing things 'properly'. This is another form of perfectionism and can be treated in a similar way. Occasionally the 'perfectionism' is not striving to be perfect but a feeling that if certain tasks are not performed in a very precise way, some other disaster may befall themselves or their family. The treatment of perfectionism of this type is described below.

Other people are slow due to the time taken with their obsessions and compulsions. For example, some people with obsessive ruminations can get so stuck in thinking over their compulsions that they become almost rooted to the spot and feel unable to move on until they have completed the ritual. To an outsider, this will appear to be just extreme slowness and only the individual knows what is going on inside his or her head. The treatment of obsessional ruminations is described in Chapter 19.

Treatment of Perfectionism

Just as in any other type of OCD, treatment for perfectionism means facing up to the obsessive thought of being 'imperfect' and not making attempts to put this right. As in all other types of OCD, it is also a good idea to go 'over the top' to some extent and to test out what will happen. So, for example, someone who is always perfectly dressed, with sharp creases in their jeans and a smart appearance, could decide to try wearing their sweatshirt inside out and take their jeans straight from the tumble dryer and wear them in a crushed state.

Some people with perfectionism do not describe seeking perfection but instead describe the need to perform an action until it feels 'just right'. Whether or not this is considered to be perfectionism is really not the point. Treatment consists of taking the risk and performing the action once, whether or not it feels 'right'.

Frequently people with perfectionism can get caught up with ensuring that they perform their treatment programme perfectly as well which, of course, can undermine the success of the programme. There are two ideas to prevent this being a problem. One is to use a 'Lucky Dip' programme and the other is to use a 'Chance' approach to the programme. These are described here and illustrated in the personal story of Edu.

Lucky Dip

For a lucky dip programme, you should write a series of 'imperfect' situations on separate pieces of paper. These may include things like wearing odd socks, wearing your top inside out, deliberately making a spelling or grammatical mistake in a piece of work, not saying good morning to someone, not replacing an item 'perfectly' after using it. The items in the lucky dip will vary with the individual's particular problem. Once you have collected eight to nine different exposures and written them on separate pieces of paper, place them folded into a mug or box. Then three times a day, without looking, take a piece of paper out from the container and that is the programme you need to do. It is important not to cheat, and so you will need to shake up all the pieces of paper after you have returned the one taken, and try not to guess or control which one you are going to pick. By selecting the programme in this way, you should find that you randomly perform all of the items.

An alternative to having pieces of paper is to write all the items in a list and put a number by them, then shake a dice, and whatever number it falls on is the number of the item you need to perform.

Chance

For people who find themselves always performing the programmes perfectly, it can be useful to play a game of 'chance'. As has been said throughout this book, programmes should ideally be performed three times a day. If someone is always performing their programmes perfectly, then this in itself may become a compulsion. To overcome this, take theprogramme that you are performing at that moment and write a number by every item you are performing during the day. Then take a dice and throw a number (or two dice if there are more items on your programme) and whatever number you throw is the item that you miss off your programme that day.

Edu's Story

Edu is an 18-year-old young man who lives at home with his parents and younger sister. He attends college and is hoping to study Law at university once he gains his 'A levels'. From the age of 16 years old, Edu had been getting increasingly slow at handing in his work and assessments. He had completed his GCSE examinations and had done well in these, but since that time the standard of his work had deteriorated, despite him spending many hours working in his bedroom. His parents were alarmed at the fact that he had stopped seeing friends and seemed to spend all his time working but this was not resulting in good grades.

When asked about this, Edu admitted that he was always trying to produce 'perfect' work. He had been quite meticulous and fussy about his appearance from a young age and his parents would note how clean and tidy Edu was compared with his sister. He would spend a considerable time in the bathroom when having a shower or doing his hair to go to college. Edu admitted that he felt he needed to try and be 'perfect' so that people would like him, he would do well at college, and make his parents proud. His parents were surprised by this and expressed how they would much rather their son was happy rather than being miserable and successful. They also commented that the more he was trying to be perfect, the poorer his grades at college were.

Symmetry Obsessions and Compulsions

Sometimes people refer to symmetry OCD. This can refer to a range of thoughts and behaviours. Sometimes, however, the fear is of things not being symmetrical and that that in itself is a portent that something bad could happen. Common types of symmetry symptoms include:

- Obsessional thoughts about symmetry
  - Obsessions and concerns that things that the individual feels should be symmetrical are not. This could lead to avoidance of geometrical designs as, for example, going into a tiled room could lead to hours of checking each tile is symmetrical. This type of obsession is seen in people with autism but does not automatically mean this is the diagnosis.
  - Worrying if items are not arranged perfectly on a shelf or are not spaced exactly the correct distance apart
- Compulsions concerning symmetry
  - Tapping items in a symmetrical pattern and equally on both sides
  - Feeling the need to finish on an even number to prevent some catastrophe occurring

Of course, this is a far from an exhaustive list, but the main message is that treatment involves facing up to the fear without putting it right. This may involve deliberately placing items in an asymmetrical pattern or varying distances apart. Alternatively, it may mean avoiding all tapping and repeating compulsions completely.

Autism and OCD

It has been found that compared with the general population, people with autism are twice as likely to receive a diagnosis of OCD. On the other hand, people with OCD are four times as likely to be diagnosed with autism than the general population.

People with autism usually have repetitive behaviours and rituals which can resemble OCD. For the outside observer, it can often be difficult to distinguish rituals due to autism and those due to OCD. The individual themselves, however, may be more able to distinguish between the two. Rituals due purely to autism are usually part of reassuring and pleasant activities which help the person to feel safe. Obsessive-compulsive rituals are, as with all OCD, linked to distressing thoughts, images, and impulses, and are generally not enjoyable at all. People with autism can successfully be treated for co-existing OCD, but it means working with the individual to establish which compulsions are linked to distressing thoughts and which they wish to change.

Although a whole range of obsessive and compulsive symptoms may be found in people with autism, certain obsessions are found a little more frequently. This does not mean that having these types of obsessions makes a diagnosis of autism more likely, or that not having these types of obsessions does not preclude an autistic diagnosis. Symmetry obsessions are more frequently found in people with autism, as are counting, repeating, and ordering compulsions. Hoarding compulsions may also be more frequent in people with autism.

Treatment for OCD in people with high functioning autism is identical to the treatments described in this book. The main differences are listed below:

1. It is important to distinguish between OCD rituals and autistic ones. Autistic rituals tend to be more stable over time. OCD rituals can change over time and are usually upsetting and distressing. Once the OCD behaviours have been identified, it is again a matter of facing up to the feared situation without the 'putting it right' compulsions.
2. Once you have identified the OCD problems that you want to change, ERP treatment proceeds in an identical way to people who do not have autism.
3. Some people with autism have difficulty using numbers to describe anxiety. If this applies then it may be helpful to devise an alternative system such as colours with, for example, green for low or little anxiety; amber for moderate anxiety, and red for the high anxiety (this can be adapted to any system which works for you.)
4. Sometimes people with autism find that their anxiety does not seem to go down in the way they hoped with graded exposure. If, however, you feel able to move up the hierarchy to more difficult items, it may be that your

autism means you are often quite anxious and therefore recording levels of anxiety with respect to your OCD may be meaningless. If this is the case, then instead of measuring your anxiety, be guided by when you feel able to comfortably move on to the next stage in your hierarchy.

5. Some people with autism find they have more side-effects with certain medications. If you find this is the case, it is worthwhile discussing this with your doctor. It may be possible to start on a very low dose and increase slowly. Of course, some people with autism find changes to their routine, such as altering the dose of medication, are always difficult and may need time to prepare for this in advance.

KEY POINTS

- Obsessive-compulsive slowness can frequently be due to a desire to perform actions perfectly.
- Perfection is generally impossible for humans. Instead, we should aim to be 'good enough'.
- Striving for perfection usually means that the end results are far from perfect, as an individual gets so slowed up and fails to obtain what they are trying to achieve.
- Treatment of perfectionism involves taking the risk and performing thinks incorrectly. Because perfectionists may try to perform a 'perfect' treatment programme, it is important to introduce random items and imperfection into the programme itself.
- Symmetry obsessions are also found in people with OCD. In this case it is a matter of facing up to the discomfort which asymmetric and 'wrong' things can cause.
- People with autism are twice as likely to suffer with OCD than the general population.
- People with autism can successfully be treated using ERP. It is, however, important to distinguish between problematic OCD compulsions which arise from distressing obsessive thoughts and those self-soothing and reassuring rituals that are part of autism.

- Sometimes, due to continually high levels of anxiety, people with autism find that their anxiety does not reduce significantly with exposure treatment. In such cases, it is important to remember that if moving up the hierarchy, progress is being made.

19

. . . .

Overcoming Obsessive Ruminations (Sometimes Known as 'Pure O')

This chapter will examine how to treat obsessions without obvious compulsions. Examples will be given of how this may be tackled. There will also be a discussion about the concept of 'Pure O', what this may consist of and how this may be tackled. Finally, there will be a discussion about distinguishing between and treating non-obsessive ruminations which can co-exist in people with OCD.

Introduction

There is considerable confusion about obsessive ruminations and how to treat them, both amongst people who have obsessive thoughts and all too often healthcare professionals as well. In reality, obsessive thoughts are no more difficult to treat than other types of OCD. The important thing is to remember the basic principles of treatment.

Obsessions are horrible, unpleasant thoughts, images, or impulses which come into the mind and cause distress. In order to deal with this distress, people with OCD perform compulsions. Compulsions are either acts or thoughts which are designed to either ward off the harm from the obsessive thought, reduce the distress, or 'undo' the bad effect of the obsessive thought, or frequently a mixture of all of these. Compulsive actions, such as handwashing in someone who has contamination fears, are familiar to all of us. People with obsessive ruminations, however, have a specific thought or pattern of thoughts which serve to reduce the distress of the obsessive thought. Although this may sound obvious, it is vitally important to remember this, otherwise confusion can occur. The foundation of exposure treatment is to bring yourself face-to-face with the anxiety-provoking thought without performing or thinking the anxiety-reducing compulsions. Examples of this type of treatment have already been given in Chapter 18. So, a short mantra to say to yourself if you have this type of OCD is, 'expose to the anxiety-provoking and stop the anxiety-reducing'.

As the compulsions are thoughts, it is sometimes difficult to stop these occurring automatically. There are two main ways of dealing with this problem. Firstly, it may be possible to induce so many obsessive thoughts that you do not have time to 'put them right'. This may be achieved by going to a place which induces many obsessive thoughts or sometimes by writing them down and reading them repeatedly. The idea here is that with so much exposure to situations which make the obsessive thoughts come so quickly, it is difficult or impossible to put everything right at sufficient speed to 'undo' the obsessive thoughts. Another way is to record the anxiety-provoking obsession in the individual's own voice and play it back on a continuous loop via headphones. In the latter case, it is extremely difficult to think about anything else when a recording in your own voice is playing in your ear. This form or treatment with a loop recording can be very stressful, and so it would be usual to start with easier items on the hierarchy before progressing to this.

'Pure O'

'Pure O' is a term which is sometimes used online to describe obsessive-compulsive disorder without any obvious compulsions. Some people have therefore thought that some people only have obsessions without compulsions. This is not a recognised form of OCD and is still quite controversial. In reality, if someone with OCD has unpleasant, horrible, intrusive thoughts, images, or impulses, they will try and push them out of their mind. Usually, this is with a compulsion. For someone with ruminations, this is another thought or image which reduces the anxiety created by the original obsession. Sometimes it can be difficult to separate out the anxiety-provoking thoughts from the anxiety-reducing thoughts. Sometimes people do not have obvious thought compulsions but may find a way of trying to push the thoughts from their mind instead. Of course, this escape and avoidance of the thought is also another form of compulsion.

The confusion exists because some therapists do not recognise that the obsessive rumination consists of two parts, anxiety- or distress-provoking and anxiety- or distress-relieving or 'putting it right' components. Once you remember this basic fact, it is relatively easy to create an exposure hierarchy.

Non-Obsessive Ruminations

Of course, not all ruminations are obsessive. People who are depressed may sit and think about upsetting things for hours on end. The difference in these cases is that the 'ruminations' have a different quality. Instead of being intrusive, unpleasant thoughts which come unheralded into your mind and are followed by a compulsion or avoidance, in depressive ruminations the thoughts are concordant with the depressed mood and are normally more varied and depend on circumstance. In depressive ruminations, there are no attempts to 'put them right'. Depression is very frequent in people with OCD, and so it can be quite tricky at times to distinguish between the symptoms of the two.

People with more generalised anxiety may also sit and go over and over particular events, either past or future, in their minds or have particular worries.

Both depressive and anxiety ruminations tend to worsen the condition and so trying to stop them occurring is the best treatment. We have already discussed treatment of obsessive ruminations through exposure to the anxiety-provoking thoughts and stopping the anxiety-relieving parts. For depressive or anxious ruminations, it is a good idea to restrict the time spent in such activity. This can sometimes be done by setting aside specific 'worry times' during the day which are shorter in duration and can allow someone to think that they will 'worry about that later' rather than getting caught up in it in the here and now. Of course, such worry times (e.g., 30 minutes at a set time each day) should be combined with a structured day and activity schedule. Activity scheduling is discussed in Chapter 11.

KEY POINTS

- Obsessive ruminations consist of the anxiety- or distress-inducing obsessive thought and then another thought or image which is designed to put right the obsessive thought.
- Sometimes this 'putting right' is purely trying to push the thought from your mind.
- Sometimes people talk about 'Pure O', not realising that there is also a compulsive component to the thoughts.
- Both depressive and anxiety ruminations are found in OCD.
- Depression and anxiety often co-exist with OCD and therefore some people may have depressive (more commonly) or anxiety ruminations as well.
- Depressive and anxiety ruminations can be treated using set 'worry times' combined with activity scheduling.

20

• • • • • • •

When the Treatment Doesn't Go According to Plan or Even If It Does, What to Do Next

---

In this chapter the principles of ERP treatment are repeated. Various problems and issues which can arise in therapy are then discussed. Even if you do not succeed at first, that does not mean that you will not in the future. It is always worthwhile rethinking your treatment programme and having another try. If in doubt, you should seek advice from the various OCD organisations or a trusted doctor or healthcare professional.

Introduction

The mainstay of treatment for OCD is facing up to the things that you fear in a gradual, reliable, and predictable way without 'undoing' this or 'putting it right' by compulsions which may be actions or thoughts. If you have any issues identifying what are obsessive thoughts, it is important to remember that obsessive thoughts are unpleasant, horrible, anxiety-provoking, or discomfort-making thoughts. The tendency when you have these thoughts in response to a specific situation is to 'run away' or avoid the object or thought which provoked the horrible thought. This running away or avoidance actually serves to strengthen the OCD thoughts and behaviour. In addition to this avoidance, people with OCD also have compulsions. Compulsions are thought patterns or behaviours which are designed to reduce or prevent the 'harm' of the obsessive thought. They reduce anxiety but only for a short while, and then the urge to perform another compulsion will come along so that the compulsions get more and more frequent and also automatic. Although compulsions seem like a good idea initially, they serve to maintain the fear and discomfort of the obsessions and can often be as problematic, and certainly as time-consuming, as the obsessions themselves. Some people ask others for reassurance, and this also becomes like a compulsion.

Treatment involves setting out a list or hierarchy of situations which you can face up to without avoidance, compulsions, or reassurance. Once the hierarchy has been developed, try and pick one or two items which you are prepared to do without compulsive activity, and which will cause you moderate anxiety. You then need to expose yourself to this ideally three times a day. As you face up to the fear without compulsive activity, your anxiety will become high, but if you stick with it, then the anxiety will reduce. This usually takes one to two hours until the anxiety comes down for a sustained time. As you continue to practise this repeatedly every day, you should find that overall, the anxiety gets less as you become used to the exposure. Of course, all of us have good and bad hours and good and bad days or weeks, so it won't always be a smooth reduction in anxiety. People vary in how quickly this adaptation happens, but you should start to see some improvements after a week or so. Once the anxiety associated with the exposure has reduced, then it is time to move on to one or two more difficult items. In this way, you work through the hierarchy.

Although the above ERP is a very well tried and tested way of overcoming OCD, sometimes people hit some difficulties, and I have tried to outline these here and how you might tackle them.

1. **All of the items in my hierarchy are extremely anxiety provoking and I cannot grade them.**

   a. Sometimes, people find that there is no easy way to start the programme. In these cases, it is probably best to just pick one item and decide to go for that one. Once you have realised that the anxiety does come down, it is easier to add in another item.

2. **I've been doing my programme and the anxiety is not coming down.**

   a. Firstly, make sure that you are not taking precautions or doing compulsions. Although they may give short-term relief, compulsions and other safety devices will prevent the anxiety coming down in a sustained way. Make sure you are fully exposing to the fear. If you find yourself doing mental compulsions which you cannot resist, it may be a good idea to record your anxiety-provoking thoughts on your phone, in your own voice, and play this back through headphones on a continuous loop.

   b. Ensure that you are performing the exposure for long enough. For example, if you are touching a door handle, make sure you grasp it properly and then rub your hands together and touch your clothes and your face with your 'contaminated' hands. Sometimes the urge is to do the exposure quickly and then escape. Remember the idea is **prolonged** graded exposure to the feared situation. If you find yourself inadvertently 'putting right' the obsessive thought after exposure and before the anxiety has reduced, try to re-expose yourself to the same item.

   c. It is important to make sure that you do the programmes frequently enough. Remember they should be done three times a day if possible, to have the best effect.

   d. Do not be tempted to do an item that is more difficult at random. Remember the key is that exposure should be **prolonged, regular, and consistent**. Sometimes people start with an easier item on their hierarchy and decide to test themselves by doing a much more difficult one and are then surprised and disappointed when they feel dreadful. The key is to progress slowly and at a rate that allows you to experience anxiety, but a level of anxiety you can tolerate.

    e. If you have thought about all of the above and still your anxiety is still not reducing, then it could be that you are too highly emotionally aroused during exposure. This can occur in people who are very depressed. It is worthwhile speaking with your doctor and asking about medication (as outlined in Chapter 4). If you are already on medication, it may be that the dose needs altering; it may be that you could benefit from switching to an alternative; or you may need an additional medication. It may also be that you will need help from a therapist, and you can ask your doctor to refer you.

3. I do my exposure and I do feel better at the end of it but after a few weeks my anxiety is still as high at the beginning of my exposure as it ever was.

    a. Again, the first thing to do is check that the exposure you have been doing has been **prolonged, regular,** and **consistent**. Make sure you are not including any 'putting it right' activities. It is worthwhile going through the steps outlined in point 2.

    b. For some people it is difficult for them to really not believe in the obsessive thoughts 100 per cent. In these situations, every exposure is seen as a new situation and the fear remains high. In such cases, it can be worthwhile speaking to your doctor and getting referred for some cognitive therapy or some medication to help.

4. I completed the programme and felt better for a while but recently I have found my symptoms are returning.

    a. Everyone who has experienced OCD will always have this tendency. When faced with major life events or tricky patches, or even changes in lifestyle, there will always be the thought that doing a little 'check' or performing a compulsion may be helpful. It is important to remember that ERP and even medication will not change your personality, and so it makes sense that the temptation will be there. This is to be expected and it is no sign of failure on your part! Once this happens (notice I say 'once' and not 'if') then the idea is to get back to doing your ERP programme as soon as you can. Maybe the fears have altered a little, in which case just switch to cover these. It is often useful at the end of your ERP programme to write down a relapse prevention plan for yourself. This means writing down the signs you need to look out for when you are relapsing and what to do about them. The sooner you implement the ERP programme and principles the sooner you will overcome the problem and the less severe the difficulties you need to tackle will be.

Finally, not everyone is able to tackle the programme alone. This is well recognised but does not mean you cannot be treated. It may be that you need help with medication, a self-help group to put you on the right track, or a therapist. In my service I saw many hundreds of people who had failed to improve on multiple trials of therapy, yet most of these people still managed to improve and return to a happier life situation. My final advice/mantra is 'Never Give Up' as you will overcome this problem eventually.

KEY POINTS

- If the ERP is not working, firstly check that the exposure is graded, prolonged, predictable, and is progressing at a pace that allows your anxiety to come down.
- Make sure you are not performing compulsions. If you are then re-expose when you find yourself doing this.
- Some people will also need medication to achieve recovery.
- Others may need help and support from a self-help group or therapist.
- Never give up. Even after several attempts at therapy, people can improve.
- Seek help sooner rather than later and don't be afraid to seek professional advice.
- There is hope and light at the end of the tunnel!

Appendix

Downloadable Self-Assessment and Self-Help Charts and Reminders of Principles of Treatment can be found in the resources tab at www.cambridge.org/ocd-drummond

The principles of treatment are to gradually, reliably, and predictably face up to your fear without putting it right by performing a compulsion or seeking reassurance. Start with an item which you feel will cause you anxiety but at a level that you are happy to stick with. Exposure should last one to two hours or until the anxiety goes down sustainably by half. This doesn't mean you need to sit still doing nothing for two hours, indeed you should get on with your usual (non-OCD) activities. Ideally, exposure should be performed three times a day.

Once you have conquered easier items on your hierarchy, you can move gradually up to more difficult items (which should seem easier as you progress).

Anxiety Scale

0 = no anxiety
2 = mild anxiety
4 = moderate anxiety
6 = severe anxiety
8 = extreme anxiety/cannot be higher/panic

Defining the Impact

If you live with others, it can be helpful to get them to help you define the impact with you as you may have developed 'blind' spots.

Questions	Answers
How does my OCD impact on my general health? Think about drinking sufficient fluid every day; eating a balanced diet; toileting without excessive straining; bathing and showering	
How does my OCD impact on my home-life? Think about cooking, cleaning etc.	
How does my OCD impact on those who live with me? Include thinking about any restrictions on children; tasks that a partner or other person may have needed to take on for you.	
How does OCD impact on my private leisure? Include how you can cope with normal hobbies such as reading; watching TV; exercise etc.	
How does OCD impact on my social leisure? Include going out and meeting friends; going to parties; meals etc.	
How does OCD impact on my work? Are you able to work or does your OCD interfere with this? Do you go in early or stay late due to your OCD?	

Once you have completed this, ask yourself what you want to do with your life and what you need to do to achieve this. Write down what you would be doing in the various areas of your life.

What I want in my life	What I need to do to achieve this
Where I would be living and with whom	
What I would be doing in my spare time	
What my social life would look like	
What I would be doing for work	

Then you will be ready to complete you plan of treatment or hierarchy. To do this, you should start with something that will cause you mild to moderate anxiety when performed without compulsions. Ideally this should be performed three times a day and should be for at least one to two hours. So, for example, if you are worried about contamination and have washing compulsions, you should touch the appropriate item on your hierarchy without any compulsions. If you do, for example, need to go to the toilet and wash your hands in the meantime, you should wash in the new non-ritualistic way described in Chapter 13. And you should 'contaminate' your hands again after this.

Problem	
Target	
Item on hierarchy (starting with easiest)	**Anxiety rating**	**How often to be performed (3x/day is ideal)**

Programmes for week commencing . . . . :

1.
2.
3.

	Programme No. 1			Programme No. 2			Programme No. 3		
	Before	During	After	Before	During	After	Before	During	After
Monday									
AM									
Lunch									
PM									
Before Bed									
Tuesday									
AM									
Lunch									
PM									
Before Bed									
Wednesday									
AM									
Lunch									
PM									
Before Bed									
Thursday									
AM									
Lunch									
PM									
Before Bed									
Friday									
AM									
Lunch									
PM									
Before Bed									
Saturday									
AM									
Lunch									
PM									
Before Bed									
Sunday									
AM									
Lunch									
PM									
Before Bed									

Glossary

Aripiprazole: This is a medication which acts to block dopamine in the brain and can be a helpful addition to treatment with serotonin reuptake inhibitors (SRIs) for some people.

Aripiprazole tends to have fewer side effects than some of the older drugs and is less likely to cause drowsiness.

Asperger's syndrome: See *autism*. A development condition which is part of the autistic disorders. This condition varies in severity from mild to severe. In general, people with Asperger's syndrome may have difficulty understanding other people and their motives and may also have difficulty interpreting other people's body language. Some people with Asperger's syndrome may develop repetitive behaviours which resemble OCD, and some will develop true OCD.

Atypical dopamine blockers: Dopamine blockers are drugs which can be used to increase the efficacy of SRIs in some people with OCD. Atypical dopamine blockers are a group of newer drugs which act on dopamine and were introduced after 1990.

They tend to have fewer side effects compared to the older dopamine blockers.

Autism (autism spectrum disorder): This is a lifelong developmental disorder (i.e., it starts in infancy). People with autism may be extremely clever, but they have difficulty understanding other people's body language and motives and consequently have difficulty in social situations. Some people with autistic spectrum disorders may develop repetitive behaviours which resemble OCD, and some will develop true OCD. Approximately 1 in 100 people have autism, and it is currently seen more commonly in men than in women.

Autoimmune: The body has many specialised protective cells which are designed to fight infection and keep people healthy. In autoimmune disorders, the process has gone wrong, and these protective cells can start to attack parts of the body they are designed to keep safe. Examples of autoimmune disorder include rheumatoid arthritis, in which the joints are attacked; type 1 (or childhood-onset) diabetes, in which the pancreas is attacked; and coeliac disease, in which the gut becomes abnormal and develops a reaction to gluten (a component of wheat).

Behaviour therapy: This is a practical form of therapy with the basic belief that many psychological symptoms are a result of behaviours which make the situation worse. As these behaviours are learned, the individual can learn to replace them with more helpful behaviours. For example, if a person has a horrible, intrusive OCD thought, the compulsive behaviour serves to fuel the obsessive thought and make it more frequent and severe. Learning to resist the compulsive behaviour results in reduced anxiety and discomfort.

Body dysmorphic disorder (BDD): This is a condition which is similar to OCD in many ways. The individual, however, is preoccupied by a perceived defect in their appearance and thoughts of it which preoccupy them throughout the day. These thoughts often lead to checking behaviours, including spending excessive amounts of time looking in mirrors. There is also frequent avoidance, and some people may totally avoid looking at themselves in the mirror and may only go out whilst concealed by wearing makeup or in darkness or, indeed, may avoid leaving the house entirely.

Cingulotomy: A form of brain surgery very rarely used to try to control the symptoms of OCD which have not responded to other methods. A very rare form of treatment.

Citalopram: A modern antidepressant drug which has a direct effect on the symptoms of OCD irrespective of whether the person is depressed or not. It works by reducing the reuptake of serotonin, a neurotransmitter which appears to be low in certain areas of the brain in people with OCD.

Clomipramine: An older type of antidepressant which was found in the 1980s to have a direct effect on obsessive-compulsive symptoms. It was discovered that this anti-obsessive effect was mainly due to its property of increasing serotonin in certain parts of the brain and appearing separate from its antidepressant action. Although a very useful drug, it tends to have more side effects than the more modern selective serotonin reuptake inhibitors (SSRIs).

Clozapine: An atypical dopamine-blocking drug. This is often used in people with schizophrenia who do not respond to first-line therapy. There is evidence that it can precipitate OCD symptoms in some people.

Cognitive behaviour therapy (CBT): A practical form of therapy used for a variety of mental health conditions.

In this therapy, the emphasis is on the 'here and now' rather than looking at the past. It involves examining thoughts and also carrying out real-life exercises to test out these beliefs or help people overcome their fears by facing them in a structured way.

Cognitive therapy: See *cognitive behaviour therapy*. This refers to the process of examining a person's thoughts and beliefs and encouraging the individual to challenge those that are unhelpful to them.

Compulsion: A thought or action which is designed to reduce or prevent the effect of an obsessive thought. However, either the compulsion is not in reality associated with the obsessive thought or it is clearly excessive. Compulsions tend to fuel obsessive thoughts and make them more frequent and more persistent. Examples include cleaning obsessions for people with fear of contamination by dirt or germs.

Covert compulsions: This refers to compulsions which are carried out in an individual's head and are not obvious behaviours. An example is someone who fears they may cause harm to others by 'lashing out' at them. After they have passed other people, they may feel the urge to imagine every movement they made to ensure they did not harm anyone. After they have done this, they will often doubt their memory and repeat the thought until their memory is muddled by repeating it so often.

Deep brain stimulation (DBS): A recently introduced potential treatment for the most profound forms of OCD that do not respond to conventional treatments. This involves inserting small electrodes into the brain and using electrical impulses to stimulate specific areas of the brain in order to reduce and prevent obsessions and compulsions. It does not cause brain damage and has therefore been thought of as 'reversible brain surgery'. It does, however, involve major surgery.

Dermatillomania: See *skin picking disorder.*

Dopamine-blocking drugs: These are drugs which act to block the action of dopamine. In larger doses, they can be used as antipsychotic drugs, but in OCD they are used in lower doses to enhance the effect of the SRI drugs. The older drugs are known as 'typical' and tend to have more side effects than the newer 'atypical' or 'second-generation' drugs.

Escitalopram: A modern antidepressant drug which has a direct effect on the symptoms of OCD irrespective of whether the person is depressed or not. It works by reducing the reuptake of serotonin, a neurotransmitter which appears to be low in certain areas of the brain in people with OCD.

Exposure and response prevention (ERP): Treatment for OCD which involves working through a structured programme of prolonged, graded exposure or, in other words, facing the anxiety- or discomfort-inducing situations for sufficient time to allow the anxiety/discomfort to subside without performing compulsive rituals.

Fluoxetine: A modern antidepressant drug which has a direct effect on the symptoms of OCD irrespective of whether the person is depressed or not. It works by reducing the reuptake of serotonin, a neurotransmitter which appears to be low in certain areas of the brain in people with OCD.

Fluvoxamine: A modern antidepressant drug which has a direct effect on the symptoms of OCD irrespective of whether the person is depressed or not. It works by reducing the reuptake of serotonin, a neurotransmitter which appears to be low in certain areas of the brain in people with OCD.

Frontal lobotomy: See *lobotomy*.

Glial cell: A type of cell found in the brain which seems to modulate or exercise some control over the neurotransmitters.

Glutamate: A neurotransmitter which has multiple effects on the neurones. It is in the brain in large concentrations, but too little or too much glutamate is not beneficial to brain functioning and health.

Haloperidol: Atypical dopamine blocker.

Health anxiety: An anxiety disorder which has many similarities to OCD. In this case, the distressing thoughts concern specific or general health issues. Once the individual has anxious thoughts about their health, they normally check in a ritualistic way. For example, some people may repeatedly check their bodies for lumps which they worry about. They may also seek repeated reassurance from friends or relatives or repeatedly visit their GP or hospitals for reassurance and to ask for more and repeated physical tests.

Hierarchy: A list or ladder of situations placed in order of increasing anxiety/discomfort.

Hoarding disorder: A disorder in which an individual collects large numbers of items beyond reasonable amounts. Individuals generally have difficulty in that they cannot resist collecting large amounts of objects and they have extreme difficulty disposing of items. Hoarding can be extremely serious, leading to social impairments as well as risk to health via inability to clean around the hoard, fire risk of a large number of items, and the risk that the individual may be crushed by a large number of objects falling.

Limbic leucotomy: A form of brain surgery very rarely used to try to control the symptoms of OCD which have not responded to other methods. Extremely rarely used.

Lobotomy: An early form of brain surgery performed in the 1940s and early 1950s to try to alleviate a number of the symptoms in severe psychiatric illnesses. The development and use of powerful antipsychotic drugs in the mid-1950s rendered this procedure obsolete. Occasionally, this has been used for very profound OCD.

Microbiome: This refers to the normal healthy bacteria found in the gut of everyone. These bacteria help to digest food and are thought to impact on the health of an individual in many ways. The healthiest microbiomes are those that have the widest range of 'good' bacteria.

National Institute for Health and Care Excellence (NICE): This body provides national guidance and advice to improve health and social care in the UK.

Neurones: These are nerve cells which transmit messages to each other throughout the brain.

Obsession: An obsession is a thought, image, or impulse which intrudes on an individual's consciousness and is anxiety-provoking and/or distressing.

These thoughts are usually totally out of character with the individual. For example, a law-abiding and caring man may have thoughts about molesting children; these thoughts are totally abhorrent to him. A devoted mother may have thoughts of violently attacking her children; these thoughts distress her greatly. A religious person may have blasphemous thoughts which can cause extreme distress.

Some people have worries about 'contamination' and the spreading of dirt or germs, and others worry that something bad may happen unless they are very careful in everyday life. Common obsessions include the following:

- Fear of contamination causing harm to self or others
- Fear of harm occurring by the individual failing to perform a vital action (e.g., switching off gas taps)
- Fear of harm occurring by performing an act of violence or similar
- Religious obsessions
- Fear of loss of objects or information

Obsessive compulsive and related disorders: These are a group of disorders which are thought to be related and include the following:

- OCD
- Body dysmorphic disorder

- Hoarding disorder
- Hair pulling disorder (trichotillomania)
- Skin picking disorder
- OCD resulting from another cause, such as brain damage, infection, or substance misuse

These disorders are sometimes also referred to as obsessive-compulsive spectrum disorders.

Obsessive-compulsive spectrum disorders: See *obsessive compulsive and related disorders*. In addition to the group of disorders categorised as obsessive compulsive and related disorders, other conditions such as health anxiety as well as eating disorders and pathological gambling are included under this term. In general, it refers to any condition in which there are difficulties in compulsive behaviours, impulsive behaviours, or both.

Olanzepine: This is one of the newer or 'atypical' dopamine-blocking drugs. Although used in people with psychotic illnesses in higher dosages, it is sometimes useful as an addition to an SRI in low doses for people with OCD.

Overt compulsions: These are compulsions which can be seen – for example, someone with extensive washing compulsions or someone who checks door locks or light switches by repeatedly touching, pulling, or switching them.

Oxytocin: This is a chemical produced in the hypothalamus area of the brain and released by the pituitary. It has a role in social bonding, sexual reproduction, and also childbirth and lactation. It is sometimes referred to as the 'love hormone'.

Paediatric autoimmune neurological syndrome: This is a controversial idea and refers to the idea that a certain type of OCD may result in susceptible children following common bacterial or sometimes viral infections. The first type of this disorder to be recognised was paediatric autoimmune neuropsychiatric disorders associated with streptococcal infection (PANDAS). These conditions start suddenly with OCD and can also be accompanied by dramatic movement disorders.

Paediatric autoimmune neuropsychiatric disorders associated with streptococcal infection (PANDAS): This represents a controversial idea that some rapid-onset OCD symptoms which can occur in childhood may be accompanied by other neurological symptoms such as an inability to control movements of the limbs or trunk or an inability to stand up and walk without falling. This condition is thought to occur in susceptible individuals following an illness such as a sore throat. Bacterial sore throats (which are less common than those caused by viruses) can occasionally be caused by bacteria known as strepto-cocci. These infections are common in childhood, whereas PANDAS is rare.

Paroxetine: A modern antidepressant drug which has a direct effect on the symptoms of OCD irrespective of whether the person is depressed or not. It works by reducing the reuptake of serotonin, a neurotransmitter which appears to be low in certain areas of the brain in people with OCD.

Personality disorder: This refers to a condition whereby the individual differs in many ways from an average person in how they think, view the world, experience emotions, or relate to others. There are many different types of personality disorder. Some examples are given here. People with obsessive personality disorder tend to be scrupulous, punctual, and rather pedantic individuals who strive for perfection and may become 'workaholics'. They tend to differ from people with OCD because they do not believe these traits interfere with their lives but tend to blame others for not being perfect. People with emotional unstable personality disorder have extreme difficulty dealing with and handling emotions and may use self-destructive behaviours as a result.

These unhelpful behaviours may include self-harm, abuse of alcohol or drugs, and binge eating.

Prefrontal lobotomy: See *lobotomy.*

Selective serotonin reuptake inhibitors (SSRIs): These are drugs which act on the serotonin system of the brain. SSRIs are known to be helpful in reducing the symptoms of OCD and tend to have fewer and less severe side effects compared to the older serotonin reuptake inhibiting drug clomipramine. SSRIs comprise the following:

- Sertraline
- Fluoxetine
- Paroxetine
- Fluvoxamine
- Citalopram
- Escitalopram

Serotonin: This is a chemical found in the brain as well as other parts of the body. In the brain, it acts as a neurotransmitter and thus helps the passage of information along the brain cells.

Serotonin reuptake inhibitors (SRIs): These are drugs which are known to be helpful in reducing the symptoms of OCD. They act by increasing the levels of the neurotransmitter serotonin in specific areas of the brain by preventing it from being absorbed quickly back into the nerve cells. SRIs comprise the older antidepressant drug clomipramine and the newer SSRI drugs.

Sertraline: A modern antidepressant drug which has a direct effect on the symptoms of OCD irrespective of whether the person is depressed or not. It works by reducing the reuptake of serotonin, a neurotransmitter which appears to be low in certain areas of the brain in people with OCD.

Skin picking disorder (dermatillomania): This is a condition in which the individual feels the urge to pick the skin to the point that they usually have visible wounds. The most common areas affected are the face and lips, but it can involve any part of the body. As with hair pulling disorder, it is most common in teenagers and young adults, and it is more common in women than men. It is included as one of the obsessive-compulsive and related conditions.

Strep sore throat: This is a bacterial throat infection in which the throat and tonsils are red and sore.

It is caused by bacteria known as streptococci. Approximately 15–40 per cent of throat infections in children are caused by streptococci; far fewer throat infections in adults are caused by streptococci. It can be treated with antibiotics. Some people believe that a tiny number of children with this infection may rarely develop PANDAS after the infection.

Subcaudate tractotomy: A form of brain surgery very rarely used to try to control the symptoms of OCD which have not responded to other methods. Extremely rare.

Tics: These are involuntary movements which the individual is aware that they are doing but which they feel unable to stop performing. Tics frequently involve the muscles of the face and can include grimacing or blinking repeatedly; such movements of the muscles are known as motor tics.

Also, people with tics frequently utter involuntary sounds, such as repetitive throat clearing. Sometimes motor tics can involve muscles which would not be visible to others, such as clenching of abdominal muscles. Tics of both types are common in childhood and may disappear spontaneously without the need for any treatment.

Tourette syndrome: This condition affects approximately 1 in 100 children and can often disappear spontaneously as they grow but can also come and go throughout childhood. It consists of muscular tics as well as vocal tics. Tourette syndrome is not dangerous, and many children and adults do not require treatment. The most profound and dramatic version, in which the individual utters obscenities, is very rare, occurring in fewer than one in ten people with Tourette syndrome. Up to half of individuals with Tourette syndrome have some OCD symptoms, and approximately one in three of these individuals will have clinical OCD.

Transcranial magnetic stimulation (TMS): This is an experimental treatment sometimes used for OCD. It involves applying strong magnets externally on the head in an attempt to 'dampen' down certain areas of the brain on a temporary basis. The magnetic fields are produced by using electric currents, and the resulting magnetism can be pinpointed to specific areas of the brain. It has been shown to be useful for major depression and also certain types of pain. Currently, there is insufficient evidence to fully recommend it for the treatment of OCD.

Trichotillomania (hair pulling disorder): This is a condition whereby the individual feels compelled to pull out their hair. This is frequently on the head but can involve other hair, such as eyebrows or eyelashes. The individual will often describe the buildup of tension and then relief when the hair is plucked. However, it often results in guilt and remorse. Many people with hair pulling disorders end up with bald patches. This condition is most common amongst teenagers and young adults, and it is more common in young women than in men.

Resources

Information Sources

General Introduction to OCD and Its Treatment

National Health Service (NHS) choices (UK) www.nhs.uk/conditions/
Obsessive-compulsive-disorder/Pages/ Introduction.aspx#treatment
Royal College of Psychiatrists (UK) www.rcpsych.ac.uk/healthadvice/
problemsdisorders/ obsessivecompulsivedisorder.aspx
National Institute for Mental Health (US) www.nimh.nih.gov/health/topics/
obsessive-compulsive-disorder- ocd/index.shtml
Description of treatment from the Australian Psychological Society www
.psychology.org.au/for-the-public/Psychology-topics/ Obsessive-
compulsive-disorder

Information from the National Institute for Health and Clinical Excellence (NICE)

A full description of the treatments that can be expected within the NHS is given at
www.nice.org.uk/guidance/cg31/chapter/1-Guidance
or can be obtained from Her Majesty's Stationery Office (HMSO) as CG31 and is
available from the National Institute for Health and Clinical Excellence,
MidCity Place, 71 High Holborn, London, WC1V 6NA

Description of Services Available in the UK

Specialist services in England: www.england.nhs.uk/wp-content/uploads/2013/
06/c09-sev-ocd- boy-dysm.pdf
Specialist services available throughout the UK: www.swlstg-tr.nhs.uk/
documents/ related-documents/our- services/336-national-service- referral-
criteria/file
Consensus statement from the British Association for Psychopharmacology.
A description of the various drugs used in anxiety disorders and obsessive
compulsive disorder: www.bap.org.uk/pdfs/BAP_Guidelines-Anxiety.pdf

Self-Help Organisations

OCD Action: a UK-based organisation providing support as well as information and meetings for people living with OCD and their relatives, friends, and carers. Available at: www.ocdaction.org.uk

OCD-UK: a UK-based organisation providing support as well as information and meetings for people living with OCD and their relatives, friends, and carers. Available at: www.ocduk.org

TOP UK: a UK-based organisation offering support and treatment groups for people with phobic anxiety and OCD. Available at: www.topuk.org

International OCD Foundation: a US-based organisation offering conferences and information for people with OCD and also professionals. Available at: https://iocdf.org

SANE: an Australian-based charity for mental health offering information and forums for conditions including OCD. Available at: www.sane.org/mental-health-and-illness/facts-and-guides/ obsessive-compulsive-disorder

Other Organisations

International College for Obsessive-Compulsive Spectrum Disorders (ICOCS): an international organisation which sets out to promote research in OCD and related disorders and to produce public statements to improve OCD treatment internationally. Available at: www.icocs.org

International OCD Foundation: A US-based organisation aiming to promote awareness about OCD, promote research in OCD, and provide information to professionals and people with OCD. Available at: https://iocdf.org

Further Reading

Autobiographical Books Written by People Who Have Experienced OCD

The Man Who Couldn't Stop: The Truth about OCD, by David Adam. London: Picador, 2015.

An autobiographical book written by a journalist which tells of his journey through treatment for OCD.

The Walking Worried: A Young Man's Journey with OCD, by Aron Bennett. Brentwood: Chipmunka Publishing, 2015.

An autobiographical book written by a young man who was studying law and who eventually received appropriate treatment for his OCD.

Self-Help Books Written by Professionals

Mindfulness Workbook for OCD: A Guide to Overcoming Obsessions and Compulsions Using Mindfulness and Cognitive Behaviour Therapy, by Jon Hershfield and Tom Corboy. New York, NY: New Harbinger, 2014.
This book concentrates on the specific approach to OCD using mainly mindfulness and CBT. It does not examine other aspects of treatment.
Break Free from OCD: Overcoming Obsessive Compulsive Disorder with CBT, by Fiona Challacombe, Victoria Bream Oldfield, and Paul M. Salkovskis. Chatham: Vermilion, 2011.
This book focusses on the CBT approach to OCD. It does not explore psychopharmacological or other NICE-approved approaches.
Obsessive Compulsive Disorder – The Essential Guide, by Joanna Jast. Peterborough: Need2Know, 2011.
This is a more general book which examines what constitutes OCD and takes a broader approach to treatment. It offers a concise overview in 120 pages.
The OCD Workbook: Your Guide to Breaking Free from Obsessive-Compulsive Disorder, 3rd ed., by Bruce M. Hyman. New York, NY: New Harbinger, 2010.
Another book purely focussing on CBT approaches to OCD.
Overcoming Obsessive Thoughts: How to Gain Control of Your OCD, by Christine Purdon. New York, NY: New Harbinger, 2010.
Another book purely focussing on CBT approaches to OCD.
Overcoming Obsessive Compulsive Disorder, by David Veale and Rob Willson. London: Constable & Robinson, 2005.
Another book purely focussing on CBT approaches to OCD.
Breaking Free from OCD: A CBT Guide for Young People and Their Families by Jo Derisley. London: Kingsley, 2008.
A CBT self-help guide for children and young people.
What to Do When Your Brain Gets Stuck: A Kid's Guide to Overcoming OCD by Dawn Huebner and Bonnie Matthews. Washington, DC: Margination Press, 2007.
A CBT self-help guide for children and young people.

Multi-author Books Written by Professionals and for Professionals

Clinical Guide to Obsessive-Compulsive and Related Disorders, by Jon E. Grant, Samuel R. Chamberlain, and Brian L. Odlaug. New York, NY: Oxford University Press, 2014.

This book is comprehensive and eclectic. However, it briefly mentions treatments and does not have any depth in any of the disorders. It is predominantly written for professionals and thus is a useful aide-memoire for this group.

Obsessive Compulsive Disorder: Current Science and Clinical Practice, edited by Joshi Zohar. Bognor Regis: Wiley, 2012.

Written for a professional audience, this multi-author book comprehensively covers the theories of OCD, its development and maintenance, and its treatment.

Handbook on Obsessive–Compulsive and Related Disorders, edited by Katharine A. Phillips and Dan J. Stein. Washington, DC: American Psychiatric Association, 2015.

This is a multi-author book written for professionals that describes various subtypes of the obsessive-compulsive and related disorders based on the DSM-5 classification. There are separate chapters on OCD and on trichotillomania, body dysmorphic disorder, tic disorders, and so on.

References

Alonso, P., Cuadras, D., Gabriëls, L., et al. (2015). Deep brain stimulation for obsessive-compulsive disorder: a meta-analysis of treatment outcome and predictors of response. *PLoS One*, 10(7), e0133591.

American Psychiatric Association. (2013). *Diagnostic and Statistical Manual of Mental Disorders* (5th ed.). Arlington, VA: American Psychiatric Publishing.

Birzele, L.T., Depner, M., Ege, M.J., et al. (2017). Environmental and mucosal microbiota and their role in childhood asthma. *Allergy*, 72(1), 109–19.

Bloch, M. H., Landeros-Weisenberger, A., Kelmendi, B., et al. (2006). A systematic review: antipsychotic augmentation with treatment refractory obsessive-compulsive disorder. *Molecular Psychiatry*, 11(7), 622–32.

Boschen, M.J., Drummond, L.M., Pillay, A., and Morton, K. (2010). Predicting outcome of treatment for severe, treatment-resistant OCD in inpatient and community settings. *Journal of Behavior Therapy and Experimental Psychiatry*, 41, 90–5.

Dell'Osso, B., Benatti, B., Hollander, E., et al. (2016). Childhood, adolescent and adult age at onset and related clinical correlates in obsessive-compulsive disorder: a report from the International College of Obsessive-Compulsive Spectrum Disorders (ICOCS). *International Journal of Psychiatry in Clinical Practice*, 20(4), 210–17.

Drummond, L.M., and Fineberg, N.A. (2007). Obsessive–compulsive disorders. In G. Stein, (ed.), *College Seminars in Adult Psychiatry*. London: Gaskell, pp. 270–86.

Fineberg, N.A., Hollander, E., Pallanti, S., et al. (2020). Clinical advances in obsessive compulsive disorder: a position statement by the International College of Obsessive Compulsive Spectrum Disorders. *International Clinical Psychopharmacology*, 35(4): 173–93. https://doi.org/10.1097/yic.0000000000000314

Fineberg, N.A., Van Ameringen, M., Drummond, L., et al. (2020). How to manage obsessive-compulsive disorder (OCD) under COVID-19: a clinician's guide from the International College of Obsessive Compulsive Spectrum Disorders (ICOCS) and the Obsessive-Compulsive Research Network (OCRN) of the

European College of Neuropsychopharmacology. *Comprehensive Psychiatry*, 100, 152174. https://doi.org/10.1016/j.comppsych.2020.152174

Heller, A.C., Amar, A.P., Liu, C.Y., and Apuzzo, M.L. (2006). Surgery of the mind and mood: a mosaic of issues in time and evolution. *Neurosurgery*, 59(4), 720–33; discussion 733–9.

Hollander, E., King, A., Deslaney K, et al. (2003). Obsessive–compulsive behaviors in parents of multiplex autism families. *Psychiatry Research*, 117, 11–16. https://doi.org/10.1016/S0165-1781(02)00304-9

Humble, M.B., Uvnäs-Moberg, K., Engström, I., and Bejerot, S. (2013). Plasma oxytocin changes and anti-obsessive response during serotonin reuptake inhibitor treatment: a placebo-controlled study. *BMC Psychiatry*, 13, 344. https://doi.org/10.1186/1471-244X-13-344

Jones, M.K., and Menzies, R.G. (1997a). Danger Ideation Reduction Therapy (DIRT): preliminary findings with three obsessive-compulsive washers. *Behaviour Research and Therapy*, 35, 955–60.

Karno, M., Golding, J.M., Sorenson, S.B., and Burnam, M.A. (1988). The epidemiology of obsessive-compulsive disorder in five US communities. *Archives of General Psychiatry*, 45, 1095–9.

McAlister-Williams, R.H., Baldwin, D.S., and Cantwell, R. (2017) British Association for Psychopharmacology consensus guidance on the use of psychotropic medication preconception, in pregnancy and postpartum 2017. *Journal of Psychopharmacology*, 31(5), 519–52.

Meier, S.M., Petersen, L., Schendel, D.E., et al. (2015). Obsessive-compulsive disorder and autism spectrum disorders: longitudinal and offspring risk. PLoS One (Online). https://doi.org/10.1371/journal.pone.0141703

Mitchell-Heggs, N., Kelly, D., and Richardson, A. (1976). Stereotactic limbic leucotomy – a follow-up at 16 months. *British Journal of Psychiatry*, 128, 126.

Rees, J.C. (2014). Obsessive-compulsive disorder and gut microbiota dysregulation. *Medical Hypotheses*, 82(2), 163–6. https://doi.org/10.1016/j.mehy.2013.11.026

Reid, J., Drummond, L.M., and Fineberg, N.A. (2021). Cognitive behavioural therapy with exposure and response prevention in the treatment of obsessive-compulsive disorder: a systematic review and meta-analysis of randomised controlled trials. *Comprehensive Psychiatry*, 106, 152223. Available at: www.sciencedirect.com/science/article/pii/S0010440X21000018

Simpson, H.B., Foa, E.B., Liebowitz, M. R., et al. (2013). Cognitive-behavioral therapy vs risperidone for augmenting serotonin reuptake inhibitors in obsessive-compulsive disorder: a randomized clinical trial. *JAMA Psychiatry*, 70(11), 1190–9.

Stern, R.S., and Drummond, L.M. Exposure and self-imposed response prevention (ERP), adapted from Stern, R.S., and Drummond, L.M. (1991). *The Practice of Behavioural and Cognitive Psychotherapy.* Cambridge: Cambridge University Press.

Tolin, D.F., Frost, R.O., and Stetekee, G. (2013). *Buried in Treasures: Help for Compulsive Acquiring, Saving, And Hoarding* (Treatments That Work). New York: Oxford University Press.

Trevizol, A.P., Shiozawa, P., Cook, I.A., et al. (2016). Transcranial magnetic stimulation for obsessive-compulsive disorder: an updated systematic review and meta-analysis. *The Journal of ECT*, 32(4), 262–6.

Turna, J., Grosman Kaplan, K., Anglin, R., et al. (2020) The gut microbiome and inflammation in obsessive-compulsive disorder patients compared to age and sex-matched controls: a pilot study. *Acta Psychiatrica Scandinavica*, 142(4), 337–47. https://doi.org/10.1111/acps.13175

Tyagi, H., Drummond, L.M., and Fineberg, N.A. (2010). Treatment for obsessive compulsive disorder. *Current Psychiatry Reviews*, 6(1), 46–55.

Tyagi, H., Zrinzo, L., Foltynie, T., et al. (2016). Deep brain stimulation for severe obsessive-compulsive disorder. International Congress of the Royal College of Psychiatrists, EXCEL, London, 27–30 June.

Uzunova, G., Hollander, E., and Shepherd, J. (2014). The role of ionotropic glutamate receptors in childhood neurodevelopmental disorders: autism spectrum disorders and Fragile X syndrome. *Current Neuropharmacology*, 12(1), 71–98. https://doi.org/10.2174/1570159X113116660046

Vaughan, R., O'Donnell, C., and Drummond, L.M. (2018). Blood levels of treatment-resistant obsessive-compulsive disorder patients prescribed supra-normal dosages of sertraline. *European Neuropsychopharmacology*, 28(6), 767–768.

World Health Organization. (1993). *The ICD 10 Classification of Mental and Behavioural Disorders: Diagnostic Criteria for Research.* Geneva: World Health Organization.

Index

Printed in the United States
by Baker & Taylor Publisher Services